THE FIRST
TOUR DE FRANCE

ALSO BY PETER COSSINS

The Monuments: The Grit and Glory of
Cycling's Greatest One-Day Races
Alpe d'Huez: The Story of Pro Cycling's Greatest Climb
Ultimate Étapes: Ride Europe's Greatest Cycling Stages
Everybody's Friend: The Life and Career of
Dave Rayner 1967–1994 and his Legacy to Cycling

THE FIRST
TOUR DE FRANCE

SIXTY CYCLISTS AND NINETEEN DAYS OF
DARING ON THE ROAD TO PARIS

PETER COSSINS

NATION
BOOKS
New York

First published in the United Kingdom by Yellow Jersey Press in 2017.

Published in the United States by Nation Books, an imprint of Perseus Books, LLC, a subsidiary of Hachette Book Group, Inc.
116 East 16th Street, 8th Floor
New York, NY 10003

Nation Books is a co-publishing venture of the Nation Institute and Perseus Books Group.

The Hachette Speakers Bureau provides a wide range of authors for speaking events. To find out more, go to hachettespeakersbureau.com or call 866-376-6591.

Typset in 12/17 pt Fairfield LH by Jouve (UK), Milton Keynes

Library of Congress Cataloging-in-Publication Data is available from the Library of Congress.

ISBN: 978-1-56858-984-8 (HC)
ISBN: 978-1-56858-985-5 (EB)

10 9 8 7 6 5 4 3 2 1

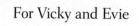

For Vicky and Evie

CONTENTS

Photographs follow page 196

AUTHOR'S NOTE

Descriptions of Marseille–Paris and each of the six stages of the 1903 Tour de France are based on details, comments and quotes reported in contemporary newspapers and magazines.

VILLENEUVE–SAINT-GEORGES, 1 JULY 1903

The keen and the curious begin to congregate from midday. By one o'clock, when the riders start to emerge from the roadside barn that has been set aside as their dressing room, allowing them some privacy as they change and have a final massage, the heat is oppressive, almost unbearable. There's hardly a breath of wind. Dust billowing up from the construction work on the Paris–Corbeil railway line hangs in the still air.

The race organisers had been praying for a good crowd, certainly more than the few hundred who are milling about in and around the Auberge du Réveil-Matin. That's more than enough to keep the proprietor, Monsieur Renard, and his staff far busier than they would normally be on a Wednesday lunchtime, but it hardly bodes well for the inaugural Tour de France. Henri Desgrange and his editorial team have been building the new race up for weeks in the pages of L'Auto, and necessarily so. If it doesn't succeed, there won't be a second, and L'Auto won't survive for much longer either.

The race officials have set up the control point for the start inside the cafe. Riders must register here over the next

90 minutes in order to compete. The first to sign in is 20-year-old Parisian Henri Ellinamour, who is handed a green armband bearing the number 64 by official starter Alphonse Steinès. He is closely followed by another rider from the capital, Léon Pernette, who walks away with his armband and square of red cloth with the number 44, which he secures to the top tube and seat tube of his bike with rubber straps.

As more riders arrive, the smell of embrocation becomes impossible to ignore. After signing in, they carry out their final preparations for the start, pressing spare parts into the square leather bags hanging from their handlebars, wrapping replacement tubes and tyres around their shoulders, always keeping their machines within eyesight to prevent sabotage, which is not unknown. This done, most flop down on their backs to rest. Two gendarmes survey them from their horses. They are almost redundant as the spectators who have been tempted out by 'the greatest race the world has ever seen' are hardly in a frenzy as they take shelter from the sun in the shade offered by the twin line of poplars lining the Avenue de Paris as it heads away from Villeneuve-Saint-Georges towards Montgeron.

Many of those gathered beneath the trees are amateur cyclists who have turned up on their bikes with the intention of following the professionals for as long as possible. Among them is a young man who has been making a name for himself in amateur races around Paris. Eugène Christophe is currently an apprentice locksmith on the Rue Chaton, but will go on to have a very illustrious future on the bike and will eventually be remembered for repairing his forks in a forge at the foot of the

Col du Tourmalet in the 1913 Tour and, in 1919, for being the first rider ever to wear the race's yellow jersey.

In his diary later that evening, Christophe will write dismissively: 'The greatest bike race the world has ever seen? It was more like a fourth-category race. There was hardly anyone there. Where were all the cars? It looked more like the start of an amateur race to me. These guys may be among the biggest names we know but they looked like riders who had won their first inter-club race . . .'

CHAPTER 1

'THE GREATEST CYCLING RACE IN THE ENTIRE WORLD'

A meeting between two friends in a cell at the Prison de la Santé in Paris's 14th arrondissement provided the surprising impetus for the foundation of the Tour de France. It took place in June 1899, a few days after the city witnessed a series of events that had almost cost the nation's president his life, had threatened the survival of the Third Republic, and provoked headlines across the world.

The man brought up from one of La Santé's 500 cells was a most unlikely prisoner. Jules Félix Philippe Albert de Dion de Wandonne was better known as Count de Dion, a French noble and co-founder in 1883 of the De Dion-Bouton automobile company that had become the world's biggest manufacturer by the end of the nineteenth century, producing the sum total of 400 cars a year. A tall, solidly built and very imposing figure with a thick moustache waxed to perfect horizontal tips, de Dion was serving a 15-day sentence for attempting to assault the president of the French Republic, Émile Loubet, during a demonstration at the Auteuil racecourse in Paris.

The count's visitor was journalist Pierre Giffard, a columnist on the best-selling *Le Petit Journal* newspaper and editor of *Le Vélo*, the leading sports title of the era. Giffard, who favoured an upward tweak on his equally luxuriant moustache, wanted to explain why he had written an opinion piece condemning de Dion's behaviour for *Le Petit Journal* and subsequently rerun it within the green-coloured pages of his own paper.

Brought together by their love of automobiles, these two prominent men were very vocal proponents of radically opposed camps on the main political issue of the moment, the Dreyfus Affair. This stemmed from the conviction in 1894 of French artillery officer Captain Alfred Dreyfus on a charge of treason after military secrets had been passed to the German embassy in Paris. Although evidence of the Jewish officer's innocence subsequently came to light, high-ranking officers suppressed it, leading to widespread accusations of anti-Semitism, as well as demands for a retrial and Dreyfus's release.

The accession of Dreyfusard Loubet to the presidency in February 1899 following the death of Félix Faure proved the turning point in the affair. The new president instigated a review of the case, which led to Dreyfus's release from the notorious Devil's Island penal colony after four years of hard labour. But his actions also infuriated de Dion and the ardent nationalists in the self-styled League of Patriots who believed that the army must be backed in every eventuality and that France was under threat from people they regarded as subversives. Loubet's appearance at the Auteuil race-course provided them with a chance to voice their dismay.

Initially vocal, the protest quickly took on a more threatening edge. The Associated Press described how Baron Christiani 'raised his cane to strike the president with all his might. The blow was averted by General Balloud, and the cane, descending on M. Loubet's hat, crushed it down, forcing it over his face like a candle extinguisher.'

After half a dozen gendarmes had rescued Christiani from a severe roughing up at the fists of irate Loubet supporters 'with blood spurting from his nose', de Dion barrelled in, swinging his cane, its jewel-encrusted end breaking off after making contact with another officer's head. 'He was promptly arrested, but his arrest was an excuse to his friends to cry, "Resign", "Down with traitors, Jews and Dreyfusards"', AP reported, adding that Loubet was 'pale and greatly cut up, but firm', and that several ladies in his party had fainted.

De Dion was happy to receive his friend in La Santé even though their political differences had been so clearly underlined. 'He was a journalist of talent with whom I was on very good terms, because we were both fervent defenders of the automobile', he said of Giffard. 'During his visit he explained his opinion to me and told me that when it came to automobiles he would remain my friend and ally, but that in politics I would find in him a committed rival.'

Freed from La Santé, de Dion soon demonstrated that he shared Giffard's double-edged approach to their friendship. In March 1900, Giffard stood for election for the parliamentary seat of Yvetot and was tipped for a clear win. Yet in the run-up to the vote, Count de Dion had copies of Giffard's *La Fin du Cheval – The End of the Horse* – distributed throughout the constituency. In it, Giffard had written about his discovery of the bicycle, how it had changed his life for the better and how, crucially in this instance, it would replace the horse in rural areas. This message did not sit well in an agricultural constituency set in the heart of rural Normandy. 'It had a magical effect and, on the day of the vote, a certain majority was transformed into a resounding defeat,' de Dion crowed gleefully.

But the defeated man had his revenge. 'Giffard couldn't forgive me and decided he would no longer mention my name in his paper and banned absolutely any kind of publicity for the De Dion-Bouton brand, which bore the brunt of the grudge that he felt towards me,' Count de Dion said. 'Due to the fact that *Le Vélo* had a large readership, the decision was bound to have a severe impact on the De Dion-Bouton company. It was as a result of this concern that I decided to establish a newspaper to rival *Le Vélo*.'

That newspaper was *L'Auto-Vélo,* and this account fits the standard narrative of its founding, which stresses the political conflict arising from the furore over Dreyfus and the anti-Semitism so evident in that affair. However, as de Dion suggested, while political issues were key to the founding of *L'Auto-Vélo*, and, in turn, the Tour de France, commercial factors were also highly significant, arguably even more so.

In that period before the mass production of motor vehicles, manufacturers like De Dion-Bouton depended absolutely on sales to those with the money and time to indulge what was still a very exclusive and expensive passion for motoring. One of the best ways to reach out to them, although its title may suggest otherwise, was through *Le Vélo*'s pages. Branded as 'the daily journal for all sports', it had, since its foundation in 1892, focused heavily on motorsport and the latest developments in vehicle production, building up a circulation of 80,000. De Dion needed to reach these readers, and he wasn't the only one.

Several other key players in the nascent automobile industry, notably Adolphe Clément, Louis Renault and Édouard and André Michelin, felt that *Le Vélo*'s coverage was becoming skewed towards the rival automobile company headed by Alexandre Darracq, who had started out producing bicycles under the Gladiator name in the early 1890s. Darracq both financed *Le Vélo* and spent considerable amounts promoting his vehicles in its pages to its wealthy readers. Consequently, as Darracq's share of the burgeoning car market blossomed, it was inevitable that his rivals would establish a title through which they could talk up their own vehicles.

They sought out a man they felt could turn a new title into *Le Vélo*'s principal rival, and didn't have to look far to find him. Henri Desgrange had already worked in Clément's publicity department. He had subsequently established a reputation as one of the most forward-thinking businessman in France's thriving cycling industry.

One of twin boys born in 1865 to wood company owner and architect Jacques Desgrange and Marie Hortense Beaurens, Desgrange was working as a notary's clerk in Paris when he witnessed cycle racing for the first time. In 1891, he was among the crowd that watched the finale of the first edition of Bordeaux–Paris, won by Englishman George Pilkington Mills. Inspired by the intrepidness of the riders who had covered the 600 kilometres in little more than 24 hours, Desgrange bought a bike and started training on the roads between Versailles and Paris. 'I couldn't go to Versailles without thinking that Mills, the giant of Bordeaux–Paris, had passed the same way as me,' he wrote.

By 1893, Desgrange was well known on the Paris cycling scene. A regular contributor to a number of cycling periodicals, he set the first UCI-recognised mark for the World Hour Record that same year, completing 35.325km on the Buffalo track, so called because it was located at the place where William 'Buffalo Bill' Cody's Western show had set up camp when it had performed in Paris.

Sitting upright on a bike that weighed between 12–13kg and was fitted with spongey tyres that were a mighty 45mm wide and not fully inflated, Desgrange's effort looks rather feeble when compared to the 54.526km achieved by Sir Bradley Wiggins at the London Olympic Velodrome in June

2015. But it was groundbreaking at the time as the Frenchman was an amateur and consequently prohibited from riding with pace-makers, as professional racers almost always did in that era.

Desgrange went on to set a number of other distance records on the track over the next two seasons, but gained a greater reputation as a coach and race organiser. In 1894, he wrote a training guide, *La Tête et Les Jambes* (*The Head and the Legs*), directing copious and often very severe advice towards his 15-year-old self. He also served as director of the riders' union, was a member of the French cycling federation's (UVF) sporting commission and had overseen the running of two Paris velodromes, a third in Bordeaux and advised on the construction of a fourth in Madrid. He was also one of the main contributors to the magazine *Le Véloce Sport de Bicyclette*, wrote occasionally for Giffard's *Le Vélo* and had produced a cycling-related novel.

In 1897, with velodromes springing up all over France as entrepreneurs realised the financial possibilities of providing a programme of races to paying audiences that were often many thousands strong, Desgrange and business partner Victor Goddet financed and directed the construction of the Parc des Princes track, a groundbreaking venue thanks to its 666.66-metre ring of cement that was twice as long as most tracks. Dismissed by *Le Vélo* as too big and too far from the centre of Paris, the Parc was a great success, attracting huge crowds to watch the best riders of the era. Very much a man of the belle époque, that period between the Franco–Prussian War and the Great War which was characterised by peace and optimism that boosted economic, technological and cultural innovation, particularly among the moneyed classes, Desgrange sensed opportunities at every turn in cycling and sought them out.

On a clear April morning in 1900, Desgrange and Goddet made their way to Count de Dion's offices on the Avenue de la Grande Armée, often described as 'L'Avenue du Cycle' because of the number of bike shops along the grand tree-lined spoke that runs down from the hub of Étoile with the Arc de Triomphe at its centre. De Dion presented them with a simple proposal: would they consider establishing and managing a title to rival *Le Vélo*? Desgrange was tempted but uncertain. While keen to avenge that paper's dismissal of the Parc des Princes, which had been compounded by Giffard's refusal to take ads promoting the Parc's events, he knew that accepting the offer could imperil their track's future. Desgrange and Goddet slept on the proposition. The next morning, they accepted it.

The new associates then turned to deciding a name for the new title, settling on *L'Auto-Vélo (Cars and Bikes)*. It was the ideal choice given the commercial interests of the new title's backers, but it would come at a cost. Initially, this was relatively insignificant. During his forensic research for the biography *Desgrange Intime*, French writer Jacques Lablaine discovered that Count de Dion had spent 1,000 francs acquiring the weekly satirical and illustrated magazine *L'Auto-Vélo*, which had been established in 1897, but subsequently published only intermittently. His intention was clear. He wanted his new title to trade on the name of Giffard's well-established paper. But would the law allow this?

The bullish and arrogant de Dion assumed so, as no one had challenged the use of the name *L'Auto-Vélo* during its three years of existence. In judicial theory, this meant that no one now could. In this assumption, though, Count de Dion and *L'Auto-Vélo*'s other backers were mistaken.*

Thirty-nine shareholders bought the 400 shares in the relaunched version of *L'Auto-Vélo,* including aristocrats such as Baronet Sir David Salomons, whose father had founded what is now Natwest bank, and prominent industrialists like Renault, the Michelin brothers, Clément and, of course, Count de Dion, who purchased 192. It was an impressively influential line-up, but if de Dion had any thoughts of using the new title's pages to push any kind of extra-sporting agenda – and it is believed that he wanted to include a political pamphlet within the first issue – Desgrange crushed

---

* Lablaine's intricate research also revealed another interesting detail about Desgrange, which suggests that he was intending to launch a title to rival Giffard's well before he had received de Dion's proposal. In the archives of Préfecture de Police de la Seine, Lablaine turned up a document revealing that a 'Monsieur Desgrange Henri has lodged a declaration of intent to publish a newspaper entitled *L'Auto-Cycle* on 4 January 1899'. Consequently, several months before de Dion's attempted assault on President Loubet that set in motion the fall-out between the count and his good friend Giffard, Desgrange was already planning for the launch of a title to rival *Le Vélo,* one that wouldn't play on, pass off or plagiarise the title of the established market leader. This discovery also supports the belief that Desgrange's desire to take on Giffard was based primarily on commercial rather than political grounds.

these immediately. In the opening column on the first page of the inaugural edition of 16 October 1900, the penultimate paragraph stated, 'there will never be, in *L'Auto-Vélo*, any question of politics . . . you can count on *L'Auto-Vélo* never talking about this with you.' Desgrange remained as good as his word until the imminent outbreak of the Great War induced an anti-German tirade in 1914.

His more immediate concern was attracting readers to the new title. One of his first moves was to exploit a split between Hippolyte-Auguste Marinoni, the editor of *Le Petit Journal*, and Pierre Giffard to take over control of the second edition of the decennial race, Paris–Brest–Paris, which had been established by *Le Petit Journal* at Giffard's instigation in 1891. The first edition had caused a sensation, turning winner Charles Terront into France's first sporting star. The second running in 1901 proved no less impressive, pitching Lucien Lesna, Terront's successor as the nation's cycling icon and winner of Paris–Roubaix just a few weeks earlier, against Maurice Garin, already a two-time winner of that same event, which had quickly become one of the racing season's most prized titles.

Lesna reached the halfway point of the 1,200-kilometre race with a two-hour lead on his rivals. At Rennes, with the course three-quarters completed, Lesna paused for what he hoped would be a revitalising bath and meal. However, it had the reverse effect. Sapped by fatigue and a strong headwind, he fell victim to *la fringale*, that moment that almost every cyclist has experienced when the body's resources are all but exhausted and legs don't respond to the mind's urging to continue. With Paris almost in view, Garin overhauled the favourite, who failed to finish as the younger man soloed to glory.

Sales of *L'Auto-Vélo* soared for several days leading up to, during and just beyond Paris–Brest–Paris, but quickly tailed off to 30,000 a day once again, which was less than half of *Le Vélo*'s total. This presented Desgrange and his backers with a dilemma that remains to a degree in the modern era: how could they make events that were free-to-view financially viable? Their initial answer was to establish another race in the same ridiculously optimistic scale as Paris–Brest–Paris.

Without Marseille–Paris there might never have been a Tour de France. Run in May 1902, it was the first road event both invented and organised by Desgrange, and proved a huge popular success. Crucially, though, it planted the idea for an even grander event in the mind of *L'Auto-Vélo*'s cycling correspondent, Géo Lefèvre.

One of several editorial staff Desgrange had poached from *Le Vélo*, Lefèvre had first-hand experience of the extent of the antipathy between his new and his former boss. After receiving a job offer from Desgrange, he went to inform Giffard he was leaving. 'I felt I had to let my boss, the irascible Pierre Giffard, know about this offer I'd had from a rival, but as soon as I mentioned Desgrange's name Giffard wouldn't listen to me for a second longer and literally threw me out on to the pavement of Rue Meyerbeer where *Vélo* had its offices,' he recalled.

*

Desgrange, Lefèvre discovered, was 'a man as hard as my first boss', but the pair quickly established a tight bond. 'He was a hard man but in the good sense of the word, that's to say hard at work, both on himself and on others. Beneath his very tough exterior, he was a lovely chap, who, when you got to know him, had a good sense of humour and, in business, was liable to show emotion . . . but after he'd won the battle,' Lefèvre explained of his journalistic mentor.

Confident Marseille–Paris would replicate the sporting and financial success that *L'Auto-Vélo* had enjoyed the previous year with Paris–Brest–Paris, the paper announced a 6,000-franc prize for the winner, clearly intent on tempting the sport's leading performers to participate and in doing so turn their backs on Giffard's Bordeaux–Paris, which was scheduled to take place just two weeks later. This objective was achieved when Lesna and Garin registered to compete, setting up the delicious prospect of a revenge match between the major protagonists in Paris–Brest–Paris.

Marseille–Paris promised to create more of a stir than the established event, and not only because the route linked two of France's three biggest cities via the third, Lyon. Like many other parts of southern France, Marseille rarely featured as a venue for major sporting events. As a result, the local press and population greeted the new race with considerable fervour. In his evocative book on the event, *L'incroyable épopée de Marseille–Paris 1902*, Didier Rapaud reveals that this enthusiasm was much needed as sales of *L'Auto-Vélo* had dropped to between 18,000–22,000 copies a day by May

1902, a quarter of *Le Vélo*'s total. In order to reverse this decline, Desgrange and Goddet decided to print six special issues in addition to their daily, hoping that these would add tens of thousands of readers.

Less importantly for *L'Auto-Vélo*'s future, but of much greater significance for the sport's, Desgrange and his organising team also opted to open the race up to *touristes-routiers* riders as well as the headlining *coureurs de vitesse* (speed racers) such as Lesna and Garin. The latter always competed with *entraîneurs*, usually very gifted racers in their own right who worked in rotation as pace-makers for the star man with the backing of a major manufacturer or supplier.

Unable to call on support of this kind, the *touristes-routiers* had little hope of competing for the biggest prizes or even demonstrating their own potential as racers. Consequently, the introduction of a separate category for these solo performers, which included a 1,000-franc prize for the first *touriste-routier* to finish – the equivalent of almost six months' salary for the average working man in France – provided them with unprecedented motivation.

As riders began to sign in for the start in Marseille, news emerged that Garin would not be starting as a consequence of a chest infection picked up while undertaking a reconnaissance of the race route. This left pre-race favourite Lesna without a serious rival for the title and imperilled *L'Auto-Vélo*'s sales objectives. Desgrange, though, responded quickly, adjusting his paper's editorial emphasis from the duel between two huge rivals to a focus on the sheer scale of the test that Lesna and the other participants were up against. Although, at 938 kilometres, Marseille–Paris was almost 300 kilometres shorter than Paris–Brest–Paris, its hillier route, rougher roads and the likelihood that the field would be racing for the opening quarter of the race into the teeth of a strongly gusting mistral made it an extremely daunting prospect for those set to take part.

'It is demonstrably clear that battles such as these are epic and the men involved in them are heroes just like those who were once acclaimed and crowned with laurels in Greece,' wrote Lefèvre, who was charged with directing and covering the new race while Desgrange remained in Paris to oversee production of the organising paper's extra editions. While undoubtedly over the top, Lefèvre's words appear less so given what lay in store for the five dozen or so racers who lined up in Marseille . . .

AVENUE DE LA CANEBIÈRE, MARSEILLE, 17 MAY 1902

Opened just a few months before and bearing the name of its proprietor, the Café Riche on the corner of Cours Belsunce and the majestic La Canebière is the extremely sumptuous setting for the control point at the start. Open between nine on that Saturday evening and one on the Sunday morning, this temple of luxury that has quickly become a favourite haunt of

Marseille's bourgeoisie, who gather there to talk business and gossip over a coffee, lemonade or absinthe, is already packed when Italy's Giuseppe Ghezzi, a touriste-routier, *arrives and becomes the first rider to sign in.*

Soon after, Lucien Lesna makes an unexpectedly early appearance, adds his signature to Georges Abran's start sheet, then just as quickly disappears, returning to his hotel to get a couple of hours' sleep prior to the start in the early hours. No sooner has the Swiss-born, French naturalised rider departed than rumours of the non-participation of his main rival, Maurice Garin, are confirmed by the organisers. The buzz of excitement within the Café Riche turns to clamour. 'Can it be true? Will there be no rematch between Lesna and Garin? Can anything beyond bad luck prevent Lesna winning in Paris?'

It's a blow to the new race, and a heavy one, but as quickly as it comes it is forgotten. The Marseillais have waited too long to witness such a momentous sporting event to allow the absence of one rider to diminish their enthusiasm, even if he is one of the favourites. Captivated by what Midi Sportif *has described as 'this gigantic exploit' in which the participants will 'defy death a hundred times', excited spectators converge on their city's most renowned thoroughfare, allaying the organisers' fears that Garin's absence might prove fatal to their race's success.*

Riders continue to appear, each of them trailed by a throng of fans. By 11 o'clock, as the bands of the 159th infantry regiment and the 9th Hussars offer a totally unexpected musical interlude, the Canebière is jam-packed. It is nothing less than a Bastille Day in May, the carnival atmosphere completed by a parade of Marseille's 17 cycling clubs.

At one in the morning, Abran calls together the 58 riders who have signed in from the 104 who had registered and, with a wave, signals for them to proceed at a slow pace through Marseille's heaving streets towards the suburb of Saint-Antoine, where the official start will take place.

At three precisely, Abran first raises and then drops his arm, and Lesna and the other coureurs de vitesse flee into the darkness with their pace-makers, the setting moon providing illumination for less than an hour of their trek northwards. Five minutes later, the touristes-routiers, spare tubes wrapped around their shoulders, some equipped with the latest innovation for a cyclist wanting to maintain his speed in the form of a rubber tube that can be fitted to allow urination on the move, follow into the blackness.

Barely eight kilometres have passed when a crash almost ends Lesna's hopes. Already leading the field with his crack team of four pace-makers, the race favourite hears warning cries from the riders he's slipstreaming, but can't see or avoid a heap of rocks piled up at the roadside to be used on works for the Marseille to Aix-en-Provence tram line. Despite somersaulting two metres through the air, he is fortunate to escape with minor cuts and grazes and is quickly under way again, having abandoned his broken bike and jumped on one offered by one of his pace-makers. The delay enables Jean Fischer to take the lead.

Frenchman Fischer is first through the flying control point at Aix-en-Provence, shouting his name at the officials as he powers by. Lesna is next through the control, a minute later. Another minute passes before Belgium's René Kuhling and Italy's Rodolfo Muller fly by, followed soon after by Constant Huret and another Belgian, Marcel Kerff, who is not aware that his brother Charles has sustained fatal injuries in a crash.

Having, like Lesna, hit a pile of rocks at the roadside, the younger of the brothers has not been anywhere near as fortunate as the race favourite. Rather than sailing over the unlit obstacle, he has ploughed straight into it, the impact causing the metal water bottle attached to his chest to stave in his ribs and breastbone.

Picked up by a Monsieur Ricard, an Algerian motorist who happens to be passing the scene of the incident, the stricken Belgian is transported to the hospital in Aix. 'He had barely passed through the door of this establishment when a weak breath came from Kerff's lips. It was his last breath, the giant of the road had just passed away,' reports Le Midi Sportif, *while his brother races on towards Paris completely unaware of his sibling's fate.*

Fischer's spell in the lead is short-lived, although he doesn't immediately realise it. The darkness is so complete when Lesna and his line of pace-makers slip by a few kilometres north of Aix that his rival is unaware that he has been overtaken. With 900 kilometres remaining, Lesna will spend every one of them with just his entraîneurs for company.

When Lesna leaves Valence chomping on a chicken thigh

and with more a quarter of the route covered, his lead over Fischer has stretched to 40 minutes. Le Vélo correspondent Robert Coquelle, who has ridden with Lesna's little band for a few kilometres, pauses to send a telegraph to his office in Paris. 'As I sat down to dine, it struck me he'd just ridden Paris–Roubaix; Bordeaux–Paris now lay ahead,' he writes.

At Dijon, 300 kilometres later, Lesna's advantage has stretched to almost two hours. Here, the weather suddenly and unexpectedly worsens, an occasional drop of rain turning into a freezing deluge that transforms the surface of the earthen country roads into sludgy gloop that has the riders skating around, barely able to gain any traction. Fischer is among many who succumb in the incessant downpour, a crash leaving him with injuries that force him to abandon and provide Lesna with a three-hour lead on the second-placed rider, the blond and very suave Italian Rodolfo Muller.

Muddied and sodden, Lesna's speed drops from 30km/h to less than 20. 'At each control point I changed my jersey, my culottes, my stockings . . . I was no longer wearing anything that belonged to me. I ended up buying two pairs of gloves, four or five pairs of stockings, socks to put over my gloves. I got through several shirts, cut down long trousers to make culottes . . . I continued on, feeling the copies of L'Auto-Vélo that I'd put down the front of my shirt being transformed bit by bit into a liquid paste,' he will tell L'Auto-Vélo, unwittingly revealing that using a copy of the organising paper to keep the cold off your chest is already a custom among riders.

As the rain continues to teem down, Lesna's competitive

spirit is close to breaking. The only thing keeping him going is the encouragement he is receiving from his back-up team and the support he is getting from fans at the roadside and accompanying him on bikes. In the final few dozen kilometres to the finish in Paris at Ville d'Avray, the road is lined almost continually with fans who, despite the driving rain, have come out to see this incredible athlete.

Between two and three thousand cyclists are following him as members of the Garde Républicaine open a passage for him through a huge throng of spectators at the finish. Victory secured, he continues on to the Parc des Princes to complete two laps of honour in front of several thousand more ecstatic fans.

Lesna has completed what he describes as by far the toughest race he has ever tackled in a little under 39 hours, with Muller a full seven hours behind him in second. Third home is touriste-routier victor Gustave Pasquier, having covered the course unassisted in 48 hours and 35 minutes. Rather fittingly, the first rider to sign in at Café Riche is the 32nd and last man home, Italian Giuseppe Ghezzi, reaching Paris 87 hours after departing Marseille.

It would be easy to dismiss Géo Lefèvre's reports of thousands of spectators cramming the roadsides and waving handkerchiefs from upper storey windows as hyperbole from the man who had effectively run the event, were it not for the evidence of Marseille–Paris hysteria provided by *L'Auto-Vélo*'s sales. On 15 May, three days before the race started, it sold 115,200 copies, that figure climbing rapidly over successive days to reach 310,429 copies on 20 May, the issue reporting on Lesna's victory. In all, *L'Auto-Vélo* sold 1,462,279 copies over the week, plus another 700,000 of its six special issues, giving a total sale of 2,117,711 for a paper that would usually sell around 150,000 over that same period. The event also generated substantial revenue for the organising newspaper in the form of 'success' ads paid for by jubilant manufacturers.

Bearing in mind these figures and the huge enthusiasm that Marseille–Paris had generated on almost every part of its 938-kilometre route, the oft-cited depiction of Géo Lefèvre coming up with the idea for a Tour de France completely out of the blue and then tentatively suggesting his scheme to Henri Desgrange over a business lunch is largely fiction. In the wake of Paris–Brest–Paris and particularly Marseille–Paris, both men and, undoubtedly, *L'Auto-Vélo* finance director Victor Goddet, would have been completely aware of the impact high-profile road races could have on issue sales and revenue generation. What they lacked was a format for an event that would sustain sales over a longer period.

Three months later, *L'Auto-Vélo*'s hierarchy received further confirmation of the lift a big cycle race could have on sales when the paper organised its own version of Bordeaux–Paris just weeks after *Le Vélo*'s well-established edition of that event. As derivative and cheeky as the use of *L'Auto-Vélo* for their paper's title, the new race achieved what

Giffard's equivalent failed to by attracting Lesna and Garin to the start. Equipped with seven and eight pace-makers, respectively, their duel failed to live up to expectations as Lesna suffered a series of punctures and two bad crashes, which helped Garin to claim victory over his rival by an hour.

Lesna, incidentally, finished the race embittered, complaining that the many punctures he and his *entraîneurs* had suffered were the result of foul play. He alleged that nails and carpet tacks had been scattered on the course in front of them. Although he didn't name Garin or any member of his rival's support team, the implication was clear.

When the frenzy of excitement and sales generated by Marseille–Paris fizzled out, *L'Auto-Vélo's* circulation dropped back to around 30,000, still less than half of *Le Vélo's* total. Consequently, as the 1902 racing season drew to a close, it seemed that, despite the boosts provided by Paris–Brest–Paris, Marseille–Paris and Bordeaux–Paris, Giffard had triumphed in his battle with *L'Auto-Vélo*, particularly as his paper's case against their rival on a charge of passing off had been vindicated by a Parisian commercial court, pending an appeal by Count de Dion. The result of this was due in January 1903.

Desgrange's plan to run a second edition of his two new events wasn't the answer to his paper's circulation deficit, as he plainly realised. He needed something much more radical, something to 'shut that the mouth of that asshole Giffard', as Pierre Chany quotes him as telling his closest confidants on his staff during a meeting in his second-floor office at 10 Rue du Faubourg-Montmartre midway through the morning of 20 November.

There are plenty of accounts of this meeting, few of which agree precisely on what was said and by whom. It is not unusual for French sportswriters to invent dialogue to fit a historical scene, and this particularly celebrated instance appears to have been a victim of both this and delayed recollection of what happened by those present. What most accounts do agree on is the identity of some of those in Desgrange's office, who included cycling correspondent Géo Lefèvre and his colleague Georges Prade, who covered motorsport.

Chany records Lefèvre as saying: 'Let's organise a race lasting several days, longer than those that exist already. Something like the six-days on the track, but on the road. Major towns in the provinces are desperate to see bike racers, they will sign up to the idea.'

A person whom Chany refers to as 'a hitherto silent witness' and is perhaps Prade cuts in, saying: 'If I understand you properly, Géo, you're talking about setting the riders the task of completing a tour of France.'

'Why not, my dear fellow?' Lefèvre responds.

In a slightly different account based on his recollection of the meeting in *Ceux que j'ai rencontrés*, which was written more than a decade later, Lefèvre relates how Desgrange asked him and Prade to join him for an early lunch in the nearby Brasserie Zimmer – later to become the Café de

Madrid, where a plaque commemorates this gathering. Lefèvre admits in his memoir that he was close to panic as the trio made the short walk to the Zimmer as he had no clear idea of what he was going to say. In the end, he confesses, all he could come up with was a list of cities starting with Paris and circling around the country to reach the capital again.

'Why not have a Tour de France? It could have stages interspersed with rest days,' Lefèvre tentatively suggested.

Lefèvre's memoir recalls Desgrange being shocked by the idea and asking his correspondent if he'd gone mad. 'Do you want to kill the Garins and Lesnas of the era?' Desgrange added testily.

All accounts agree that Desgrange, Lefèvre and Prade returned from their lunch at the Zimmer and went straight to Goddet's first-floor office to seek his opinion. Many propose a rather theatrical scenario of this gathering where, rather than answer the question of whether they should organise the Tour or not, Goddet went to his safe, opened the door and simply gestured to its near emptiness, effectively saying we've got nothing to lose.

A conversation Desgrange had with a fellow journalist at the 1921 Tour supports the unavoidable impression that a good deal of this story has been embellished over subsequent decades. Speaking to *Sud-Ouest's* Léo Delberge during the Tour's stopover in Bayonne, Desgrange admitted that, 'the idea to organise the great cycling race that we know came from the record set by Théodore Joyeux, who lived at Castillonnès.' In 1895, Joyeux, a barber and part-time racer from Tonneins in south-west France, completed a 5,500-kilometre tour of the country.

Joyeux was no mug on a bike. He had finished ninth in the inaugural Paris–Brest–Paris won by Charles Terront and was a regular participant in other long-distance road events. For his tour of France, he received 2,200 francs from La Métropole to ride their revolutionary Acatène bike, which featured a drivetrain comprising a rack and pinion rod connecting the pedals to the rear wheel. He completed the epic test, carried out almost inevitably in appalling weather, in 19 days, averaging almost 300 kilometres per day.

An official history of the Tour published in 1908 provides further evidence of Desgrange's awareness and even obsession with Joyeux's exploit, recounting how he spent long hours plotting the rider's route on a huge map of France to the bewilderment of his colleagues. In addition, a monument erected in Tonneins in 2008 to commemorate Joyeux's extraordinary feat bears a plaque with a quote from Desgrange that states: 'It was Joyeux's exploit that provided me with the inspiration to create the 1903 Tour de France.'

While the most popular account of the moment that inspired the Tour now appears to lack substance, there is no absolutely no question regarding Desgrange's expectations about the court case his paper was embroiled in with Le Vélo. From the moment that the commercial court had issued its judgement on the case in January 1902, declaring that the former would have to change its name and pay fines amounting to 11,000 francs, Desgrange had been sure that an appeal would fail. He had voiced this opinion in a meeting of all of his paper's principal shareholders, where the confrontational Count de Dion had been equally adamant that he would not accept the court's decision and would appeal.

Indeed, so convinced was Desgrange of the futility of this appeal that on the day after the court's judgement, he registered a new title for a paper in order to prevent anyone else securing it first. Rather than switching to *L'Auto-Cycle*, his initial preference, he'd opted for the simpler title of *L'Auto*. It's not clear why he decided to drop the reference to cycling, although the court case may well have made him reluctant to choose any title with a cycling reference, fearing a further legal action by *Le Vélo*.

What is also beyond dispute is that Desgrange and Lefèvre spent a great deal of time shaping plans for their new race in between their Zimmer lunch on 20 November 1902 and the supreme court's verdict of 2 January 1903. When this came, the court ruled, as Desgrange had long suspected, that *L'Auto-Vélo* was legally obliged to remove the word 'vélo' from its title. Exactly two weeks later, the first edition of *L'Auto* appeared on the news-stands. Identical in every way apart from its title to *L'Auto-Vélo*, its staff and backers clearly hoped the change wouldn't affect the size of its readership.

Confirmation of the change meant that Desgrange could finally start to announce the new title's racing calendar for the coming season. Consequently, the very next day, 17

January 1903, *L'Auto* hinted at 'a great road cycling race that will be of such interest that we will make special mention of it in the days ahead'.

Two days later, the first column on the opening page of *L'Auto* provided the first details of the new race. Under the headline 'Le Tour de France', the first time that name had appeared anywhere, the sub-head announced: 'The greatest cycling race in the entire world. A race lasting more than a month. Paris–Lyon–Marseille–Toulouse–Bordeaux– Nantes–Paris, 20,000 francs in prizes. Start: 1 June. Finish: 5 July at the Parc des Princes.'

Further down in the small and very dense text that was typical of newspapers in that era, *L'Auto* revealed that a general classification would be established based on cumulative time recorded on each stage, that riders would be able to change their bikes if they were damaged, that the winner would receive 3,000 francs and, perhaps picking up on the success of the *touristes-routiers* in Marseille–Paris, the use of pace-makers would only be allowed on the final stage.

But could Desgrange and his staff turn this groundbreaking proposal into reality?

CHAPTER 2

'THE PHANTOM RACE' TAKES SHAPE

Now long established as one of the great events on the sporting calendar, the Tour de France was born in a period of rapid industrial, social and economic change, comparable to the dotcom revolution that would reshape the industrialised world a hundred years later at the turn of the millennium. The belle époque was a golden age of progress and prosperity that featured the invention of the telephone, telegraph and cinema. Electric lights illuminated city streets. Trains were making travel easier and bringing far-flung destinations within reach of Europe's major cities, most famously Constantinople with the establishment of the Orient Express. Motorised vehicles were becoming more commonplace, and bicycles substantially more so.

Driven by the thirst for knowledge, innovation and adventure, there were advances on all sides. As *L'Auto*'s staff set to work on organising the Tour, the Wright Brothers were making final preparations for the first powered flight, the Ford Motor Company was working on its first vehicle, the Model A, and the Trans-Siberian Railway was nearing completion. The start of Norwegian Roald Amundsen's three-year voyage to negotiate the North-West Passage highlighted the enthusiasm for polar exploration, which *L'Auto* underlined with a report on a rich American couple, the Goldens, setting out on an expedition to drive from northern Canada to the North Pole in a heavily adapted car, hoping to make the return trip in ten hours. Although no update of their attempt appeared in Henri Desgrange's paper, their quest highlighted the sense of intrepidness, invention and often plain lunacy that marked that era.

At the centre of all this optimism and progress was Paris. Revitalised during the Third Republic that had been established during the course of France's demoralising defeat in the Franco–Prussian War of 1870–71, the French capital's status as 'the city of lights' and as one of the world's great centres had been cemented by its hosting of the World Fair in 1889, which saw the construction of the Eiffel Tower as the entrance to the exhibition area.

Described by Italian writer Paolo Facchinetti as 'the epicentre of an earthquake of upheaval that also transformed into a philosophy for life', Paris was a magnet for entrepreneurs and artists from all over the world. It was, according to Facchinetti, 'studded with concert-cafes, music halls, a kind of free zone where anything was possible and everything

was permitted . . . to go to a boxing match between a kanga-
roo and a man or a show featuring a Burman family who
were covered with hair or the incredible Joseph Pujol, "Le
Pétomane", a flatulist who appeared at hugely popular ven-
ues such as the Moulin Rouge and the Folies-Bergère with
an act in which he sucked air into his rectum and blew a
candle out from several yards away, and farted the tune of
La Marseillaise or *O Sole Mio*.

Within this context, the Tour, which was both groundbreaking and exceptional, was very much in line with the
zeitgeist for extraordinary innovation. Although initially
viewed as rather madcap even by some of those most closely
associated with it, the Tour was broadly welcomed in the
French press, *Le Journal* hailing the 'colossal cycling event
that is going to be organised by our colleagues at *L'Auto*',
while *Le Figaro* described it as 'a monstrous race . . . that is
guaranteed to cause a sensation due to its enormity'.

Only *Le Vélo* remained silent, a fact that didn't escape
Géo Lefèvre's attention. Two days on from the announcement in *L'Auto*, he pointed out: 'The only paper that's now
called *Le Vélo* won't deign to devote a single line – yes, you
understand me perfectly – not a single line to this bicycle
race, the most sensational organised since the invention of
cycle sport.' This did, finally, prompt *Le Vélo* into producing
an 11-word story on the new event.

Yet *Le Vélo*'s mulish disregard for the Tour was never likely
to have much of an impact on press and popular interest in
the new race. It took shape at a time when an increasingly

literate population with more spending power and free time was eager for new experiences, and cycling had already proved well capable of fulfilling this desire for entertainment and adventure.

Ever since Englishman James Moore won the first significant place-to-place cycle race on 7 November 1869 between Paris and Rouen, cycling had been a focus for the French public's search for competitive and leisure diversion. Riding a velocipede built by the Michaux company that was equipped with a larger, pedal-driven front wheel, Moore completed the 123-kilometre course in 10 hours and 40 minutes. Among the 32 finishers behind Paris-based Moore were two women. The first of them, placed 29th, was using a pseudonym, Miss America, which betrayed not only a sense of humour but also awareness of the often hostile attitude towards the growing push for female emancipation in the second half of the nineteenth century.

Set back by the outbreak of the Franco–Prussian War, bicycle production in France picked up again after 1871, when the desire for greater speed led to the rapid growth in size of the front wheel and the emergence of the 'ordinary' or 'penny-farthing'. The obvious flaw in a design that set the rider high off the ground was safety. Strike a pothole, of which most roads had plenty, or a rival competitor and a rider was very likely to 'come a cropper', as a newly coined English phrase had it.

The ordinary was anything but that in terms of price. During the 1870s and into the mid-1880s, the bicycle was very much the preserve of the moneyed classes, an item of conspicuous consumption. In 1885, French periodical *Véloce Sport* commented that racers were 'a sect to a certain degree' and quoted a Rouen councillor as saying that 'to be a cyclist you require a small fortune'. That situation began to change, however, with the development of the safety bicycle, which featured wheels that were equal or close in size and a chain-driven rear wheel. The template for the modern-day bike, the safety bicycle quickly superseded the ordinary, its security and comfort aided by the invention of the practical pneumatic tyre by Scot John Boyd Dunlop in 1888.

Previously little more than a means of diversion for those with plenty of spending power, the bicycle quickly transformed into an affordable means of transport and leisure for those on far more modest incomes and became a viable alternative to the horse or Shanks's pony. Existing manufacturers flourished and many more emerged to fill the demand for this new steed, costs tumbling as worldwide production increased from a few tens of thousands a year to millions. Between 1890 and 1900, the number of bicycles registered for taxation in France alone rose from a little more than 50,000 to 975,878, with similar growth recorded in Great Britain and other European countries, as well as the United States. In 1903, the French government's 4.50-franc tax on 1,416,666 bikes yielded 6,375,000 million francs. Many tens of thousands more were employed in public service and therefore not eligible for taxation.

As sales boomed, manufacturers used racing to promote

their products, focusing primarily on the huge popularity of track events as velodromes sprang up in cities across the industrialised world. By the end of the century, Paris had more than half a dozen, including the Buffalo, suggested by the great British racer H. O. Duncan, financed by Folies-Bergère director Clovis Clerc and featuring Desgrange as its technical director during construction, the Charenton, and later on Desgrange and Victor Goddet's Parc des Princes. London had a similar number. Interest in the star names who competed on them was such that sports papers such as Le Vélo and L'Auto published not only results from track meetings across Europe and the United States but also reports on track training sessions, which were often well attended.

In some cases, this hugely popular and very commercial-ised means of mass entertainment extended to running novelty events alongside the serious racing. Scantily clad actresses, clowns and acrobats appeared on bikes in an attempt to boost profits. However, the public responded in far bigger numbers when offered greater spectacle, speed and endurance rather than more trivial fare such as this. As a result, out went dancing girls on bikes and in came brutally tough six-day and 100-hour races, which pushed participants right to their physical limits.

The first notable event of this kind in France took place in 1893 at the Vélodrome d'Hiver, better known as the Vel d'Hiv, which was then located within the Galérie des Machines that had been created for the World Fair four years earlier. It featured France's first sports star, Paris–Brest–Paris victor Charles Terront, who had recently completed a 3,000-kilometre ride from Saint Petersburg in Russia to the Buffalo Vélodrome in 14 days. The now veteran champion's opponent was Breton Valentin Corre, third in that year's Bordeaux–Paris. Corre challenged 'Napoterront' to a 1,000-kilometre, 2,500-lap endurance race that would last for the best part of two days.

Organiser Paul Meylan later said of the contest that 'The most important feature of that event was the nature of the crowd it attracted and the effect such spectacles had on the masses. This was the beginning of cycle racing as a popular spectacle.' Yet, the event didn't have the most promising of starts. Each rider was able to call on no fewer than 40 pace-makers. However, rather than employing them to race flat out, the two men sat in behind their pacers with the sole aim of waiting for the other to crack.

After a first night with little to report on, some papers railed against 'this unhealthy exhibition' and the 'idiotic and useless race', but the public's interest grew as the hours passed and neither Corre nor Terront stopped to pee. Three times Terront slowed, apparently in order to answer the call of nature. Corre slowed too, desperate to do so, only to see Terront speed up and return to his former steady pace.

After 27 hours, Corre couldn't hold on any longer. He rolled to a stop. His pace-makers and soigneurs surrounded him on the track's infield, allowing him to relieve himself as Terront gained six laps. The next morning, as the contest continued, the papers unearthed Terront's secret: a section of inner tube that had been cut open on one side. When the seasoned pro needed to use it, he slowed and his pace-makers gathered around him, sheltering him from view. Once he'd completed the business in hand, Terront would pass the tube to one of his pace-makers, who would surreptitiously empty it as he circled the track. The revelation caused such a rush for tickets that the police had to be called, Terront eventually completing the duel in a shade under 42 hours, with a lead of nine kilometres on the embittered Corre.

Gripping as this was, promoters and the public wanted a more intense and varied spectacle. For the next two years they got precisely that from American sprinter Arthur Zimmerman who won his own national title and then added the British crown. Hailed as unbeatable, 'Zim' generally was, Europe's top riders lining up to challenge him on tracks across the continent, and most often in Paris. As his period of dominance ended, another huge draw emerged on the track scene, Marshall 'Major' Taylor, regarded as one of the greatest sprinters of all time and one of the tiny few in that period at the end of the nineteenth century who was African-American.

Taylor caught the eye of French journalist Robert Coquelle during a six-day race at New York's Madison Square Garden. Unlike their modern equivalent that feature racing across six consecutive evenings, the original Sixes ran non-stop, day and night. Attendances were biggest on the final three days, when riders would often collapse on the track, zig-zag or even ride in the wrong direction on the track due to exhaustion. No wonder, then, that Taylor leapt at the chance to take on Europe's best in match sprint contests that stretched to seconds rather than days.

Taylor was initially pitted against Edmond Jacquelin, the French sprint champion who was reputed to have the fastest acceleration among all track riders. In the weeks building up to their contest, the press covered the preparation of both riders in intricate detail and marvelled at Taylor's muscular physique. A week before the match at Desgrange's Parc des Princes, tickets were selling on the black market for three times their advertised price. Unfortunately, on the day, the American's relative lack of experience shone through. Surprised by Jacquelin's phenomenal acceleration coming out of the final bend, Taylor lost by a distance. 'If we do this all over again, the result won't be the same,' he promised. Ten days later, the American lived up to his word, countering Jacquelin's burst and then outpacing the Frenchman easily at the line.

Over the next two years Taylor had continued to compete regularly at Desgrange's Parc des Princes, becoming the biggest draw in cycle sport. During the 1899 season, however, the pair fell out after Taylor approached Desgrange and told him his next appearance at the Parc would be his last because he had been offered more to race at the Buffalo. When Taylor returned to collect his fee, Desgrange paid for it with a sackful of 10-centime pieces, for which a carriage had to be hired to transport it to Taylor's bank.

Although Taylor's contests with Europe's elite sprinters

continued to generate headlines for the next four seasons, track racing's headlining status was almost at an end. In 1899, a weekly sporting periodical, *La Vie au Grand Air,* which stood out over its rivals thanks to its evocative photographs of sporting events and those watching them, suggested interest in track-racing was waning 'after the fantastic and exaggerated passion for cycling spectacles two or three years ago'. In the wake of Jacquelin's duels with Major Taylor, the public's focus began to switch towards road racing, which was more unpredictable and compelling, and tied in far more with the experiences of the increasing number of people who were using a bike to explore the countryside around them. It also cost nothing to watch and by its nature reached out to a new audience in rural areas.

One event particularly highlighted this change of emphasis: Paris–Roubaix. First run in 1896 in order to promote the opening of the new velodrome in the textile city hard against France's Belgian border, it initially had a supporting role, offering paying fans the sight of muddied and exhausted riders slogging around the new arena as a prelude to events featuring clean and sprightly trackies. Yet, from its very first edition, won by French-based German Josef Fischer, it drew a strong field and had considerable prestige.

Comprising 50-odd kilometres of riding on cobbled roads and paths, with the remaining 230 kilometres run on yellowish earth roads pocked with holes rather than the well-surfaced roads of today, it followed established practice in allowing the use of pace-makers, enabling the leading road performers to use it as preparation for Bordeaux–Paris, which ran a month later and at that time had higher status. What these two races shared with each other and also had in common with six-day and other long-distance track events was what Richard Holt describes in *Sport and Society in Modern France* as 'fin-de-siècle fanaticism', still very much in evidence at Roubaix these days, when it remains the most obvious throwback to road racing's early days and is arguably the sport's most popular event after the Tour de France.

As ticket sales for six-days and for contests such as that between Terront and Corre repeatedly underlined, the public craved excess and the only limit on this was the imagination of race organisers. Prior to the birth of the Tour, their recipe for sating this craving was an increasingly meaty diet of place-to-place races: Paris–Rouen, Paris–Brest–Paris, Bordeaux–Paris, Paris–Roubaix and, seemingly the most over-the-top and crazed of all, Marseille–Paris. Yet, these events essentially reprised the same format, which provided a spike of interest and, consequently, higher sales for newspaper proprietors and bike manufacturers, but did not maintain interest in what were two extremely competitive markets.

The Tour, though, promised to have a far more sustained impact, drawing in readers not only across the five weeks over which the race was scheduled to take place, but also in the lead-up and subsequent to it. However, the weeks that followed *L'Auto*'s announcement on the innovative format didn't augur well for the revamped title and its exceptional event.

Most worryingly for Desgrange, Count de Dion and the paper's other backers, sales dropped, often falling below the 20,000-mark as two new dailies, *Le Monde Sportif* and *Les Sports,* entered this niche market. *L'Auto*'s content may have remained the same following its court-enforced name change, but a daily entitled called 'The Car' was never likely to have as broad a reach among readers as 'Car and Bike', despite Desgrange's plea to readers to show loyalty to his title.

In the month following Desgrange's announcement of the Tour de France, *L'Auto* barely mentioned its new cycling event on page one of what was generally a six-page paper. There was news of Paris–Roubaix, of the Paris–Madrid automobile race, but very little about the Tour. Even though Desgrange wrote in his editorial column on 14 February that his intention was 'to give people, who haven't already witnessed it, a spectacle providing the most beautiful demonstration of cycle sport and to the winner fame equal to that of Charles Terront,' *L'Auto* appeared to be holding back from complete commitment to the race, perhaps through fear of impending fiasco or, more probably, as a result of the huge logistical task required to organise this unprecedented sporting event, which was set to be far bigger in scope and duration than the second Olympic Games in Paris three years earlier.

While the Tour de France remained in the background,

the ongoing feud between *L'Auto* and *Le Vélo* took a bizarre turn that same month when a correspondent from each title fought a duel stemming from a dispute relating to the recent foundation of a French boxing federation. Widely reported in the press, the contest was between Léon Manaud, athletics correspondent at *L'Auto*, and Frantz Reichel, a senior figure at *Le Figaro* as well as *Le Vélo*, who had won a gold medal at the 1900 Olympics as a member of France's winning rugby team and was, coincidentally, the writer responsible for the criticism of Desgrange and Goddet's Parc des Princes track six years earlier.

The pair settled their argument using swords in a duel at a private property near Neuilly, not far from the Bois de Boulogne in eastern Paris. Writing in *Le Sport Univers Illustré*, one of their peers described their contest in detail, pointing out that 'it is naturally always dangerous to play with knitting needles when your rivals are present because when they cross each other it can easily lead to a conclusion that we would all deplore', and then went on describe duels that had ended tragically, including for those looking on or acting as seconds.

Noting that the two rivals showed very correct fencing form, which would have been expected of gentlemen in that era, the writer continued: 'Thankfully, this wasn't the case in the duel that I've just been talking to you about today as the contest was stopped after M. Léon Manaud received a wound that lightly penetrated his right forearm.'

Manaud's defeat presaged another for his newspaper.

L'Auto had set the eve of the Tour, 31 May, as the deadline for registration. Yet at the start of that month little more than a dozen riders had signed up to compete. The length of the race was the most common criticism, especially among *touriste-routier* riders who couldn't afford to be away from their day jobs for that amount of time, particularly as most would return out of pocket due to the cost of lodgings, food and other supplies that would be incurred. Marseille–Paris winner Lucien Lesna was also dismissive of the format that allowed riders to opt in and out of stages, while other observers wondered how it would be possible to prevent riders being paced and receiving other support during night-time riding, *Le Vélo* deriding it as 'not a race but a free-for-all'.

Within *L'Auto*'s offices, other issues had emerged as a result of a reconnaissance of the route undertaken by one of the paper's reporters, who informed Desgrange and his editorial team of roads that were unfit for racing, local officials who couldn't grasp the concept of the event and of a lack of financial resources in some areas scheduled to welcome it. As they went up and down the spiral staircase that connected their offices to discuss the growing mountain of difficulties, Desgrange and Goddet came close to calling off the Tour de France, 'the phantom race' as *Le Vélo* witheringly described it. But these barbs spurred them on. Rather than abandoning the scheme, Desgrange opted to rein it in with the aim of making it more manageable for his team and more attractive to potential competitors.

On 6 May, Desgrange hinted at the change about to come.

'These last few days we've seriously considered abandoning the Tour de France in the face of the racers' lack of interest in this event . . . We are hesitating, they tell us, because we are fearful of the consequences of being away from home for six weeks. And it's not just the length of that absence, but the costs of the race as well!' A few days later, Desgrange announced a shorter event, starting in Paris on 1 July and returning to the capital to finish on 19 July.

He backed up this revamp by applying pressure to the teams and manufacturers that supported the leading riders, and encouraging his paper's powerful backers to adopt the same policy. Count de Dion, in particular, must have been difficult to resist. Restlessly busy, confrontational, immense in stature and character, he had recently been elected a member of parliament and his attention was turning much more towards politics. However, like Desgrange, who 'wasn't short of lucidity, malice, nor of cunning', according to Pierre Chany, Count de Dion could still not resist the craving to obliterate Giffard's paper, even though Giffard himself was devoting much more time writing about politics for *Le Matin*.

Although Desgrange's hopes for a second rematch between Lucien Lesna and Maurice Garin were scuppered when the former crashed while training and sustained injuries that prevented him from starting, Garin was among those who signed up for the Tour, along with Hippolyte Aucouturier, who completed the Paris–Roubaix/Bordeaux–Paris double that spring, and Léon Georget, runner-up at Bordeaux–Paris and winner of the prestigious Bol d'Or 24-hour endurance race at the Buffalo track. More registrations followed.

On 11 June, Géo Lefèvre announced another coup, confirming that Germany's Josef Fischer would be lining up along with compatriot Ludwig Barthelman, the 48th and 49th riders to commit to the Tour. Winner of the inaugural edition of Paris–Roubaix in 1896 and Bordeaux–Paris four years later, 38-year-old Fischer may have been in the twilight of his career, but his name would have been very familiar to sports fans. In what would become *L'Auto*'s stereotypically hyperbolical style for introducing the Tour's riders, Lefèvre signalled that the German veteran 'has been training for two months and that he is in top form'.

The fact that Fischer was no longer backed by a bike manufacturer didn't faze the Tour's originator either. Lefèvre presented this as an opportunity, explaining that, 'Being free of any commitments at the moment, the German champion has asked us to announce that he would be at the disposition of any brand that would like to lend him the bikes required for the whole race. Let notice be given to the big "teams" that would like to take advantage of the German ace's services. They only need let us know and we will pass on their offers to Josef Fischer.'

Further details of the prizes and payments that would be available to riders appeared on the same page, emphasising to those who were still considering registering to race that 'an indemnity of five francs per day will be given by *L'Auto* to all those who finish in the first 50 places and haven't won 200 francs in prize money and have completed all of the stages at a speed in excess of 20 kilometres per hour.' For those unsure of the maths, the paper helpfully pointed out that completing 19 days of racing would earn them 95 francs.

When Parisian Julien Girbe became the 50th competitor to register, Lefèvre couldn't resist penning a waspish opinion piece clearly directed at Giffard and *Le Vélo*. 'This time we've achieved our target and the list is still not closed,' he began, referring to the false start little more than a month earlier. 'We were completely certain that we would reach the figure of 50 registrations that we thought was necessary to put on the Tour de France. Yet, my good friends, those who only like sport when it is in their interests, were already hailing the probable abortion of the most beautiful road race that has ever been imagined . . .'

In the days running up to the start of the Tour, *L'Auto* offered insight into the enormity of the logistical task its staff, correspondents and many thousands of volunteers had undertaken to get the race off the ground. The paper's correspondent in Orléans, who signs himself 'Harry', described a meeting at the city's Hotel de Berry, where, 'The inspector-general of *L'Auto*, Monsieur Abran, has just given a very interesting talk on the genesis of the Tour de France and on the organisation of this race that is destined to revolutionise all of sporting France for two weeks.' Also present was one of the pre-race favourites Hippolyte Aucouturier, looking 'resplendent with good health' according to 'Harry', who concluded by noting that all of the organisation relating to the race with the city would be undertaken by the members of a single cycling society.

Meetings of this kind took place in every village, town and city that would feature a stage start or finish, or a fixed (requiring riders to dismount and sign their name before proceeding) or a 'flying' control point. Thanks to reconnaissance of the route undertaken by the paper's staff, riders, correspondents and, in many cases, readers, *L'Auto* was also able to provide substantial detail on the conditions of the roads in every area, where possible danger points might lie in the form of steep descents or sharp bends, and what influence the elements might have.

When registration closed in mid-June, 80 riders had signed up to tackle the 2,428-kilometre route, while another 24 registered for individual stages. With two weeks remaining to the start, *L'Auto* could now turn its attention to raising the status of these racers, many of whom were complete unknowns, and drawing in new readers – the fates of both the paper and the race depending on this.

CHAPTER 3

'A GREAT EVENT BEYOND OUR IMAGINATIONS'

Once Henri Desgrange and Count de Dion had cajoled, per-suaded and twisted the arms of riders and their teams, *L'Auto* had a very mixed bag of racers signed up for the first Tour de France. Half a dozen – Maurice Garin, Léon Georget, Hip-polyte Aucouturier, Jean Fischer, Rodolfo Muller and Josef Fischer – had a palmarès worthy of star billing. Another half dozen or so had obtained decent results in professional races or shown the potential to do so, while the rest were mostly complete unknowns, even to experts such as Desgrange and Géo Lefèvre. Like the Goldens undertaking their return trip to the North Pole, many were completely unprepared for the challenge that they were about to take on and had been drawn in by the tantalising lure of prizes well in excess of their wages as butchers, smiths, carpenters and office clerks: 'With a few francs you could win 3,000!' *L'Auto* had proclaimed.

In the week leading up to the start, *L'Auto* listed the CV of every competitor who registered for the opening stage, its listing on 26 June typifying the paper's editorial line, which was clearly to inflate any essence of ability and to always highlight every rider's courage.

JAY (Paris), 24, on leave from his regiment. Without the assistance of pace-makers he finished fifth in Bordeaux–Paris 1899, behind Huret, Garin, Fischer and Rivierre. Also fifth in Paris–Roubaix 1899. In the last Bordeaux–Paris he finished eighth after numerous punctures. Great endurance, will certainly be one of the dangerous competitors.

GUILLARME (Troyes), 26, endurance champion of the Aube, regional record-holder for 6 hours, for the 100km (2hrs 40). Lacking soigneurs and pace-makers, and after numerous punctures, he finished 14th in *L'Auto*'s Bordeaux–Paris 1902.

DARGASSIES (Grisolles, Tarn-et-Garonne), 30. Has never raced, but is an experienced rider and hopes to finish among the leaders. Over the course of two months, he's covered more than 3,000 kilometres.

CATTEAU (Tourcoing). An excellent roadman who will be in his pomp in the Tour de France.

MOULIN (Belle-Isle-en-Terre), 40. Winner of the Coupe des Routiers in 1900, of the *routiers* category in Paris–Épernay, Paris–Dieppe. Figured very honourably in Paris–Brest–Paris and Marseille–Paris. Consequently, an experienced and solid roadman.

This list was typical of those that appeared in the days before and after, and encapsulated the talent that would be on display between 1 and 19 July. For every Jay, there were four Moulins or Dargassies. Yet Lefèvre, who put together these pocket profiles, quickly turned the presence of these unknowns to his paper's advantage. He talked up the possibility that one of them might emerge from complete obscurity to threaten the established names and pointed to the prohibition of pace-makers on all but the final stage as a good reason to believe the playing field would be levelled between the stars and those expected to do no more than make up the numbers. It would be 'a race with equal weapons', he regularly repeated.

The example of Jean Dargassies, a blacksmith from a small town close to Montauban in south-west France, is particularly noteworthy given the way he had caught the attention of Lefèvre when he had signed in at *L'Auto*'s offices the day before this list appeared in its pages.

'Yesterday I met a competitor who delighted me,' Lefèvre begins, before going to present Dargassies' extraordinary tale. 'A very nice chap, not very big, but stocky with wide shoulders, thighs and calves like pillars, a weather-beaten face, smiling eyes, a long blond moustache, and a goatee beard.

— I'm Dargassies, from Grisolles, and I've come to ask you for information on the Tour de France.
— But haven't you read *L'Auto* yet? You're already signed up to ride.
— Oh! They read *L'Auto* in Monnetaubanne [writes Lefèvre, taking off Dargassies' southern accent], but I don't have the time. It was Gladiator's agent, the one who sold me my bike, who told me one day that there was going to be a race known as the Tour de France. So I said to myself: 'Dargassies, that's right up your street!' And I asked the agent to sign me up. And here I am now, so please let me have the details.
— Have you already raced?
— Oh, just the once. A brevet, as they call them. A hundred kilometres in three hours. But that doesn't count. It only featured 'clowns' who finished an hour and a half later. However, on five occasions over the past three months I've done Montauban and back in one go, which is almost 500 kilometres [in total]. And that without eating much for training purposes.
— So do you know who your rivals will be?
— No, but I'm not bothered by that. They will know me soon enough.
— You've never heard talk of Garin?

— Garin? No, I don't know him.

— And Aucouturier?

— No, him neither.

'So I filled Dargassies in on the details . . .' Lefèvre concludes, his glee at finding a neophyte ready to take on all
comers, and never mind what their reputations were, very
apparent in his story.

There were plenty more in the same mould as Dargassies,
such as 19-year-old Elie Monge from Pierrelatte, who Lefèvre
describes as 'a very good roadman but without any previous results'; 28-year-old Parisian Lucien Barroy, 'a former
clown acrobat who has turned to cycling, a gentleman of
truly royal manner, but also the king of unfortunates. If
he has a little bit of luck, he will figure very strongly in the
Tour de France'; Parisian A. Lassartigues, who is 'a very good
roadman. He finished second in a four-day race in Buenos
Aires in 1902 and knows the route very well'; and Benjamin
Mounier, 'an experienced rider who has never raced. He has
arrived on the Tour de France route via Nantes.'

As well as Lefèvre's overstating of the ability of many of
the riders, the inclusion of their hometown or region was
also hugely important in boosting *L'Auto*'s potential sales.
Like most of the paper's readers, a significant percentage of
the riders either hailed from Paris or had spent a considerable part of their life in the French capital, where literacy
rates and interest in cycling were at their highest. Yet in
order to encourage the success of the Tour in the provinces,

Lefèvre played up regional links, underlining the fact that this was not only a Tour de France but a race for men from all across the nation.

It was essential for *L'Auto* to highlight riders in this way as this would guarantee interest in the local papers and encourage spectators out on the roadside as the race worked its way around France. This would, in turn, increase sales of the organising paper, which aimed to be the most up-to-date source of news. This policy continues in the current era, when *le régional de l'étape*, the stage's local rider, is still guaranteed to garner considerable attention in the French media, and especially the provincial papers.

The editorial policy of over-exaggeration, which was vigorously encouraged by Desgrange, extended to the invention of nicknames that either played up some physical characteristic or rooted the riders to their origin, adding to their aura. Consequently, Alexandre Foureaux was anointed and consistently referred to 'The Flying Carpenter', Lucien Pothier became 'The Butcher of Sens' and Émile Pagie 'The Prince of the Mines'. Desgrange also insisted on adjectival exaggeration, so that Maurice Garin was often described as 'a giant' despite being just 1.60m (five foot, three inches). His main rival, Aucouturier, was 'The Hercules of Commentry', but only stood a few centimetres taller.

It followed that similarly florid descriptions were also applied to the Tour de France. Two days prior to the start, Lefèvre explained the extent of the challenge, 'which is going to light up the whole of France not for a few hours but for 19 days. I'll repeat once again, tell you once more that men just like us are going to be grappling on consecutive occasions on routes that are almost all as hard as Bordeaux–Paris, remember the feelings of stupefaction and admiration that you felt on the arrival of a Maurice Garin or an Aucouturier in Paris, when men finished covered in dust and mud having ridden for hours and hours, climbed hills, tumbled down descents, had seen the moon replace the sun in the sky, then seen it return in the east after it had set in the west, and all that while we were all going about our ordinary everyday business, yes remember all of that and see now the full extent of the task that these human beings are going to undertake.'

Delivered in a sentence that's as epic as the event being described, this magnification of the test ahead continued day after day. Subsequently, Lefèvre evoked 'this enormous ring of white road that runs all around France with Paris as the knot at its centre,' and affirmed that 'the Tour de France is a great event that goes beyond all imagination'.

L'Auto had received reports from riders training on the route such as Muller and Aucouturier, the latter admitting his astonishment at passing through some places where the locals had never seen a bicycle. 'A dozen times I heard peasants exclaiming about my "makine" or my "varicopete" as I was passing by,' he told Lefèvre. 'And there are also still towns and villages where they have no knowledge at all of cycle sport. Your Tour de France is going to create a real revolution among people like those.'

Picking up on this, Lefèvre pointed out the commercial and moral benefits of the Tour, making it clear to manufacturers that, 'The Tour de France . . . completes a tour of France. The curious folk who will have inspected the machine of a competitor who has stopped for a moment on the road, at a village auberge or at the hotel that's acting as a control point, those inquisitive folk are future purchasers. And when the victorious manufacturer launches a poster-based publicity campaign, it will find it just as productive.'

The commercial prompting is well demonstrated by another piece of Lefèvre hyperbole in the run-up to the start, as he pointed out that, 'Anyone who has seen a race wants to race. There are still places where they don't know what a bicycle race is. Next month they will find out just about everywhere.' If that wasn't clear enough, he immediately went on to emphasise his point by declaring: 'And in all areas, L'Auto will also have spread its reach more widely. Reading our beloved paper, which has such an elevated goal, will convert many of those who have remained unexposed to it up until now . . . because they didn't know about it . . . Everyone will understand that the Tour de France is a thing of greatness and much more than a gigantic sporting event.'

Equally important, though, to Desgrange as L'Auto plugging itself as the ideal place for manufacturers to promote their products was the moral aspect of the Tour de France. This was a nation still struggling to reassert its power and identity in the wake of the defeat in the Franco–Prussian War three decades earlier, when France had suffered the humiliating loss of the provinces of Alsace and Lorraine.

Through the Tour, Desgrange hoped to achieve a fundamental desire to 'rebronzer la France', to get his compatriots out into the countryside, to encourage them to be fit and active. Rather than having a Jim Fixx-like desire to promote fitness and well-being on an individual basis, Desgrange's objective was to reassert French manhood and even to prepare France's youth for any future war.

This could be taken as a demonstration of his allegiance to the pro-military, right-wing policies of Count de Dion and the League of Patriots, but no evidence exists of Desgrange sharing a platform with them or propagating their views. Indeed, as he made clear in his very first editorial in L'Auto-Vélo, he saw no place for politics within the sporting press. Yet, he was undoubtedly a nationalist, an extremely proud Frenchman determined to do whatever he could to restore his nation's fortunes and defend its borders, which is best highlighted by his decision to volunteer for frontline service in 1917 at the age of 52.

Prominent Italian fatigue researcher Angelo Mosso described the traumatic defeat to the Prussians as 'the triumph of German legs', leading to a long debate about the need to reform French physical education. As part of this, the military increased its influence over gymnastic training in secondary education in order to improve French youth's readiness for the mandatory three-year national service.

Sport was regarded as having a role to play in this too, even though some, including Mosso, dismissed it as the answer to France's dilemma, regarding the exhaustion physical exercise brought on as being detrimental to the body's natural rhythm.

Despite these naysayers, cycling gained a key role in supporting the French military, underpinning the widely held belief among nationalists that *'il nous faut du muscle'* – we need muscle. The many *associations vélocipédiques* established at that time were, according to Christopher S. Thompson in *The Tour de France,* 'committed to supporting military cycling. The rides they organised would help to produce a generation of healthy, strong, and determined patriots, ready to make the ultimate sacrifice in a future war with Germany.'

Details of these *brevets militaires* appeared in *Le Vélo, L'Auto* and other titles. The objective for participants was to complete a set distance within a specified time, usually based on an average speed of 20 kilometres per hour, the same speed that Desgrange laid down as the lower limit for the payment of the daily stipend during the inaugural Tour. For many, these events were their path into racing, as Dargassies had revealed to Lefèvre.

The establishment of a bicycle-borne regiment based at Longchamps also revealed the importance of the bicycle to the French military. Intended to compensate for France having a smaller cavalry force than Germany, their regimental song proclaimed: *Les cyclistes nouveaux soldats seront les premiers au combat. Pour nous votre baïonnette sera sera sera la bicyclette* – 'The new cycling soldiers will be will be will be the first into battle. For us your bayonet will be the bicycle.' Concerned by this innovation, copied by the British army, the Germans trained dogs to attack them.

Presented as superhuman, the descriptions of both the Tour and participants chimed with this far more widespread affirmation of French renaissance and progress. They offered, according to *L'Auto,* another clear signal that France was not only revitalised but leading its rivals. The paper's insistence that 'the battle between these giants of the road is being awaited with feverish anticipation' bolstered this impression of vigour and action.

During the week running up to the start of the race, *L'Auto* offered substantial details on what lay in store for the intrepid competitors, as well as interesting insights into the organisational task being undertaken by Desgrange and, particularly, Géo Lefèvre and their assistants. A large part of this information came from the paper's correspondents. Akin to stringers, the freelance journalists who supply reports or photographs to news outlets although they generally received no fee for their work, these correspondents supplied a good deal of *L'Auto's* content, covering all manner of sports, from cycling to pétanque, and cricket to pelota.

In one, 'our correspondent from Langon, Monsieur G. Dubourg Junior', reports on preparations in this small town on the banks of the Garonne that was set to be the site of a control point during the fourth stage between Toulouse and Bordeaux.

'You can rest assured that everything will be ready and marvellously organised at Langon. The Café du Sport, the location of the control, and I are in the midst of getting everything ready,' Monsieur Dubourg writes. 'The mayor of Langon, M. Papon, has put a team of six men at our disposal on the eve of the race to put out the poles and banners as well as ensure the smooth passage of the competitors, who are very eagerly awaited and will receive the warmest of welcomes from the local population.' His brief report adds that several local cycling clubs will be collaborating with L'Auto Vélo Langonnais club to ensure that all runs smoothly.

In the absence of *Le Livre du Tour de France*, the route 'bible' that every rider, team member and journalist now turns to for information on the state of the roads, the nature of the climbs, and even the length of the finishing straight and its width at the line, these details provided most of the riders with all of the information they had about the inaugural Tour's route. Others, though, went to far greater lengths to obtain insight into the challenge in store for them.

Thanks to the backing of well-funded teams or manufacturers, the race's biggest names inspected the route for themselves, some of them covering it in its entirety in the hope that it would give them an edge on their rivals. The most high-profile of them is Italian Rodolfo Muller, younger brother of renowned Franco-Swiss painter and sculptor Alfredo Müller and a long-time friend of Henri

Desgrange, who explored the route in the weeks preceding the race and supplied *L'Auto* with precise and often very entertaining descriptions of his journey.

L'Auto published these in the days immediately prior to the start, setting the scene quite wonderfully both for the contest ahead and for the readers' discovery of the many variations of the French countryside and terrain. Leaving Marseille for Toulouse to recce the third stage, Muller picks out critical aspects for riders, such as the high number of tram tracks crossing the road, flocks of sheep being driven to market that force him to a halt, and, perhaps most important of all, the condition of the highway – 'a superb road, wide and delightfully flat,' he says of the initial stretch beyond the deneutralised start at Saint-Antoine, where the racing would begin in earnest following the neutralised parade of riders away from Marseille's Vieux Port.

After going on to detail instructions at various crossroads and junctions – 'there are two roads and you have to take the one on the right' – Muller diverts into describing what he can see around him as he makes for Salon-de-Provence. 'A harsh landscape, with a very rustic look and overwhelmingly monotonous. Not a single house, not a single peasant, nothing except a road of blinding whiteness that winds back and forth like a great sleeping serpent. It climbs the slope up to the horizon. From there, the horizon looks the same again as far as Salon.'

His lyricism continues as he heads into the Crau, a pan-flat, sun-baked region between Salon and Arles that still continues to be a severe test due to the winds that frequently barrel across it that can sweep away the best-laid and most scientific of plans. 'From Salon to Arles there are 40km of road that are perhaps the most beautiful in France. Not a turn, no undulations. Sickly little cypress trees line the road; in the distance, you can see the mountains,' says Muller.

Tour favourites Garin and Aucouturier also looked over the route, although the pair differed on their approach to this. Able to call on the backing of the powerful La Française team he headed, Garin checked some sections of the route, but left the bulk of the reconnaissance to his team manager, Monsieur Delattre[*], who covered the whole course and was stunned to come across Aucouturier doing precisely the same.

Their meeting highlighted a critical difference in the approach the two favourites had to the race. While Garin could count on the support of several teammates during the race, as well as Delattre looking after his every need, including the precise location of control points, where the La Française manager ensured that spare equipment would be on hand for his leader, Aucouturier was left almost to his own devices by the American Bicycle Company for whom he was the star turn. Delighted and apparently very satisfied with his victories in Bordeaux–Paris and Paris–Roubaix

---

[*] M. Delattre, who is 'Garin's manager' or 'my friend Delattre', is likely to be Lucien Delattre, who finished 9th in the 1899 edition of Paris-Roubaix. However, no clear confirmation of his identity has been located.

earlier in the year, the American bike manufacturer offered Aucouturier no support beyond one of their Crescent bikes.

Lefèvre details Delattre and Aucouturier's meeting in *L'Auto*'s 28 June issue and reports the La Française manager telling him: 'I've just met one of the Tour de France's most fearsome competitors, training "for as long as is possible" and doing so between Montélimar and Avignon on the same day that his mother-in-law is being buried in Paris. Bowled over, I asked him why he wasn't there and do you know what this glorious sportsman replied? He simply said this: "My dear Delattre, it is true that today I should be attending my mother-in-law's burial, but as I'm racing the Tour de France, I simply have to train. By heavens, you understand that work comes first and pleasure comes later!"'

CHAPTER 4

'LET US FIGHT WITH THE SAME WEAPONS'

On Tuesday, 30 June, the eve of the Tour de France's start, *L'Auto*'s focus switched suddenly and perhaps, given the extent of the hype it had hitherto lavished on the new race, rather surprisingly. For days, the Tour had dominated its front page, but Henri Desgrange's paper completely lived up to its recently acquired title with an edition dominated by the fourth running of the Gordon Bennett Cup, the forerunner of Formula 1.

Thanks to Selwyn Edge's victory in 1902, when the cup had been disputed on a course between Paris and Vienna, Britain was hosting the event. Since motor racing was banned on roads on the British mainland, this fourth edition of the Gordon Bennett was taking place in Ireland on a 527-kilometre course featuring three loops starting and finishing in Ballyshannon, south-west of Dublin.

Line drawings depicting the cars and drivers representing

the four competing nations of Great Britain, France, the USA and Germany filled two of the four editorial pages, which comprised half of the paper, with the other half given over to advertisements. Beneath, there was a recap of the three previous editions and extensive details on the course – a closed circuit for the first time – and the vehicles taking part.

There was much else besides: a reminder that cars would be travelling on the left- rather than the right-hand side of the road; a suggested four-day travel itinerary for French spectators wishing to see the action; and a translation of a story from *Correspondencia España* reporting on the outcome of the race fully two days before it actually got under way, which stated that several cars had failed to start and that the German cars had dominated the race run in cold, wet and stormy conditions. Bizarrely, the most significant detail in this story proved to be entirely accurate.

Looking back now, when the presence of cyclists on the roads elicits so much debate and, sadly, anger, it is illuminating to realise that motor vehicles and their drivers were viewed with much the same level of disdain in the early part of the twentieth century. Mainstream newspapers across Europe were calling for limits to be placed on the speed and access allowed to cars and other motor vehicles, which were generally viewed with fear due to innumerable reports of crashes and mechanical failures. These frequently resulted in fatalities. There was condemnation too for the noise and pollution they produced.

The motoring title *L'Autocar* attempted to counter this type of criticism by comparing deaths over the previous nine months that had been caused by motor vehicles, 329, with those that were the result of incidents involving animal-powered vehicles and carts, 3,011. However, the article omitted to mention there were only 10,000 or so motor vehicles on French roads in 1903, when most of the country's 40-million people still depended on horsepower to move themselves and goods around.

The council in the Paris suburb of Saint-Germain responded to public antipathy towards the car by banning them from its streets. This was a move that *L'Auto*, backed, it should be remembered, by some of the world's leading car manufacturers of that period, could not ignore. Desgrange's paper urged drivers to boycott the town and its businesses, even suggesting diversions enabling them to do so.

A glance at the advertisements in that 30 June edition of *L'Auto* both underlines the importance of the automobile industry for Desgrange's yellow-papered title and explains its sudden and overwhelming focus on the Gordon Bennett Cup. Several large ads trumpet the successes achieved by different manufacturers in motor races at the Semaine d'Aix-les-Bains and the Circuit des Ardennes, including those taken by the De Dion-Bouton brand headed by *L'Auto*'s principal backer and its main rival Darracq. There is only one for a cycle-related brand – Pâris tyres, 'unbeatable on the track – as the famous Black Cyclone Major Taylor was cruelly made aware on Thursday evening at the Buffalo.'

Just as the Tour would revolutionise cycle racing, the closed circuit employed for the Gordon Bennett Cup was set to change the face of motorsport. For the first time, security mattered as much as speed, and the move could not have been better timed. The event took place just weeks after Paris–Madrid, which had been organised by the French and Spanish automobile clubs, the former headed by *L'Auto* shareholder Baron de Zuylen. Featuring many of the great and good of motor racing and early twentieth-century society, including Renault brothers Marcel and Louis, Charles S. Rolls, William K. Vanderbilt and Vincenzo Lancia, the race drew huge crowds out on to France's dusty roads. The result was a fatal mix that led to more than a dozen deaths, including that of Marcel Renault, and hundreds of injuries. Meeting in emergency session, the French government shut down the race in Bordeaux and ordered its transfer to the Spanish border. Competitors arrived there to find the Spanish government had imposed a similar ban.

Broadly declared as 'the death of motorsport', Paris–Madrid ultimately led to the formulation of rules and limits on racing. Baron de Dion and *L'Auto* were among the standard-bearers, the paper and its main backer calling for courses that offered safety guarantees for drivers and spectators. To this end, more than 2,000 British soldiers were drafted in to marshal the Ballyshannon course in Ireland, where fans, that prescient Spanish paper may subsequently have noted, saw the German Mercedes driven by legendary Belgian Camille Jenatzy claim the cup.

Henri Desgrange's sidelining of the bike race his paper was organising in deference to coverage of the Gordon

Bennett Cup offers fuel to the oft-heard argument that his initial commitment to the Tour de France was far from total. Widely portrayed as a man who was quick to delegate responsibility for risky stunts such as the establishment of the Tour or, several years down the line, the introduction of the high mountains into the race itinerary, but very quick to take credit for their success, Desgrange has been painted as something of a chancer. According to Pierre Chany, his rivals 'respected his doggedness, but hated him in equal measure', and that antipathy has certainly coloured his reputation. Even those who worked with him and knew him well acknowledged he was tough and prone to anger, Lefèvre even describing him as 'merciless'.

Yet, as Lefèvre pointed out, 'Desgrange always won. He went into battle without being impetuous, after having always weighed up the pros and cons.' With just two days remaining to the start, no one could have had the slightest idea what the Tour's impact might be. While Aucouturier, Muller, Delattre and others who had carried out reconnaissance of the route had marvelled at the response from locals in *la France profonde* to their passing, even the most far-sighted of business people wouldn't have envisioned the hysteria the new race was about to provoke.

As a result, *L'Auto* relegated 'the most incredible road battle that has ever been encountered', as Lefèvre described the race in the first sentence of his article on the Tour, to the sixth and final column on page three. Yet, within it Desgrange's right-hand man offered what was hitherto the most instructive insight into the race. Having laid out the length and extent of the challenge facing the 80 riders who had signed up to compete and admitted to 'a bizarre sensation' at finally being on the brink of an event to which he and his associates had devoted the previous three months, he outlined the magnitude of what had been achieved during that period, insisting their task had been as arduous as that of the riders who had trained and prepared for the Tour.

'Kilometre by kilometre, we've had to prepare for every eventuality, organise controls, a system of surveillance, put up posters along the immense itinerary, seek out grassroots support among the [cycling] societies, attract innumerable volunteers who will be responsible for helping to ensure that the organisation of the Tour de France is perfect in all places,' wrote Lefèvre. He confessed to his relief at putting this task behind him, but also to 'a touch of nervy concern' that, he acknowledged, the racers must also have been feeling. Finally, after months of what was almost certainly the most intensive organisational effort that had ever been devoted to a sporting event anywhere in the world, bearing in mind the extent of the race and the size of the team involved, who all, it should be remembered, had to keep up their other tasks at *L'Auto,* Lefèvre was able to turn his attention from the organisational aspect of the race to the competitive.

It must have been a wonderful moment for this young but already very experienced sports journalist to direct his attention to an event that had been nothing more than a flight of fancy just seven months earlier. Now, as the racers ventured into *L'Auto*'s offices to confirm they would be starting and renew acquaintance with members of the paper's staff, Lefèvre was able to report their hopes and fears. Naturally, he focused on the few names that his paper's readers were sure to know, starting with Maurice Garin.

The first of nine children born to a peasant family in the French-speaking Aosta valley in north-west Italy, Garin had been dispatched to France at the age of 14 to earn his keep. Legend has it that his parents swapped him for a round of cheese, although the exchange of custody was certainly a temporary one as he later rejoined members of his family in France. The cheese may have been offered to Garin's impoverished parents by smugglers who trafficked children into France to work in factories and other places to do jobs suited to their small stature. In the case of the diminutive Garin, after being led across the mountains to northern France, he worked for some years as a chimney sweep before discovering his ability as a cyclist. His past stuck with him, though, as the papers dubbed him '*le petit ramoneur*' – the little sweep.

A pro at the age of 21 and very quickly a successful one, he earned enough money to open a bicycle shop in Roubaix with two of his brothers in the mid-1890s. Third in the inaugural Paris–Roubaix of 1896, he won the following two editions. In common with most of the leading pros of his era, he gained a reputation for almost unbreakable mental and physical toughness, but stood out both for his speed on two wheels and his unyielding resilience in the face of any challenge. Of one victory in a 24-hour track race affected by severe cold, he said: 'When you've had to sweep chimneys for a living, 24 hours on the track in 15 degrees of frost doesn't bother you.'

Hard-nosed and savvy, Garin may have had very humble beginnings and little formal education but he was, as Lefèvre regularly made clear, very intelligent. 'I realised that after Paris–Brest–Paris when he described to me, with a precision that highlighted a prodigious memory, all of the different turns in the battle. And he delivered this account in such beautiful fashion, using such evocative words, expressions that were intended to have an impact on readers and made them fully aware of what he was putting across, that it was clear Garin was far from being an imbecile.'

The only one of the big names to build his whole 1903 season around the new race, Garin, described by *Le Matin* as 'small, squat, but of lean build, a little head divided by a blond moustache, blessed with insurmountable energy and ceaseless courage', had honed his speed by riding as a pace-maker for La Française teammates, notably for Gustave Pasquier at Paris–Roubaix. He had filled the time in between these commitments with training on the Tour route, which meant he was better equipped than most for what lay ahead, particularly as La Française were ready to provide him with every possible means of support allowed by the rules, which stressed that riders would be competing as individuals and that alliances, by team or mutual convenience, were prohibited.

'I know it's going to be hard. But that's what I want,' Garin told Lefèvre when he called on him in *L'Auto*'s offices. 'The sun is going to burn us, and so much the better. The short rest between each leg will make the first hundred kilometres of each stage terrible, and so much the better! In a race such as this, you can't be sure who the winner will be, as the road can prove so treacherous, but I assure you that I will have to be carried back to Paris if I don't return there as the winner.' He added that he was happy in the knowledge that the riders would be carefully monitored and the rules strictly enforced, although he would soon show that more than a decade of professional racing had resulted in him acquiring all manner of ruses through which he could bend both the race's rules and his rivals in his favour.

Garin's adversaries, almost every one of whom had followed the fashion for a bristling moustache, were equally bullish. German veteran Josef Fischer, renowned for his iron constitution and called 'Joseph' in *L'Auto* after many years of racing in France, felt the Tour was his kind of event, even though his career was on the decline. 'I've always loved tough races and this one, I believe, will be the ultimate of that type,' he declared. 'Maurice Garin, my old rival, will be there, but remember our last head-to-head finish in the 1900 Bordeaux–Paris: Garin couldn't drop me for some six hundred kilometres of racing . . . and I beat him in the sprint. Yet I think I've got even greater endurance than I had in 1900. Without pace-makers Garin will never drop me . . . and I will always beat him in the sprint. And as for the stage from Nantes to Paris, we will see who has conserved enough energy to follow his pace-makers. As for Aucouturier, I don't know him as well, but I can't believe he will beat Garin. And if he can't beat Garin, he won't beat me.'

Hippolyte Aucouturier, fresh from his victories in Paris–Roubaix and Bordeaux–Paris, informed Lefèvre he was more confident and faster than he had ever been, and that his only fear was being thwarted by an accident. Looking the image of a villain from a Buster Keaton comedy in contemporary photos with his thick moustache waxed rakishly upwards at the ends, thick eyebrows almost hiding his eyes, and wearing a hooped jersey and flat cap, he too picked out the absence of pace-makers as a reason to be confident of victory.

Indeed, this was a very consistent theme. When Rodolfo Muller breezed into the paper's offices with a boater barely keeping his lustrous, 'too blond hair' in check, the Italian evaluated this innovation in typically lyrical fashion, telling Lefèvre: 'There's no doubt that all of the clever clogs who are talking about eating their rivals up will be more full of themselves at three o'clock on Wednesday than they will be a few days afterwards . . . I'm expecting them to get tired. And remember this: you won't only see Muller at the start, but at the finish as well.'

It's impossible to underplay the importance of the prohibition of pace-makers from all but the final stage of the Tour. In a similar way to motor racing, the overriding emphasis within cycle racing in that era had been on speed. Consequently, just as the car manufacturers went well beyond the boundaries of safety relating to both drivers and spectators as they searched to outpace each other, cycling teams gave their leading riders an increasing number of pacers, often using tandems or triplets. Inevitably, they then took advantage of advances in motor vehicle technology to replace human pacers with motorbikes and even cars, the advent of the former still evident nowadays in the keirin event on the track.

'With a car, I could ensure that my mother won the race,' complained Dutchman Mathieu Cordang after he'd lost out to Frenchman Gaston Rivierre in the 1897 edition of Bordeaux–Paris. A week before the Tour got under way, Lefèvre harked back to Cordang's griping, highlighting to *L'Auto*'s readers that, 'In cycling's primitive era, in the times when the likes of Terront and [Henri] Béconnais battled on their own on huge bikes, pace-makers were unknown. They were completely unaware of what kind of an advantage a cyclist could gain from riding on the wheel of the machine in front; it can't be contested that pace-making is one of the principal elements of speed.'

It perhaps won't surprise many on the northern side of the English Channel that Lefèvre placed the blame for the obsession with pace-making on France's old enemy, and specifically on George Pilkington Mills, winner of the first edition of Bordeaux–Paris in 1891 who had inspired Desgrange to take up the sport. Realising the extent of the advantage a rider could gain by sitting on another's wheel, 'We then saw Mills drop his rivals in the first Bordeaux–Paris, thanks to the English sprinter Lewis Stroud, who waited for him at the top of a hill and then pulled him along behind him at a terrible speed . . . When every

Bordeaux–Paris hit the road, it featured an army of pace-makers and hundreds of machines specially created with this in mind.'

Lefèvre concluded that the use of pace-makers had resulted in two critical issues for cycle racing. It had become impossible for a good racer to mix it up with the big stars, unless he was able to pay the lofty price for a decent group of pace-makers. As a result of this, the number of racers was progressively falling, leading to a consequent decline in the number of races. 'The wonderful blossoming of town-to-town races is nothing more than a memory; only Paris–Roubaix and Bordeaux–Paris survive,' Lefèvre lamented.

While the second statement was an exaggeration, although not completely so as there were very few road races of note prior to the Tour's establishment, there is no doubt that pacing had removed almost any element of unpredictability from the outcome of races. As Lefèvre put it, 'the battle remains unequal between competitors who have made their name and those who are still to achieve this. At the end of every race, the same chorus of complaints goes up: "It's unfair. It's impossible to continue in these conditions. Let us fight with the same weapons."'

By giving the underdogs the opportunity to battle on a level-playing field with the star names, Desgrange and Lefèvre returned the sport to its roots. Lefèvre described the move as 'the resultant logic of a 20-year evolution that has brought us almost all of the way back to cycling's primitive era'. He went on to suggest that pace-makers might be banned completely the following year. In the end, the suppression of pace-makers didn't even take that long.

As they came into *L'Auto*'s offices in the final days of June, rider after rider hailed this overhaul of established wisdom. 'The cracks can go faster than us at the start, but the incredible distance will enable us to get on terms with them again. It will be a race where endurance counts, and only endurance,' they told Lefèvre, who was further boosted by the support voiced by rival publications for the move. In *Paris Sportif Illustré*, A. d'Herdt bemoaned how 'men of real class are left to their own means, eclipsed by stars from the second rank who have the advantage of a "regimen-like" deployment of masseurs, soigneurs, pace-makers and spare bikes. This suppression of those who falsify race finishes, which has been so well received by everyone, will give everyone just about the same chance of success.'

Desgrange and Lefèvre hoped they could increase the egalitarian competitive aspect by introducing a number of other innovations, which were primarily designed to prevent racers cheating. In addition to an armband bearing their race number, each rider would have a piece of red cloth bearing their race number attached to the frame of their bike using strong elastic ties in order to make identification of riders easier at 'flying' checkpoints. The frame number, which had to be attached to any new bike used by a racer in the event of a swap necessitated by breakdown, also made it easier for officials carrying out secret checks to see who might be bending the rules.

For obvious reasons, these misdemeanours often occurred

when racing took place at night, which was essential in most long-distance events in order to ensure an early-afternoon finish. As race officials rarely had access to a reliable motor vehicle from which they could monitor competitors, they were reliant on racers playing fair, which, of course, they seldom did. There were innumerable tales of riders being knocked from their machines by other racers or their fans in the dead of night, but it was impossible for officials to assess who the miscreants might have been.

L'Auto's competitors made hay with this long-standing issue, suggesting that a race run over such distances and so many stages would be a free-for-all, encouraging every kind of shenanigans. Yet, the Tour's organisers responded with a ruse of their own, which, according to Lefèvre, would result in 'extremely rigorous surveillance along the whole course, especially at night.'

In addition to the race officials identified by a blue armband, the rules stressed there would be an equal number of 'absolutely secret officials on the race route who will be provided with a letter by *L'Auto*. If these officials have any observation to make to a rider, they will show him said letter.' In effect, like the 'vampires' who now call on athletes in the early hours to undertake blood and urine tests in order to prevent doping taking place, the Tour's organisers were making it clear that although they couldn't monitor their race in absolutely every place, they could do so at regular intervals, but only they would know how frequent this surveillance would be.

Other measures, such as the use of control points to monitor the progress of competitors were already well established. For the Tour, each *contrôle fixe* was set up in towns and cities that were both stopping points for express trains, enabling Lefèvre and his assistants to keep ahead of the riders, and, crucially, also had a telegraph office, enabling rapid dispatch of race news back to Paris. With the telephone still in its infancy as a means of communication – installation cost 400 francs at that time and only a few thousand offices and businesses had them – the rapidly developing telegraph network was vital to news gathering, its importance highlighted by US president Theodore Roosevelt's involvement during the opening week of the Tour in sending the first transglobal message. Sent from Oyster Bay, Long Island, his message of congratulation took 12 minutes to reach Clarence H. Mackay, president of the Pacific Cable Company, who was standing at Roosevelt's side.

On the first stage from Paris to Lyon, for instance, there were three fixed control points, at Nevers, Moulins and Roanne. Riders had to dismount and sign their name or make their mark on a sheet at a table usually set up under an awning at the roadside. Failure to sign meant disqualification. The *contrôles volants* tended to be manned by *L'Auto*'s local correspondents or by volunteers. Riders had to shout their names out as they passed, which was sure to result in confusion if they were grouped together. This is where the numbers on the frames came in particularly useful, if it wasn't too dusty or dark.

As race day neared, *L'Auto* provided details of final tweaks to the route and warnings about potential dangers along it – a switch of approach heading into Nantes to avoid five kilometres of cobbled road that 'would trouble the riders', a sharp hairpin bend on a descent near Audance early on in the second stage from Lyon that would be marked with lamps and lanterns. The paper noted almost in passing that, 'It therefore seems likely that the competitors will have to have a brake.'

For the most part, bikes were *pignon fixe*. In other words, there was no freewheel that would, for instance, enable a rider to stop pedalling and allow a bike's wheels to spin freely on a descent. Instead, as with track machines and many children's bikes nowadays, racers regulated their speed via their pedalling cadence. Consequently, braking required a slowing in cadence or, in extreme circumstances, complete locking of the legs, a manoeuvre best avoided at high speed because a concurrent degree of control is always sacrificed, sometimes with very dramatic effect, as first-timers on the track soon realise and then remember very well. Engaging a back-pedal band brake of this type when descending a rutted road with a slippery surface on a heavy bike would have been terrifying and taxing, especially when racing at night.

In races such as Paris–Roubaix and Bordeaux–Paris this wasn't a major concern as the courses were essentially flat. However, the Tour de France featured plenty of ups and downs, even though the route steered clear of the country's mountain ranges until it ventured into the Vosges massif in 1905. Consequently, before the Tour got under way, some riders and manufacturers admitted to Lefèvre that they were likely to fit a single hand-pulled brake on the front wheel. Constructed using metal rods and fitted with either wooden or rubber brake blocks, these brakes weren't overly effective on the wooden rims all bikes were shod with, and many competitors shunned them. Some of them compensated by carrying ballast on descents to provide downward force and, therefore, stability on steep gradients on the gravel- and dust-based roads.

Although the major manufacturers were always investigating new methods to improve their bikes and reduce their weight, they were still a world away from the sleek and twitchy thoroughbred set-ups that are now sculpted with carbon-fibre and weigh in at seven kilos or even less. Star performers such as Garin and Aucouturier were inevitably able to insist on the most cutting-edge technology, which meant a bike that weighed in at between 12 and 14 kilos. Most, though, had to rely on steel-framed bikes of 16 kilos and more that would be described as 'bombproof' in the modern era. They needed to be on roads that would now only be tackled on a cyclo-cross or mountain bike. Like those off-road machines, the seat-tube and head-tube angles were more relaxed than modern-day road frames, which helped to absorb the bumping of rough roads.

The riders selected the single gear with which they would tackle each stage by choosing a chainring and a rear sprocket with a certain number of teeth, with that gear measured in terms of distance covered with one rotation of the pedals.

Consequently, Lucien Barroy, the former clown acrobat, had a gear of 6.80m, blacksmith Jean Dargassies one of 5.80m, and Tour favourite Maurice Garin opted for an even smaller one of 5.25m, which meant he could pedal at a faster cadence and made climbing easier. The only way to change gear was to stop at a control point and fit a rear wheel with either more or fewer teeth, or, as Garin was able to do thanks to La Française's impressive logistical assistance, swap to a new bike with a different gear.

Naturally, tyres were a subject of great debate. Ever since John Boyd Dunlop's breakthrough work on the pneumatic tyre in the late 1880s, Édouard Michelin's perfecting of the removable tyre in 1891, and the introduction of rubber inner tubes in that same decade, punctures had become far easier for all bike riders to deal with. Racers carried several spares, either wrapped around their shoulders or stuffed into saddle bags. They also carried patches and glue to carry out repairs. Vulcanisation of tyres in powerful hydraulic presses had delivered another significant advance as it radically improved the extent by which the rubber impregnated the tyre's woven fibres, making them, according to Michelin's regular Monday bike maintenance tutorial in *L'Auto*, 'watertight and unlikely to rot'. Rather than being rounded, these tyres could also be shaped to have sidewalls, improving their rigidity and cushioning, and also putting more distance between road and rim.

The other significant feature of the racers' bikes was the leather bag that hung off the front of their bars or the back of their saddle. As well as spare equipment, this contained bottled water and often wine or beer. Riders swigged alcohol not only for its supposed pain-relieving qualities, but also because these drinks had gone through a fermenting process that removed impurities often found in tap water, which often came from tainted springs and polluted rivers until the gradual introduction across France of *eau potable* in line with the law on public health passed in 1902.

Favourite foods for the bags were chicken, rice and eggs, with chocolate often slipped in as well to deliver a fast sugar hit. They also contained spare clothes, including a woollen jersey and tights for the cold of night-time riding, which were exchanged for shorts and a lighter sweater or jacket during the day. Caps had a peak to keep out the sun and often a neck-protecting flap on the back to ward off its rays, with goggles used to keep their eyes free of dust. Most riders also packed lights to make them visible in the dark, although the beam from these oil lamps was too weak to pick out perils in the road.

They may well have been carrying more suspect items as well. Ever since the Greeks established the ancient Olympics, athletes have been turning to all manner of products in search of a competitive edge. In the late nineteenth and early twentieth centuries, the pick-me-ups of choice were caffeine, strychnine, brandy, cocaine, arsenic and capsules containing nitroglycerine, which was used by doctors to stimulate the heart after cardiac arrest and to improve breathing.

Heaven help those who overindulged in some of these products, though. At a time when anti-doping organisations weren't even a consideration, athletes often went too far. The most infamous case involved Welshman Arthur Linton, who finished fourth in the first edition of Paris–Roubaix as preparation for the bigger prize of Bordeaux–Paris, where he suffered terribly in almost every way. He sustained severe wounds in two crashes and, when leading on the final run-in, took the wrong route into the finish as a result of a late change due to roadworks. He finished second to Frenchman Gaston Rivierre, with many noting his poor health. Although the race officials later promoted Linton to joint winner of the event with Rivierre, the Welshman's health did not improve in the same way. He died two months later.

Speculation has long surrounded the role played in Linton's fate by his manager and trainer, James 'Choppy' Warburton, who was widely reported as carrying a bottle containing a magic elixir that revived his riders when they were flagging. It has been suggested the bottle contained strychnine. Although Linton and Warburton were no longer working together at the time of the racer's death, the Welshman was almost certainly using a potion of his own to boost his performance. Indeed, in a 1997 study, the International Olympic Committee listed him as the first athlete to die as a result of doping during competition.

In spite of Linton's sad demise, racers were still taking risks. American track star Major Taylor quit a race in New York because, he said, 'there is a man chasing me around the track with a knife in his hands'. Such hallucinations were a side-effect of strychnine use. In 1898, Frenchman Jean Fischer earned the nickname 'Le Grimpeur' (The Climber) not for his exploits on a bike in the mountains but for running out of the Parc des Princes during the 72 Hours of Paris, climbing a tree and refusing to come down, which was surely not the action of a man in control of his faculties.

It is almost certain that many of the first Tour's racers were doped in some way or another. Almost all of them hailed from very humble backgrounds from which their ability as riders offered them an escape, in a few cases a lucrative one. In addition, the competitive conditions they faced were brutally extreme. The roads were rotten, their bikes were heavy, the races often incredibly long, and no one was much concerned with their well-being. Their job was to entertain and sell bikes and other merchandise, and to do so uncomplainingly. Some of their successors would argue that little has subsequently changed.

With 24 hours to the start, *L'Auto* rounded up its preview by listing the odds for the race. Garin was priced at 6/4 for victory on the opening stage, with Aucouturier 2/1, and Josef Fischer and Paris–Roubaix runner-up Claude Chapperon at 5/1. The organising newspaper put Garin at evens for the title, Fischer at 2/1 and Aucouturier at 4/1. The accuracy of these odds would now be put to the test.

CHAPTER 5

'THESE RIDERS WILL NEVER REACH THE FINISH'

'LA SEMENCE'. The headline on Henri Desgrange's editorial on the first page of the 1 July edition of *L'Auto* doesn't translate easily or well into English. Sitting alongside a hand-drawn map of the Tour de France route detailing each of the six stages and the position of the control points within them, it perhaps works best in its most obvious translation, 'The Sowing', especially as Desgrange goes on to describe the 'unknowing and rough sowers of energy that are our great professional riders' and compares them to the labourer depicted by novelist Émile Zola in *La Terre* (*The Earth*).

The style is typical of Desgrange in its lofty reference and erudition, floweriness and lyricism, and, perhaps to many English-speaking sports fans, pomposity. He may not have been the originator of this style, but Desgrange certainly popularised it, to the extent that French sports journalists, and particularly those covering cycling, have replicated and developed it over subsequent decades and it remains very evident today.

The opening sentence of 'La Semence' is just as significant, though, in what it says about class within French society in the early part of the twentieth century. As the head of a newspaper financed by members of the ruling and upper class, read largely by those in the growing middle class and reporting on the exploits of athletes almost entirely drawn from the lower classes, Desgrange and his staff had to achieve a fine balance with regard to their editorial slant at a time of political, economic and social emancipation, which included loud and frequent demands for greater rights for workers and women. Consequently, L'Auto's writers had to reassure their established readership, but avoid appearing elitist. With the literacy rate at 97 per cent thanks to increased investment during the Third Republic and interest in sport also rising rapidly, L'Auto's potential market was far bigger than its fluctuating and often worryingly low circulation.

With his nod to Zola, whose hugely popular works often highlighted the travails of members of the lower class and increased awareness of the issues they faced, Desgrange was elevating the importance of his new race, while his reference to the 'unknowing and rough' riders emphasised the civilising effect he believed that sport and particularly the Tour would have. Indeed, Desgrange was doing nothing less than playing down the fears of many of his moneyed readers, who feared rising agitation on all sides – from their employees, from their wives and daughters. What Desgrange wanted to demonstrate, above all, was that his race would transform the riders and their fans into responsible members of society.

Having portrayed the race's itinerary 'from Paris to the blue waters of the Mediterranean, from Marseille to Bordeaux via pink-tinted and dreaming towns sleeping in the sun . . .' Desgrange revealed his two greatest hopes for the race: no less than the revitalisation of French manhood and vitality, and the introduction of high-level sport to French provinces hitherto almost totally ignored by it.

He came at the former in his flowery but direct fashion, hailing the racers about to undertake an unprecedented challenge and adding that, 'they will encounter the useless, the inactive and the lazy, on whom a gigantic battle is going to be declared to rouse them from their torpor, a battle during which they will become ashamed of allowing their muscles to atrophy and be embarrassed at having such a large paunch'. The Tour was nothing less than his answer to humiliating scars on the national consciousness.

He also hoped to remedy indolence in another way, by taking top-class sport into regions where it had rarely been witnessed. 'We want to penetrate into every area, to see everyone, to prevent anyone from being able to say one day, "I've never seen that stunning expression of energy and motivation that you've delivered."' Desgrange's paper would, of course, benefit from this if the race proved a success.

However, although no one could yet know this, cycle sport would too, as the Tour cemented its place as France's national sport, a position that was only eroded in the 1980s as the popularity of football, tennis and other sports grew, and innumerable doping scandals tainted cycling.

Once Desgrange had had his say, *L'Auto* turned its attention fully to the race. Following his boss's high-blown words, Géo Lefèvre opted for a simpler approach. *'Qui?'* his article began. Who will win the Tour de France?

Before delivering his predictions, *L'Auto's* chief cycling correspondent declared that the name of the Tour winner would be forever fixed in the memories of fans in the same way Charles Terront's had been since he'd won the Paris–Brest–Paris a dozen years earlier. He added, with far greater insight, that, 'A race such as this, even more so than all of the great track events, will have an impact on people, because it delivers itself directly to them.'

Like his journalistic peers, Lefèvre was well aware that track-racing's popularity was declining. Here, he signals one significant reason why, and the timing of his prophecy is key. The morning of the first Tour marks the end of track-racing's hegemony. Since 1 July 1903, road racing has ruled the roost.

Lefèvre divided the contenders for the 'cake they are going to be sharing' into three categories: those who were certain to challenge for victory; those who hoped to; and those who were targeting places of honour.

Into the third category, he placed the large majority of the 60 or 70 riders he expected to start. Predicting who will perform well in a race as long and wearing as the Tour remains a devilishly difficult task, and it was far harder for Lefèvre with no previous stage races to use as an indicator. As a result, he included within this selection a number of riders who were to emerge as veritable Tour contenders. Given his predilection for Jean Dargassies, it is also worth noting that he omitted the blacksmith from Grisolles from this list, effectively dismissing him as a complete no-hoper.

Turning to those who hoped to challenge for victory, he listed eight names, beginning with Gustave Pasquier. Save for a crash during Bordeaux–Paris just a few weeks earlier that left him with his knee cut open to the bone, Pasquier would have been a top contender, explained Lefèvre. Léon Georget was described as 'one of the race's big outsiders' due to his tenacity and cool temperament, although, Lefèvre added, his best years were still to come.

Next up was Jean Fischer, 'a furious competitor who complains about everything and everybody, but then makes the gallery chortle when he recounts his misadventures'. Thanks to 'solid lungs and a very accommodating stomach', Fischer was rated a dangerous and durable contender, although lacking in flair. The winner of the 1902 Bordeaux–Paris race Édouard Wattelier was described as 'a climber of undoubted class and a fast racer', but Lefèvre questioned his endurance in such an arduous test.

The three main Belgian challengers, Marcel Kerff, Jules Sales and Julien Lootens, aka Samson, were lumped together as robust and dependable roadmen likely to challenge for high positions in the final overall classification. Lootens, incidentally, gained his nickname not for the length of his hair or strength, although he was a typically powerfully built Fleming, but from his desire to prevent his family's good name being associated with a sport that was regarded as not fitting for the upper classes and bourgeoisie.

Finally, Lefèvre picked out Paris–Roubaix runner-up Claude Chapperon, pointing out he had the speed and endurance to trouble the favourites, and had opted out of Bordeaux–Paris in order to focus fully on the Tour. 'It's only because he hasn't confirmed his ability with a big victory that I've decided against including him in my final and very rigorously made selection, which comprises just four names,' Lefèvre revealed, going on to name Maurice Garin, Hippolyte Aucouturier, Josef Fischer and Rodolfo Muller as the quartet from whom the Tour champion would emerge.

L'Auto's correspondent then became emphatic. 'I will say straight away – because my mind has been made up, and for quite a time – that I believe final victory in the Tour de France will go to Maurice Garin,' he stated, backing this up by pointing to his victories over Lucien Lesna in Paris–Brest–Paris in 1901 and in Bordeaux–Paris a year later. 'From the very first time I saw him climb hills and plunge down descents, I've admired the unfailing robustness of this stocky athlete, crouched over his machine ready to forge ahead, crushing the pedals with his power . . . For me, Maurice Garin will arrive in Paris as the winner or he won't arrive at all: he will have fallen at the roadside, victim of one of the injustices of the road.'

Lefèvre admitted he could imagine Aucouturier's wry smile on reading these words and added that he fully expected Garin's main rival to win the opening stage to Lyon. However, he was afraid for him, 'afraid that he will succumb in the end in the face of this infernal and enduring machine that we know as Garin.'

Lefèvre recognised that his last two picks were more debatable, but reminded readers that, although much heavier than his rival, Josef Fischer had beaten Garin in the past and claimed to be in the shape of his life. Curiously, he also wondered whether being foreign might handicap the German. Perhaps, having read Henri Desgrange's pronouncements about the Tour revitalising French manhood and playing on memories of the humiliating defeat to the Germans just three decades earlier, Lefèvre sensed there would be repercussions for Fischer if he did beat France's principal aspirants for victory. *L'Auto* too needed that home victory in order to wring every possible benefit out of its new race.

Oddly, Lefèvre didn't offer a similar assessment of Muller's prospects. That may have been because the man from Livorno had spent so long in France that he was commonly known as Rodolphe. Plus, Italy wasn't France's traditional rival. Instead, Lefèvre justified his controversial choice of a rider who was yet to win a major road event by emphasising his endurance and suggesting that the Tour might finally be the race that was totally suited to his qualities. 'I'm convinced that he will be dropped at the start, but stage by stage he will improve his position to finish among the leaders,' he said.

Just as news of the Gordon Bennett Cup had done a couple of days previously, details of the Tour de France filled almost the entirety of the opening two editorial pages, beginning with a list of the 80 riders registered to start and instructing them that they would have to present a licence from the French cycling federation, the UVF, or from a federation affiliated to the international federation, the UCI. Registration would take place on the edge of Villeneuve-Saint-Georges at the intersection of the Route de Melun and the Route de Corbeil, where the control point would be situated inside the Auberge du Réveil-Matin.

The control point, manned by Alphonse Steinès, would open at one in the afternoon and close at 2.30. Twenty minutes later, the riders would be called to the start. 'At three o'clock precisely, the start of the Tour de France will be given, under the guidance of our director Henry [sic] Desgrange, by *L'Auto's* inspector-general Monsieur G. Abran, who for the past three months has devoted himself to the organisation of the route of this incredible event,' the paper reported, before detailing the route, timetable – which was based on Muller's projections from his reconnaissance of the route – and itinerary of the opening stage, as well as the location of the controls and points where caution was advised, notably on a short and steep descent towards a level crossing coming out of Myennes where a fatality had recently occurred.

L'Auto went on to outline every little piece of information that may have been of even the slightest interest to readers, from the many names of the officials overseeing the control points, to the donation of a 100-franc prize by 'a generous sportsman from Nevers, Monsieur Philippe de la Case of 61 Rue d'Anjou in Paris' to the first rider to reach his home city. There was also a reminder of the rules, which stated that bikes of any type were permitted 'as long as they are moved by muscular force', that any drafting behind a car or acceptance of mechanical or nutritional support outside control points were forbidden, and that the control point at the finish at the Brasserie Comte on the Quai de Vaise in Lyon would close 39 hours after the start in Paris, based on an average speed of 12 kilometres per hour.

The detail went well beyond what would now be expected of the Tour's road book. In addition to stock information such as the prize list, which promised the stage-winner 1,500 francs, close to a year's wages for the average working man, it informed that a masseur, a Monsieur Mingot, would be offering his services gratis to riders in Lyon, that the Diorama des Variétés on the Boulevard Montmartre in Paris would be showing the stage results between nine in the evening and midnight on its 'immense luminous screen', and that *L'Auto* would be printing a special edition with the very first results within minutes of the stage finishing. The organising paper also announced it would telegraph the results of the stage to readers who paid a 50-centime fee – ten times the cost of the paper itself.

L'Auto's sporting rivals may not have been happy about doing so, but they also devoted considerable coverage to the new race. *Le Vélo* didn't stint at all, although news of the latest action from the Gordon Bennett Cup and the prospects for a clash between French sprinters Edmond Jacquelin and Henri Cissac and Britain's Tommy Hall at the Buffalo Velodrome were given precedence. The Tour didn't escape the notice of the mainstream press either, *Écho de Paris* giving the race significant space beneath news of the health of the pope and rumours of a British defeat in Somaliland to religious leader Sayyid Mohammed Abdullah Hassan and his Dervish forces in what is now Somalia.

The main question that needed to be answered now was whether the French public would respond in the same positive manner.

RIDERS WHO REGISTERED TO RACE
(WITH AGE, HOMETOWN AND BRAND
OF BIKE WHERE KNOWN)

Riders in italics pre-registered but did not start

1. Maurice Garin, 32 (Lens, France) La Française
2. Gustave Pasquier, 25 (Paris, France) La Française
3. Lucien Barroy, 28 (Paris, France) Herstal

4. *Charles Prévost (Lens, France)*
5. Alexandre Foureaux (Paris, France)
6. Henri Gauban, 23 (Muret, France)
7. Louis Barbrel, 25 (Paris, France) Roussin
8. Hippolyte Aucouturier, 26 (Paris, France) Crescent
9. Marcel Kerff, 37 (Sint Peters Voeren, Belgium)
10. Léon Georget, 23 (Châtellerault, France) Aiglon
11. Eugène Brange, 33 (Belleville-sur-Saône, France)
12. Jean Fischer, 36 (Boulogne-sur-Seine, France) La Française
13. *G. Dorlin (France)*
14. Isidore Lechartier, 32 (Paris, France) Gladiator
15. Benjamin Mounier, 36 (La Rochelle, France) BSA
16. *Adolphe Dorion (France)*
17. Émile Pagie, 32 (Tourcoing, France) La Française
18. *Marcel Vallée-Picaud (Paris, France)*
19. *Gabriel Baraquin (France)*
20. *Auguste Laprée (France)*
21. Jean Dargassies, 30 (Grisolles, France) Gladiator
22. Émile Moulin, 40 (Paris, France) Primo
23. *Émile Fichtner (France)*
24. Jules Sales, 28 (Brussels, Belgium) Jules Sales
25. *Paul Émile (France)*
26. Édouard Wattelier, 26 (Paris, France)
27. Claude Chapperon (Paris, France)
28. Julien 'Samson' Lootens, 26 (Wevelgem, Belgium) Brennabor
29. René Salais, 28 (Angers, France)

30. *François Julien (France)*
31. Léon Habets, 26 (Paris, France) Humber
32. Victor Dupré, 19 (Roanne, France) La Française
33. Rodolfo Muller, 26 (Italy) La Française
34. *Paul Rosa (France)*
35. *Georges Leblais (France)*
36. Jean Bédène (Paris, France)
37. Lucien Pothier, 20 (Cuy, France) La Française
38. Armand Perin, 20 (Paris, France)
39. Fernand Augereau, 20 (Châtellerault, France)
    La Française
40. Eugène Jay, 24 (Paris, France) La Française
41. Ernest Pivin, 33 (Rocheservière, France)
42. Paul Mercier (Lausanne, Switzerland)
43. Pierre Desvages, 36 (Paris, France) Champion
44. Léon Pernette, 18 (Paris, France) NSU
45. François Beaugendre, 22 (Salbris, France)
46. Anton Jaeck, 21 (Geneva, Switzerland) La Française
47. François Poussel (Nice, France)
48. Josef Fischer, 38 (Munich, Germany) Brennabor
49. Ludwig Barthelmann (Munich, Germany)
50. Julien Girbe (Paris, France) Cycles JC
51. Charles Laeser, 23 (Geneva, Switzerland)
52. *Louis Trousselier, 22 (Levallois, France)*
53. Georges Borot (Paris, France)
54. Léon Durandeau, 30 (Angers, France)
55. Léon Riche (Sens, France)
56. A. Lassartigues (Paris, France) Primo

57. L. Fougère (Paris, France)
58. Émile Torisani (Paris, France)
59. Henri Charrier, 29 (Neuilly, France)
60. *I. Vermuelen (Brussels, Belgium)*
61. *Pamateur (Switzerland)*
62. Ferdinand Payan, 33 (Alais, France)
63. Paul Trippier, 18 (Paris, France)
64. Henri Ellinamour, 19 (Arles, France) Primo
65. Jean-Baptiste Zimmermann, 17 (Paris, France)
66. Marcel Lequatre, 20 (Yverdon-les-Bains, Switzerland)
67. Arsène Millochau, 36 (Chartres, France)
68. *Léonard Vandendaelen (Valenciennes, France)*
69. François Monachon, 32 (Paris, France)
    Le Métais NSU
70. *Yvel (Nice, France) Peugeot*
71. Aloïs Catteau, 25 (Menen, Belgium) La Française
72. *Louis Constant (Saint-Étienne, France)*
73. Victor Lefèvre, 21 (Tours, France) Griffon
74. *Lucien Petit-Breton, 20 (Paris, France)*
75. Auguste Daumain, 25 (Paris, France)
76. Gustave Guillarme, 25 (Troyes, France) Primo
77. Charles Quétier (Versailles, France)
78. Philippe De Balade, 20 (Agen, France)
79. *Margot (Ancenis, France)*
80. *Walter Madorin (Basle, Switzerland)*

VILLENEUVE–SAINT-GEORGES, 1 JULY 1903

By two in the afternoon, with the inescapable heat at its most intense, an unmistakeable sense of torpor has descended on the disappointingly spartan crowd that has been drawn to the Auberge du Réveil-Matin. Rather than the race, the oppressive conditions are the main topic of conversation among the groups of spectators pressed together in the shade beneath the trees. People have been dying simply going about their everyday business, some are saying.

No one, not even the growing number of riders making their way to and from the control point in the cafe, is dressed for such a temperature. Some of the ladies are displaying the new fashion for skirts to be pleated below the knee rather than from the waist. But all are suffocatingly constricted by tight bodices that conceal any fullness of the bosom and high-necked blouses with double sleeves, the outer one flared from the elbow, ensuring modesty is guaranteed but adding to the stifling effect that frilly-edged parasols do little to deflect.

The gentlemen, meanwhile, are uniformly in three-piece suits, their contrasting coloured waistcoats single-breasted, fully buttoned and sitting high on the chest, their trousers creased front and back, with turn-ups over leather, above-the-ankle boots. A straw boater is the only allowance made for the heat, although many have opted for a topper, bowler or flat cap.

The racers too look rather ill-prepared given the conditions. With no assistance allowed along the route from soigneurs except at control points, they have to be prepared for the extremes of day- and night-riding, as well as the constant battle with choking dust. Light cotton jackets, long-sleeved cotton shirts or wool jerseys are worn according to preference, the latter heavier but less liable to chafe and more of an insulator in a night-time chill. Legs are hidden from the dust and protected as best as possible from the potential wounding effects of crashes by cotton plus fours and knee-length socks. The flat cap is the headgear of choice, although the towering Fernand Augereau is hard to miss with a linen covering over his head and neck that suggests he's about to go collecting honey.

There is audible excitement as Hippolyte Aucouturier appears at the control point having spent the last few hours resting in a nearby hotel room he had presciently reserved some time before. Sporting his distinctive woollen jersey with red and blue hoops, dark racing tights, a flat cap and with his moustache waxed to perfection, Aucouturier wheels his ABC Crescent bike very casually through the spectators to the control point, looking so relaxed you'd be mistaken for thinking he's about to set off on a Sunday morning training ride.

At the control point he encounters his arch-rival, Maurice Garin, who is offering some words of advice to his young La Française teammate Lucien Pothier, a 20-year-old butcher's assistant from Sens whose introduction to the bike was as a delivery boy in the town, riding with one hand on the bars and the other clutching a meat-filled wicker basket balanced on his head. The two favourites exchange a few friendly words, but their demeanour changes when Alphonse Steinès hands each of them the large square of red cloth bearing their race numbers. Henri Desgrange tells them the number must be fixed to their bikes or they will be disqualified.

'We've already got an armband. If the wind gets up we're going to be pedalling with our bikes between our knees, which is going to be a picture,' they complain. Desgrange's word is final, however, and Aucouturier winds his way off into the crowd in search of a coco vendor who can fill his bottle with the refreshing mix of water, lemon and liquorice, while Garin continues his griping in Italian with another teammate, his good friend Rodolfo Muller.

There's more anger when Jean Fischer reaches the control point. There is no obvious reason for it. This is simply how 'The Climber' behaves. Number and yellow armband claimed, he stalks off through the crowds to a neighbouring cafe that he insists has a better reputation for its food. There he comes across Le Monde Sportif correspondent Jean Lafitte, whom Fischer berates for omitting him from his list of Tour favourites.

His spirits apparently lifted by the delivery of this roasting, he returns to the throng to buy a cup of barley sugar water from 'Boum-Boum', an African gentleman belting out a catchy ditty to attract custom, his colourful jacket and voluminous pantaloons ensuring that he is absolutely unmissable. There are several other vendors hawking their wares in similar sing-song fashion. One, Ali Baba, is selling an elixir that, he says, cures all ills and is no doubt a variation on Vin Mariani, the tonic created by mixing alcohol-suffused coca leaves with red wine that has been glowingly endorsed by Pope Leo XIII.

Just before three, and almost half an hour later than scheduled, Steinès, his boater pushed back on his head, peers over the top of his gold spectacles at the throng around the control point and prepares to announce the closure of registration when two very late arrivals appear in the Au Réveil-Matin. The first is Claude Chapperon, who is well tipped for success. Running up to Steinès, the gasping racer explains that he has ridden almost 20 kilometres from the centre of Paris after missing his train to the start. No sooner has Chapperon completed sign-in formalities, than Émile Moulin, at 40 the Tour's oldest starter, hurries up shouting, 'I'm here! I'm here!' His registration guarantees a round total of 60 starters, almost three times as many as Bordeaux–Paris a few weeks earlier, and including all of the favourites apart from upcoming stars Louis Trousselier and Lucien Petit-Breton.

The moment has finally arrived when the action can begin. But immediately another issue arises. Riders are complaining about a hazardous section of road 600 metres from the start. Wear caused by the wheels of the carts transporting rubble from the Paris–Corbeil railway construction works has left a humped spine along the centre of the road. There's confusion. Some riders and spectators start to walk along the road, expecting the start to be moved, only to find the organisers have not come with them. A car arrives to summon them back to the crossroads on which the Au Réveil-Matin stands, where the officials are gathered in discussion.

The chatter ends when all those milling about are brought to attention by the official starter, Georges Abran, who sports an expansive but neatly trimmed moustache and is immaculately turned out in a lightweight suit topped off with a broad-brimmed panama. Distinguished and authoritative, he calls for quiet and the hubbub subsides.

'Gentlemen, because of the building works currently being carried out, the start will take place 600 metres from here, towards Draveil,' Abran bellows above the construction noise, which even he can't quell. There are groans and laughter from the curious spectators at the roadside as Steinès sets off along the middle of the road with the pack of riders on his heels.

When Steinès and the 60-strong peloton are beyond the rough section of road, Abran calls the entourage to a halt and indicates the new start point. He stands on the left-hand edge of the road, while Steinès takes up a position on the other side next to an almost listless pennant in the same yellow shade as L'Auto's pages that has been hurriedly fixed into the ground at the end of a small branch.

Abran signals for the riders to mount their bikes. He takes out a starter's pistol with his right hand and pulls out his pocket watch with his left. As he points the pistol skywards, he follows the second hand as it ticks round for a few moments, the riders and the crowd gazing at him in silent anticipation. At exactly 3.16, he fires the pistol. The Tour de France is under way. With no thought of saving themselves with almost 500 kilometres ahead, the peloton races away at high speed. Within a few seconds they have all disappeared into a billowing cloud of dust.

'It seemed quite fantastic to those watching, but I bet deep inside we're all thinking that these riders will never reach the finish,' *Eugène Christophe will write that evening. Henri Des-grange may well be thinking precisely that as he walks briskly back to his car, which then turns around and heads in the other direction, towards Paris. He is not planning to see the race before its return to the capital on 19 July. He knows better than anyone that the paper's future is likely to have been decided well before then, and the rather disappointing turn-out for the start does not augur well. In the meantime, he has other commitments to think about. His first child, Denise, is a month old today. However, rather than heading home, his route takes him straight to L'Auto's offices on the Rue du Faubourg-Montmartre to prepare the first special edition of his paper.*

CHAPTER 6

'A BEAUTIFUL BUT TERRIBLE BATTLE'

One of the most obvious differences between the first Tour and the modern-day editions was evident from the very moment the opening stage to Lyon got under way: the poor state of the roads on which they were racing. Within seconds of the riders starting, the spectators and officials gathered at the start would have been able to see no more than a huge cloud of dust swirling in their wake as the peloton hared away on a surface of hard-packed earth.

Unlike the cobbled surfaces that had been laid in most of France's towns and cities, these dirt roads did offer a fairly consistent surface. However, too much sun and too little rain, or vice versa, rendered them hazardous. Road users ended up either blinded by dust or slithering through sludge. The dust was easier to deal with, as long as it was your bike or motor vehicle that was kicking it up. For anyone behind, successful forward progress was a lottery.

That this issue desperately needed resolution had become even more apparent due to the growing numbers of motor vehicles, which were restricted in theory by a speed limit of 20 kilometres per hour in built-up areas and 30 in the countryside. However, the only actual limit was each driver's common sense. Gendarmes depending on bikes or foot power were almost completely unable to enforce these regulations, to the dismay of pedestrians and, most particularly, those who lived alongside busy roads and were unable to open their windows in warm weather because of the all-pervading dust.

Articles on the poor state of the roads and the many accidents resulting from this appeared regularly in both the mainstream and the sporting press, usually demanding the introduction of a formal *code de la route* that laid down speed limits for all vehicles. Yet, the legislation implementing rules of the road did not go through until 1922.

Resurfacing France's roads, though, occurred much more quickly. In August 1903, C-M. Gariel, the inspector of bridges and roads, wrote an article for *La Révue du Touring Club du France* giving his impressions of an experiment in *goudronnage*, the laying of coal tar, over a section of road at Porte Dorée in south-east Paris. 'At first glance, the coated section seemed clean and well-sealed and, looking even more closely, you could see that there wasn't any appreciable amount of dust lying on it,' he reported, adding that the bikes and motor vehicles that passed when he was inspecting it didn't kick up the usual irritating and blinding cloud. He concluded by saying it was desirable for further tests to be carried out across France and over a longer period in order to confirm the efficacy of tarring roads to quell the plague of dust for road users.

Within a few years, the Tour would feature a lot of riding on roads of this type, but for the hopefuls at the 1903 race there would be no escape from the dust. Goggles kept it out of their eyes, but it coated everything else. The best they could do was try to avoid it, which to a large extent explained what may seem to be rather madcap tactics.

The individual stages of a modern multi-day race tend to stick to a very formulaic pattern. From the start, an early break will form comprising a small group of riders. The racers don't have a realistic ambition of being contenders for the overall title and either don't have the sprinting speed to win a bunch finish or are not specialist climbers. The peloton will allow them to build a lead, before beginning to chase them down to ensure a bunch sprint or a battle between the pick of the climbers depending on the terrain at the finish. Although there are slight variations to this, the one unchanging guarantee is that the best sprinters and climbers will sit in the midst of the peloton, saving all of the energy they can until the last and, hopefully, decisive moment. Any appearance by them at the front of the pack before this would be strategic suicide.

In the first Tour, where, it should be remembered, the rules laid down that the riders had to race as individuals even though several of the bigger names did belong to teams, there was absolutely no question of the favourites sitting back. Instead, they attacked each other right from the very first moment. Establishing a gap over your rivals meant having a clear road ahead of you and leaving a dusty trail in your wake, so those following behind could not clearly see the ideal line to take in order to avoid potholes, debris or animals in the road or the best approach to corners.

Then there is the question of how the suppression of pace-makers affected tactics. Firstly, the star names would have been used to going off hard from the gun, but doing so while sitting in behind well-paid pace-setters who were effectively doing most of the work for them, just as a team leader's domestiques now do. They simply weren't used to sitting in a pack in order to preserve their physical resources. Consequently, after Abran had fired the starting pistol on stage 1, they raced flat out as they always did.

A nagging concern about 'the levelling of the playing field' brought about by this change to the well-established rules also had an impact. Sprinting away from the start, the leading names wanted to impose themselves on less-renowned riders who sniffed an opportunity to upset the established hierarchy, determined to quash suggestions that their dominance was about pace-makers more than ability.

STAGE 1, PARIS–LYON, 467 KILOMETRES, 1–2 JULY 1903

As soon as Georges Abran pulls the trigger on his starting pistol, the race is on, reports Géo Lefèvre, the first in L'Auto's relay of 542 correspondents and reporters. 'What is most important in a road race of the importance and scale of the Tour de France is undoubtedly the start,' he says, which explains why he is not planning on catching an express train south until he reaches Fontainebleau after watching the opening 50 kilometres of racing. Travelling in one of the few cars tracking the riders, Lefèvre can get some idea of what is happening at the front of the race.

With a tailwind encouraging them along, Hippolyte Aucouturier, Jean Fischer, Paul Trippier and Maurice Garin lead the charge towards Montgeron, with Gustave Pasquier also towards the front. A few of the favourites, including Rodolfo Muller, Josef Fischer and Léon Georget, lose ground because the start is so frantically fast, but they are quickly back on the pace of their rivals. Within a kilometre the peloton is already spread over a considerable distance.

Pasquier surges to the front, setting a tremendous pace that lines out the riders behind him, Garin still prominent among them, reluctant to attack but quick to respond whenever another rider attempts to break clear. Pasquier, who caused a sensation when he finished third at Paris–Brest–Paris in 1901 despite riding without pace-makers and is now one of the string of La Française team members who will be able to count on comprehensive mechanical support at fixed control points, is sure that the Tour will be the race where he will upstage his more illustrious rivals, even after the heavy crash at Bordeaux–Paris that opened up his knee.

Coming out of Corbeil, where L'Auto's correspondent says he has never seen so many people turn out to watch a road race, the first hill brings Garin to the front, but he's doing no more than monitoring the competition. Although consistently close to the front, the Tour favourite is one of the few who is prepared to bide his time, to allow fatigue to take a toll. 'The start was bewildering, tumultuous, but I managed to keep myself out of trouble. I heard someone clattering down behind me and someone shouted out that Josef Fischer had fallen. Poor guy! But we saved ourselves, which is how it is in war,' he will later explain to Géo Lefèvre.

At Melun, 25 kilometres in, Le Vélo correspondent Alphonse Baugé is confounded when a peloton of around 40 riders, with the favourites gathered near the front and apparently going hell for leather, charge through 16 minutes later than scheduled. He calculates they are averaging just 25 kilometres per hour, not aware that the start had been delayed by 16 minutes. In fact, they are riding at close to 35 and showing no sign of tempering their pace or tactics. Garin is still prominent, with Claude Chapperon and Georget also in the vanguard. 'It is impossible to recognise the others in the whirlwind of dust whipped up as they pass,' Baugé reports.

Chapperon, Trippier, Georget and Aucouturier continue to

press, their objective clearly to unsettle and drop Garin if pos-sible. 'They want to see me off, but they won't manage it,' the Tour favourite tells himself. There's another acceleration, to which Garin and his protégé Émile Pagie respond.

At every little town and village, large crowds are awaiting the riders' arrival, lining both sides of the road. Initial concerns about the pulling power of the race appear unfounded as the leaders cross the Seine heading for the first 'flying' control point at Fontainebleau, where the Café de l'Union in which the offi-cials are waiting has been besieged by eager onlookers. By now joined in his car by Compagnie Dunlop director Monsieur Price, Lefèvre slows on the approach to the town to assess the damage wreaked by the incessant speed. With less than 30 kilometres covered, almost a third of the riders are trailing the lead pack.

It's 4.50 in the afternoon when the lead group containing 11 riders flashes past the control point, each racer yelling out his name as they pass. Two minutes later, Marcel Kerff charges by, and six minutes after that another five come into view. Paris-ian Claude Chapperon, one of those who almost missed the start, is at the rear of this little group. Struggling with injuries sustained in a crash, he becomes the first rider to abandon the Tour de France. Soon after, Léon Riche also quits having injured his knee.

Léon Manaud, now recovered from the wound he sustained in his duel with rival journalist Frantz Reichel a few weeks before, takes up the reporting baton from his colleague Lefèvre. Comparing the Tour with the other great races of the era, he *suggests that, 'Generally, once 53km have been covered there are just two men at the front, but on this occasion there are eight riding well grouped, fighting with equal arms . . .' All of the favourites are present, including the unflappable Muller, who, noticing Manaud, shouts across, 'Bonjour les enfants!'*

Climbing again coming out of Fontainebleau, Georget, who is far from alone in believing wine delivers a boost to the muscles and is known as 'The Brutal', thanks to the astounding amount of red, preferably Bordeaux, he can quaff at one sitting, sets the pace ahead of Aucouturier, his back bent due to the effort required to push the large gear he's using. Garin, of course, is in close attendance as the leaders press on towards the second 'flying' control, almost a quarter of the way to Lyon, at Montargis, where the crowd has been building since the late afternoon. Manaud estimates there are almost a thousand people gathered around the Café des Glaces when Dunlop's Monsieur Price arrives at six to announce that the leaders are right on his tail.

Half an hour later, Georget leads the first group through at an impressive rate. There are as many as 15 in it, but, following Chapperon's early abandon, another of the favourites is absent. Several minutes later, Édouard Wattelier halts having ridden for the last 18 kilometres on a rim after puncturing. He becomes the third man to abandon. With time to spare before he can catch a train back to Paris, he seeks consolation in consumption, buying 'a superb pair of blue worker's trousers'. He informs L'Auto that a lady's hairpin was the reason for his predicament. 'Oh, what are women like!' declares the organising paper.

Montargis also sees the abandon of the only rider in the field from the Midi, François Poussel from Nice, another crash victim. Germany's Josef Fischer is also struggling, apparently set back by age as much as misfortune. He hasn't been able to stay with the pace of the strongest, who are still averaging more than 31 kilometres per hour. 'This is superb for a race without pace-makers,' notes Manaud, who also points to the presence at the front of riders such as Eugène Brange, René Salais, Léon Habets and Samson, 'who would certainly have been eliminated [from contention] if pace-makers had been used . . . The Tour de France is definitely a race that gives real encouragement to young riders.'

Riders trickle through Montargis for the next 90 minutes. One of the last is Parisian Lassartigues, who is groggy after crashing not long before. After receiving attention from a doctor, he becomes the latest rider to abandon. Most onlookers are distracted from his predicament, though, by a gentleman ranting about defects in the organisation of the race. He is, Manaud relates, a Monsieur Fouquin, secretary of the local cycling club that has been responsible for the organisation of the control point. It appears the excitement of the occasion has got too much for him.

Darkness is beginning to fall when the first riders approach Cosne where another huge throng awaits them. Still pushed along by a northerly wind, Garin in his white jersey and Aucouturier in his blue and red are the easiest to pick out in a group that also contains Georget and the surprising figure of Pagie, victor in a minor race at Ypres the Sunday before and now competing with the sport's very best.

Riled by the fact that an agreement between the leaders to halt at Briare to freshen up was ignored by everyone and angered by the constant attempts to attack him, Garin has been waiting for the right moment to respond. Aware that Aucouturier is toiling, Muller is weakening and Pasquier is audibly blowing due to his exertions, he decides to tighten the screw as several members of the group lobby for a brief halt in Cosne. 'Listen to me, I forbid you from getting off your bike in front of an inn,' he instructs Pagie.

Believing a deal has finally been struck between them for a temporary cessation of hostilities, most of the lead group roll to a halt, only to see Garin and Pagie persist with their pace. Georget splashes himself with water and charges after them, but is the only rider to regain contact with the two La Française teammates. 'Aucouturier has lost the Tour de France as he's been dropped and I've won it!' Garin says later of this moment, yet the opening stage is still only half run.

His statement looks a little less ludicrous when Georget tells him he thinks he's got a rear wheel puncture. Clearly expecting Garin and Pagie to stop and wait for him because they will gain more ground working as three than two, he instead finds himself alone at the roadside as his merciless rivals continue on into the darkness.

At Nevers, the fixed control point overseen by L'Auto's Fernand Mercier at the Café Bussy is lit up like a Christmas tree. Thousands of expectant locals are craning for a sight of the table where every racer is required to stop and sign his name. At four minutes to eleven, Garin and Pagie emerge from the blackness, the former winning the 100-franc prize on offer to the first rider to cross the line chalked across the road 100 metres short of the control. They come to a halt and grab for the pens on the table, then dunk their heads in buckets of water to sluice away some of the grime from the road.

La Française manager Delattre has a bowl of broth ready for Garin. His star rider describes it as 'a kind of soup that I like a lot and which contains huge amounts of sugar'. Although its contents are otherwise a mystery, the revitalising effect of this foul-smelling liquid is very well known by his rivals. Seeing Garin drinking it down, Pagie, the stage's surprise package who has no food of his own ready and waiting, asks to try it. He gags when he tastes how bitter it is, the officials laughing uproariously at his reaction.

Before they are away again into the night, Garin spots Mercier and tells him, 'You'd better believe how well this little chap is hanging on, but now we're going to see what he's made of.' Mercier works out that the two leaders are 80 minutes ahead of the expected schedule having averaged more than 25 kilometres per hour from Paris. At this rate, they will arrive in Lyon at eight in the morning, three hours ahead of the predicted time.

A dozen minutes later, a truculent Georget signs the paper. Eight minutes on, the Belgian Catteau, young Lucien Pothier and Italy's Muller do the same. Another four riders and almost a quarter of an hour pass before Aucouturier adds his signature to the sheet, his deficit widened by an enforced stop to carry out a repair on his disintegrating saddle with a piece of twine.

Prominent early on, Parisian Paul Trippier abandons at the control point. Former acrobat, trapeze artist and clown Lucien Barroy looks set for the same fate when he arrives seriously injured as the result of a crash. With the new moon only just starting to wax and providing very little illumination of the dirt roads, these night-time hours present the riders with their most severe test. They must maintain a good pace, but the lights most have fitted to their front fork offer almost no help in revealing hazards in the road.

After waiting an hour and receiving some medical attention, Barroy manages to continue on his way. Hungry, tired and unable to see more than a few metres ahead of their front wheel in the darkness, most of the other riders languishing in the second half of the field are also pausing for an hour or more under the bright lights of the Nevers control where they can replenish themselves, their saddle bags and receive a fortifying rub from local masseur Monsieur Alliot. 'The Flying Carpenter', Alexandre Foureaux, receives an extra lift as his wife is waiting there for him, and the recently married couple embrace tenderly.

With the leaders now well on their way towards the second fixed control point at Montargis, a message is dispatched from the telegraph office in Cosne by L'Auto's correspondent Monsieur Walter announcing the disqualification of Jean Fischer. Suspicions about his progress had already been aroused, and further surveillance by Desgrange and Lefèvre's undercover officials has resulted in 'this strapping man being caught in flagrant abuse of the rules on pace-making behind a vehicle and being towed'. Although the officials stopped the irascible Fischer and informed him of his disqualification, he has protested his innocence and is continuing to ride.

This news has yet to reach Géo Lefèvre. Having arrived in Nevers on an express train from Paris, L'Auto's special correspondent, who is also the race director, lead commissaire and finish-line judge, has viewed the control point at the Café Bussy, and then moved on towards Moulins, another 60 kilometres down the course. Yet, rather than continue all of the way to the control point, he asks his driver to stop short of the town. He takes his bike from the car and sits down at the roadside beneath an avenue of large trees, the tops of which are hidden in the darkness.

He's expecting six or seven riders to emerge from the night, but at almost one in the morning he sees just two white forms hurtling towards him. He leaps on his bike and sprints to catch up with the two phantoms.

— Who are you?

— Garin, Monsieur Géo!

— What's become of the rest? Where are Aucouturier and Josef Fischer?

— I don't know. This race of yours with no pace-makers and soigneurs is incredibly tough, but I will win it! I will win it! I will win it!

Pagie says nothing. The pair of them take turns to set the pace, swapping on and off, pushing out their advantage over the rest of the field and quickly distancing Lefèvre. They reach the cobbled roads on the outskirts of Moulins, then its lamp-lit streets, and finally the control point where, despite it being past one in the morning, an immense crowd is waiting and applauds thunderously as the two men rush in to sign their names.

Once again Delattre is ready for them. He has chickens, chocolate, broth, oranges and Vichy water, and Pagie eagerly tucks in, encouraging Garin to do the same. But the race favourite, who has blood trickling from a knee, flies into a shameful rage, shouting orders at his manager. 'Get me cold water! Get me this to eat! Get me that to drink!' Delattre sucks up the verbal battering, wiping down his star man, handing him a bowl of broth that he slurps down, then a bottle of milk and another of Vichy water, which Garin stuffs into his jacket pockets. He fills the little leather bag hanging from his belt with oranges, then slowly remounts and is pushed away into the night by Delattre, with Pagie scuttling after him, the pair of them trailed by chief race controller Léon Collet on his motorbike.

Le Monde Sportif correspondent Léopold Alibert reveals the reason for Garin's anger. A few kilometres outside Moulins, surprised by Pagie suddenly slowing to avoid an obstacle, he had clipped his teammate and somersaulted over his bars. His arms and legs were bloodied, but the wounds were superficial. However, his bike was a write-off. Helped back to his feet by Pagie and a Monsieur Bourassier from Moulins, he used the latter's bike to reach the control point, where a new one was ready for him. Fortunately for Garin, what could have been a serious incident has had few repercussions.

The crowd's applause has barely died down following Garin and Pagie's departure when there's hubbub again. Georget, looking remarkably fresh, arrives at the control point, calling for cold water. He plunges his head into a bucket full of it. His hair dripping, he demands Bordeaux and biscuits. He mixes a lot of water with the wine and swigs it down as he crams in a dozen biscuits. Within moments, he is away again, continuing his pursuit of the two leaders.

Jean Fischer, disqualification hanging over him, is next to emerge from the darkness and flit away again, then Marcel Kerff, Muller and several more before, an hour behind the leaders, Aucouturier rolls in and flops down on a chair. He starts chewing mechanically on the roast beef and eggs his soigneurs have ready for him, big tears creating furrows through the dust encrusted on his face.

'I've never felt like this. My head is good, my legs are good, but I'm making no progress. My stomach is churning. It's over! It's all over!'

Distressed by the sight of 'The Hercules of Commentry' reduced to a wreck, Lefèvre tries to encourage him, and eventually the great champion throws his leg back over his bike and recommences his pursuit of glory. He persists as far as La Palisse, another 50 kilometres along the route, and abandons there, complaining of severe stomach cramps.

Day is beginning to break, the sun starting to burn off a light mist, as Garin and Pagie approach Roanne, just 80 kilometres from Lyon. It's just after five in the morning, but it appears the whole town is out waiting for them. Ahead of them lies the final significant test of this opening stage, the Charolais hills, where the Côte de l'Hôpital and the 10-kilometre ascent of the Col du Pin Bouchain are the most challenging ascents.

Approaching the top of the former, Garin starts to feel hunger pangs. Spotting a cherry tree, he calls Pagie to a halt and clambers into the branches to fill his pockets with the fruit. Spurred on by the sugary pick-me-up, they breeze on to the summit. Now for the descent. Downhills are more complicated and physically demanding for riders using a fixed gear, as all the racers are, apart from Paris gentlemen's outfitter Pierre Desvages, whose bike· is equipped with a BSA freewheel. Garin admits that the strain this puts on his muscles takes more out of them than the climbs.

After juddering down the Côte de l'Hôpital, they start up the bigger Pin Bouchain. Topping out at 760 metres, it's a steady climb, averaging less than 4 per cent, the gradient rarely rising much above that. Standing on the pedals, the two leaders conquer it and take the descent carefully, well aware that they have a large advantage over Georget.

The road drops into Tarare, 43 kilometres from the finish, where another great throng has filled the streets. Pagie has a scare when an overexcited fan stumbles into his path, knocking him to the ground. Thankfully, the young racer is unhurt and, helped by the apologetic fan, he's quickly back aboard and sprints to catch up with Garin.

While the racers continue on the almost eternal road to Lyon, Lefèvre joins several fellow scribes and Delattre on the train from Moulins to France's third city. The La Française *manager is ecstatic with how the race is unfolding. His star man is heading for victory and no fewer than nine of the dozen riders backed by his team are in the contest for high finishes at the conclusion of stage 1 – the two leaders, plus Augereau, Muller, Pothier, Jaeck, Catteau, Pasquier and Jean Fischer. All on the train are destined for disappointment, however, as none of them will witness the finish, such is the pace being set by Garin and Pagie.*

Allies for most of the night, the two teammates become rivals as they approach the finish on Lyon's Quai de Vaise on the banks of Saône, where a trumpet signals their arrival, sending the spectators rushing into the road. Two hundred metres from the line, just as they are sizing each other up for a sprint, they encounter a series of tram tracks and two farmers' carts blocking the direct route to the line. Drawing on his experience, Garin, 'jumping like a cat over the large cobbles on the Quai de Vaise', manages to weave his way between them while Pagie dismounts and trots past. The contest is over, the opportunity for a fascinating duel between mentor and acolyte lost, for now at least.

Garin trundles across the line with dozens of local cyclists in his wake cheering him on. He has covered the 467 kilometres in a little less than 18 hours, averaging 26 kilometres an hour, an astounding feat considering he and Pagie have raced right through a near-moonless night. He dismounts and signs in at the control point located at the Brasserie Comte with an 'Ouf!' of satisfaction as L'Auto's Fernard Mercier and Georges Abran look on. The completely unheralded Pagie rolls in a minute later. He signs the control sheet and the two teammates embrace, the less experienced rider telling his mentor, 'Thank you, Maurice. You encouraged me the whole way, you allowed me to eat your food and, thanks to you, I've finished second.'

Mobbed by fans, the pair shake dozens of hands, offer innumerable bonjours and recount their race to the handful of journalists within the throng. Géo Lefèvre arrives just as Garin and Pagie are being driven away, but manages to see Georget's arrival half an hour or so later. 'The face of this son of Châtellerault is a mask of rage,' he reports. 'He signs in and, without saying a word, allows himself to be driven the nearby bathhouse to which Garin and Pagie have already departed.'

Having seen Augereau finish fourth and Jean Fischer fifth, Lefèvre follows them to the baths, where he finds Garin stretched out naked on a bed of thick wool. The stage-winner shows the race director his derrière, pointing out that all signs of wear caused by his saddle have already disappeared. He's finished with just a few minor cuts and grazes on his knee and elbow, which won't trouble him on the second stage. Pagie, having washed and had a massage, looks 'as fresh and pink as a little baby'. Georget is still distraught, constantly repeating: 'I punctured twice! I punctured twice!'

As Lefèvre gauges reaction from the early finishers, riders continue to arrive through the rest of the morning, the afternoon and into the evening, each of them announced by a trumpet call. Josef Fischer's pre-race optimism looks very misplaced when he reaches Lyon in 19th place, more than four hours behind Garin, after puncturing five times. Blacksmith

Dargassies, who crashed heavily soon after the start and spent three hours receiving treatment to his knee and arm, has bravely carried on to arrive at three in the afternoon, six hours after the winner. A couple of hours behind him is 18-year-old Philippe De Balade.

As night falls, the crowd dwindles to just a few captivated souls, the rustling of the leaves in the trees now audible in the calm evening. Each time a rider emerges, dusty and almost unrecognisable, they are greeted with near silence, the specta-tors appearing to sense their disappointment. They look demoralised, some weeping, their defeat total.

Thirty-seventh and last in before the closure of the control point at the Brasserie Comte is one-time cabaret singer Eugène Brange, who arrives just three minutes before the closure of the control point at six on Friday morning. More than 21 hours in arrears, he explains that, stricken by hunger, he lost contact near Cosnes and later spent several hours sleeping in a meadow. Dismayed by his performance, he declares he will quit the race if he doesn't finish in the first five in Marseille.

Brange is not the last to finish, though, as Léon Durandeau rolls in three hours later, but receives no reward for his persist-ence as the rules make clear he is outside the time limit. However, the plucky Durandeau insists he will start the second stage, as the rules allow non-finishers and new entries to com-pete on individual legs of the race.

L'Auto's staff couldn't be more delighted. There have been only one or two minor organisational hiccups, lots of impres-sive performances and an unbelievable turn-out in all parts *after Paris. 'Let's just take note of the fact that this great race without pace-makers has been a lot better sporting contest than Bordeaux–Paris run with pacers. It has placed men on a completely equal footing with riders of great class, even though the stand-out roadman has triumphed,' Lefèvre concludes.*

'It was a near unknown, Pagie, who finished second. All of the rest performed very well . . . There is no doubt that this first stage of the Tour de France has been a beautiful, but terrible, battle.'

STAGE 1 RESULT

1. Maurice Garin 467km in 17-45-13 (average speed 26.304km/h)
2. Emile Pagie (Fra) at 55 seconds
3. Léon Georget (Fra) at 34-59
4. Fernand Augereau (Fra) at 1-02-50
5. Jean Fischer (Fra) at 1-04-55
6. Marcel Kerff (Bel) at 1-42-55
7. Aloïs Catteau (Bel) at 1-48-57
8. Ernest Pivin (Fra) at 1-49-49
9. Léon Habets (Fra) at 2-08-16
10. François Beaugendre (Fra) at 2-08-27
11. Rodolfo Muller (Ita) at 2-58-00
12. Henri Gauban (Fra) same time
13. Anton Jaeck (Swi) same time
14. Lucien Pothier (Fra) same time

15. Marcel Lequatre (Swi) same time
16. Gustave Pasquier (Fra) same time
17. Charles Laeser (Swi) at 4-03-07
18. 'Samson' (Bel) at 4-05-53
19. Josef Fischer (Ger) at 4-22-52
20. René Salais (Fra) at 5-57-27
21. Georges Borot (Fra) same time
22. Isidore Lechartier (Fra) at 6-04-07
23. Jean Dargassies (Fra) at 6-17-07
24. Julien Girbe (Fra) at 7-56-57
25. Alexandre Foureaux (Fra) at 8-22-07
26. François Monachon (Fra) at 8-22-59
27. Philippe De Balade (Fra) same time
28. Henri Ellinamour (Fra) at 8-34-07
29. Ferdinand Payan (Fra) at 9-01-01
30. Gustave Guillarme (Fra) at 9-01-03
31. Léon Pernette (Fra) at 9-43-34
32. Lucien Barroy (Fra) same time
33. Arsène Millochau (Fra) at 9-52-12
34. Émile Moulin (Fra) at 10-25-57
35. Ludwig Barthelmann (Ger) at 11-35-55
36. Pierre Desvages (Fra) at 13-28-57
37. Eugène Brange (Fra) at 20-55-49

CHAPTER 7

'AN HONEST AND CLOSELY CHECKED CONTEST'

Prior to the start of the Tour, Henri Desgrange had made it clear to *L'Auto*'s staff that they had to ignore or minimise any organisational flaws and, on the other hand, should not skimp on hyperbole and over-exaggeration when writing about the race and those taking part. Consequently, it is not surprising that the paper's post-stage coverage of the opening leg between Paris and Lyon is extremely upbeat and features not a single mention of any kind of issue relating to the event's organisation.

Of course, there were what, to modern eyes at least, seem like significant problems. The reports in *L'Auto* and other newspapers record several incidents of riders being knocked from their bikes by over-eager fans, there was clear evidence of cheating, and, most obviously, the final face-off between Maurice Garin and Émile Pagie was ruined by the two carts blocking the route to the line. However, this is nitpicking when one considers both the unprecedented scale of the Tour de France for that era and the spectator turnout.

The race may have started with a degree of Parisian apathy, which is understandable given the intense competition among sporting events and other entertainments for the attention of the city's inhabitants. But outside the capital, the French population could hardly have been any more enthusiastic. Even in the middle of the night, racers from the frontrunners to the backmarkers found themselves riding between a corridor of spectators in every town and village, while, as Garin found to his benefit when he crashed and wrote off his bike, there were fans even in the heart of the countryside throughout the night-time hours.

Therefore, it is no wonder that Henri Desgrange hailed the opening stage of his new race as 'a success that surpassed all expectations'. He added, 'What a beautiful start for the Tour de France and how happy we are to see the success of a race that we judged from the start would be supremely interesting.'

Desgrange may have been crowing, but the verdict from other sports papers supported his right to do so. Having branded the Tour 'the phantom race' when Desgrange had postponed the start only a couple of months earlier, *Le Vélo* began its report with an introduction lauding 'the golden age of road racing' and 'a success without precedence'. Robert Coquelle, the rival paper's chief cycling correspondent, suggested that there wasn't another country anywhere in the world that felt so much passion for bike racing, whether on the road or on the track, declaring that, 'The gigantic ran- donnée that is the Tour de France has taken this to its apogee, and the undeniable success of this event, which has been so very well organised by our colleagues at *L'Auto* and has sparked the interest and enthusiasm of the Lyonnais towards the competitors, is such an eloquent testament in itself that there is absolutely no need here for me to make the case in favour of great road race events.'

La Vie au Grand Air, one of the few illustrated periodicals that covered the race, was equally impressed, praising 'the grandeur of the event' and hailing its organisers for 'their considerable financial sacrifices and the gigantic organisa- tional and surveillance task required for such a race'.

Although the mainstream press wasn't as gushing, report- ing the unfolding of the action but rarely offering any description or analysis beyond these basics, their lack of interest was more the result of a general antipathy towards sport than towards the Tour or cycling in particular. They gave the Gordon Bennett Cup a little more coverage and in more prominent locations, but that was already a well- established competition and had renowned, wealthy and well-connected backers. For the main part, though, high- circulation dailies such as *Le Petit Journal* and *Écho de Paris* stuck to the main political, economic and diplomatic news, and this would remain the case for many decades to come. Sport had its place in the French press and, for the most part, that was within its own particular niche, which suited *L'Auto* and its rivals perfectly.

Those captivated or intrigued by the Tour had very few options if they were seeking greater detail, and essentially three if they wanted the fullest of details. Consequently, sales of *L'Auto's* special edition reached 93,000, more than 400 per cent higher than its average circulation, while those of *Le Vélo* and *Le Monde Sportif* jumped considerably too. Strangely, no sales figures were reported for *L'Auto's* main daily edition, but based on these figures and the paper's sales during Marseille–Paris the previous year, it seems likely that each sold more than 200,000 copies. Despite very large print runs, a variety of contemporary reports describe how vendors at stage starts, finishes and the control points in between rarely had enough copies such was the demand for these titles. Taking advantage of that, they often sold those five-centime copies they did have at twice, three or even four times that price, an action *L'Auto* was quick to condemn.

With just a single stage of the race completed, it's easy to imagine how delighted Henri Desgrange and Victor Goddet must have been. Beset by despair earlier in the year, the future of their newspaper suddenly looked rosy. That optimism would have been buoyed too by the immediate boost in advertising revenue the Tour yielded. La Française (Garin, Pagie), Crescent (Aucouturier), Aiglon (Georget) and Dunlop were just the most prominent brands to respond to the accomplishments of riders they backed with large 'success' adverts. Initially, these ads shared space with those generated by the Gordon Bennett Cup, but as the Tour went on cycling-related advertising filled a very significant part of *L'Auto's* content, and not without good reason.

Bikes had long been taxed in France, and the numbers being so were rising very rapidly, reaching almost 1,500,000 in 1903. During this same period, the cost of a new bike fell from around 500 francs, a price that put them within reach of only the wealthy, to 100 francs and below, making them available to most of the population.

Although mass production meant manufacturers had more of these cheaper bikes to sell, the obvious cut in their profit margins meant they were always looking for ways to boost their volume of sales. Hitherto, piggy-backing on track-racing and exploiting the feats of stars such as Major Taylor had been the best way of achieving this. Yet the Tour offered manufacturers something different and much more useful. It took place on the same rough highways familiar to millions of Frenchmen and -women, who could much more easily identify with these 'giants of the road'. In the weeks following the Tour, road-cycling clubs reported rapid growth in interest.

There were also cultural reasons for cementing this sense of identification with the Tour de France. Since the Middle Ages, the artisans and craftsmen who were members of the Compagnons du Tour de France had been conducting their own tours of the nation in order to learn their trade, and were well known for doing so. Apprentice masons, smiths, carpenters to name but a few of the *compagnon* professions would spend between six months and a year learning their trade before moving on to the next place, gradually working their way up through the *compagnonnage* hierarchy to become master craftsmen who were able to establish a business where they wanted and welcome touring apprentices into their own workplace.

As a result of compulsory primary education, which was introduced across France in the early 1880s, literacy was almost universal among French children. One of the textbooks they used during this period and well into the twentieth century was *Le tour de France par deux enfants* (*A Tour of France by Two Children*). Written in 1877 by Augustine Fouillée using the nom de plume G. Bruno, the book tells the tale of two boys, André and Julien Volden, who, as a result of the German annexation of Alsace-Lorraine and the death of their father, set out on a journey around France to search out other members of their family. Their adventures bring them into contact with hugely diverse people, as well as local dialects, regional food and stories about French heroes and history.

Hugely successful and extremely patriotic, which would have made it doubly attractive to Henri Desgrange, the book's annual readership was between six and seven million copies, and it continued to be used in French schools until the 1950s. Its significance can be gauged by the fact that its centenary in the 1970s was marked by a television adaptation by Jean-Luc Godard, arguably the greatest of all French film directors.

Evidently, *L'Auto*'s Tour de France didn't so much bring a concept to life, but borrow from one that was already firmly entrenched in the French psyche. The Tour is the Tour, it is often said, and even in 1903 that was already the case

Oddly, given the modern-day obsession with thrusting a microphone or recorder in front of panting athletes as soon as they have crossed a finish line, the reaction of the riders to the challenge they had just completed was often not sought. Aside from Maurice Garin's insight into how he had won the Tour's opening stage and remarkably complete reports on how many punctures or crashes individual riders had suffered, the competitors remained mute as far as the press was concerned.

Reports on the Gordon Bennett Cup and other major sporting events were equally neglectful. While correspondents were given often very ample space to report on and offer their analysis of the action, those who best knew what had been happening were largely ignored. It is clear from the articles written by Géo Lefèvre and his journalistic colleagues that they had a very close relationship with competitors and were able to describe the state of form, hopes and complaints of the cyclists, but almost none of this appeared in the first person. To a degree, this reflected the general perception of the riders' lowly status, but was more the result of a clear division of roles – sportsmen (and they were almost always men during this period) competed and journalists reported their feats. Like racing strategy, sports reporting was very much in its infancy.

At the same time, journalistic devices that are still commonplace were already very apparent, and none more so than the high-brow editorial offering a seasoned expert's evaluation of the action. In future years at *L'Équipe*, *L'Auto*'s post-Second World War successor, this role would be taken up by Pierre Chany and, in more recent times, Philippe Bouvet, their knowledge and expertise enabling them to provide a beautifully described, humorous and pithy reflection on the Tour's latest stage. Inevitably during the inaugural Tour and for most of those that followed prior to the Second World War this task fell to Henri Desgrange.

Unlike Chany and Bouvet, who were writing for a newspaper that dominated the cycling landscape, Desgrange was fighting to ensure his paper's survival. As a result, his editorials were persistently upbeat. There was no question of him dwelling on the race's failings. He had instructed his correspondents to focus on the positive, and he stuck firmly to this himself.

In *L'Auto*'s 4 July edition, for instance, he alludes to pre-race concerns about a race without pace-makers becoming as monotonous as most 24-hour track events without pacers, where 'competitors were literally sleeping and used to ride at ridiculous [slow] speeds after a few hours'. Desgrange points out that rather than becoming a bore-fest of this nature, 'The race can clearly be seen as a battle between men, where all physical means needed to be functioning well in order to triumph. It was the first time that the stomach, resistance to thirst and to hunger featured as crucial

factors.' After praising Garin for demonstrating these qualities to the full, Desgrange concludes: 'The revolution taking
place in road racing is therefore complete and the success of
events without pace-makers is now assured . . . [the racers]
will be happy and proud to be able to say in future that they
have taken part in the greatest event in cycle sport.' His
words may be overblown, but they are prescient too.

With the benefit of hindsight, the only area in which the
analysis of Desgrange and his correspondents clearly failed
was in their response to cheating, although they would be
far from the last to be come up short in this domain. To the
credit of the Tour organisers, to an extent the measures they
implemented to dissuade racers from looking for an unfair
advantage worked. Two of their secret officials caught Jean
Fischer being paced behind two motorbikes close to Cosne.
The officials imposed the penalty set down by the race and
disqualified Fischer, but were unable to prevent him continuing on to Lyon, where he finished fifth, insisting on his
innocence.

Desgrange, a stickler for the rules but, at this early point,
ready to believe that racers approached his event with the
intention of behaving in honourable fashion, conducted an
inquiry with race director Lefèvre into Fischer's wrongdoing.
Their first step was to request that the two officials involved
send them a detailed account of the incident via telegraph.
Once they had received this report, they combed through it
and found 'an ambiguous phrase' that they felt required further explanation, although they did not specify what this

phrase might be. It appears, though, that Fischer was riding in the slipstream of two motorcyclists wearing red armbands of the type given to Tour officials, 'who procured them we know not how'.

That offered Fischer an opportunity to excuse his behaviour and he almost certainly claimed that he was doing no more than complying with orders given by these bogus officials. His case was helped by Gustave Pasquier and Marcel Kerff, who between them completed most of the stage with him and declared they had seen him involved in no wrongdoing.

Fischer then offered further information that initially appears foolish but may have been a canny ruse with which to deflect attention from his rule-breaking. He confessed to taking a drink while riding from a person he claimed he did not know. This broke article six of the race rules, which laid down that racers could not receive outside assistance when racing – they could only do so at control points. *L'Auto* announced that this made Fischer's ejection from the race much more likely, but added that he would be allowed to continue on the second stage to Marseille 'at his own risk'. If further evidence of rule-breaking emerged, he would be tossed out.

After the finish in Lyon, information reached the race officials that third-placed Léon Georget was also guilty of taking pace behind a motor vehicle, in his case a car bearing the registration 418 X that was being driven by the Darragon brothers, Louis and Arthur. 'One of them subjected one of our controllers, from whom we have received a complaint, to a revolting series of insults,' *L'Auto* reported, adding that the vehicle contained a bike that appeared to be for the use of Louis Darragon, a young professional who would go on to become a double world champion in Derny racing, the implication being that Georget had also been receiving pedal-powered assistance. Once again, though, the allegation of rule-breaking came to nothing.

Accusations were also made against 'two of the race's principal riders' in an anonymous letter, but *L'Auto* completely dismissed this until such time as the informant revealed both their identity and the specifics of the alleged rule-breaking. The paper added that the case against Fischer was the only serious one, and that anyone concerned about further indiscretions should calm their worries because three of the remaining five stages would be run entirely in daylight hours.

It is interesting to note that there was no suggestion in *L'Auto* that the stomach complaint that afflicted Aucouturier was the result of a sinister hand. The rider himself didn't make too much of his unexpected alimentary breakdown. *L'Auto* put it down to the fact that he wasn't receiving the same level of support as his rivals from La Française, who would jump from their bikes at control points and immediately start eating the pre-requested food that La Française manager Delattre had ready and waiting for them.

Aucouturier, on the other hand, had to scuttle around at the controls to find and prepare his food and drink. This may have resulted in him being handed something that had been deliberately tainted with the precise aim of nobbling him – Gustave Pasquier later revealed he had been offered lemonade that had been tampered with in precisely this way. Yet, it was more likely that Aucouturier had simply eaten or drunk something that was past its best, or that the intense heat had brought on sunstroke.

There were easier ways of ensuring a rival rider's hopes were scuppered than tampering with food that they might not even eat. Throwing tacks on the road was a simpler and more effective means of waylaying a rider, and something that many of those racing in the Tour would have been familiar with as it was so commonplace. Races organised by manufacturers were renowned for this kind of underhand behaviour, which was intended to ensure that the riders backed by the organiser would fill the top places, enabling their sponsor to laud its products in 'success' ads.

Yet, *L'Auto* went out of its way to say of its race that, 'The dominant feeling is one of satisfaction from not having found any tacks because, rather incredibly, none were thrown and as a result the race has been contested in an honest and closely checked manner.' However, that certainly would not remain the case.

CHAPTER 8

'I'VE BEATEN GARIN!'

Rest days during the inaugural Tour de France were much the same as those in the modern race. With no race action to focus on, the papers turned to forecasting what would happen on the stages to come, offered insight into the form of key competitors, and served up any gossip that had come their way. Much of the conjecture focused on the condition of Hippolyte Aucouturier. Having arrived in Lyon by train a completely beaten man rather than roaring in at the head of the race as he had very loudly predicted in Paris, Maurice Garin's principal rival wasn't expected to start the second stage between Lyon and Marseille.

According to the rules, riders who had failed to complete the opening leg of the race and those who had missed it due to other reasons could line up in the 374-kilometre run to France's biggest port and subsequent stages, although they would not be classified in the overall standings. During the rest day, many of the racers whose hopes of overall success had ended on stage 1 signed up in Lyon for a second crack at glory, including pre-race favourite Édouard Wattelier and the unfortunate Léon Durandeau, who had made it to Lyon on two wheels but not within the time limit.

Aucouturier hedged on his decision. Initially reluctant on arrival in Lyon, he woke refreshed on the rest day, which he spent wandering through the centre of Lyon, receiving regular encouragement to continue. By that evening, he had committed to the race once again and added his name to the 27 others registered to contest stage 2 alongside the 37 remaining in the longer battle for the overall prize.

While Aucouturier relaxed, stage-1 victor Garin and runner-up Émile Pagie took the train south to Saint-Étienne in order to reconnoitre the first section of the upcoming stage in reverse. Their outing extended to less than 60 kilometres of riding, but underlined the professionalism very apparent among the star names of that era. They recognised not only that all knowledge of the route was useful, but also that it could be folly to avoid the bike on a rest day by allowing tired muscles to tighten.

The La Française pair almost certainly ventured further than any of their rivals, who were variously described as spending the day meandering Lyon's sweltering streets or catching up on lost sleep in the swanky Hôtel de Russie, which had halved its rate in exchange for a few lines of puffery in *L'Auto*'s pages. Many undoubtedly spent considerable time reviewing what was being written about their performances in the Tour as well as the latest news from elsewhere, which included a hippopotamus delivering a fatal bite to its keeper at the Jardin des Plantes in Paris and an explosion in a coal mine at Hanna, Wyoming, that had cost the lives of 175 miners.

On the sporting side, details of a new Italian race may also have caught their attention. Due to take place on 11–12 July, Milan–Bologna–Padova–Brescia–Milan amounted to 603 kilometres of racing. There were updates on training sessions from the Buffalo and Parc des Princes tracks, news that 'The Black Cyclone finds form again' as Major Taylor recorded victories over notable rivals Thorwald Ellegaard and Willy Arend at the Brunswick track in Germany, and the latest from the Americas Cup in the United States, where the home nation was on course to retain the trophy.

Almost every sporting event, save for football, which had its own specialist publications and was anyway in its off-season, was ripe for coverage in *L'Auto* and other sports papers. Offering readers a comprehensive review was an essential part of maintaining and boosting readership. Consequently, these papers featured anything and everything from the track results at London's Canning Town and New York's Madison Garden, to the latest news from the world of pétanque and reports on 'pig-sticking', an event where a car would drag a 'pig' around an arena while drivers in other cars would attempt to score points by spearing it with a lance tipped with a padded cover. 'Given the difficulty of this event, the jury decided to annul the competition,' *L'Auto*'s Édouard Nobilé reported from Le Gymkhana Automobile in Paris.

There was, though, a much more effective way of attracting readers from other publications – scooping them. The Tour may have been *L'Auto*'s race, but it wasn't always the best source of up-to-date information on it. *Le Vélo* generally offered more detail, thanks to their well-established network of correspondents and the experience of writers such as Robert Coquelle, Alphonse Baugé and Victor Breyer. Yet both *L'Auto* and *Le Vélo* were upstaged by *Le Monde Sportif*, which only been established earlier that year.

Not initially regarded with seriousness by either of the more established titles, *Le Monde Sportif* quickly demonstrated that it merited more respect. Founded by former *Le Vélo* editor Paul Rousseau, it featured not only hand-drawn illustrations of riders – the use of photographs was still not possible in daily publications that had tight deadlines – but also a very impressive editorial team working beneath Rousseau, notably Frantz Reichel, the former Olympian who had fought a duel with *L'Auto*'s Léon Manaud, Jean Lafitte and Léopold Alibert.

Firstly, the upstart publication outwitted the more renowned papers by delaying the printing of its 2 July edition until 2.30 in the morning of the opening stage, allowing its correspondent to deliver the latest update on riders' positions as they raced through the night towards Lyon.

This gave the paperboys selling the paper a considerable advantage over other vendors. *Le Monde Sportif* backed this up by securing the first in-depth interview with stage-winner Garin and by printing *L'Auto*'s map of the route, which apparently came into its possession because the two papers used the same printer. The race to report on the Tour was just as fiercely contested as the battle to win it, and with such shenanigans was also well worth following.

For Géo Lefèvre and his organising team, the halt in Lyon was far from restful. They not only had to produce the copy required by Henri Desgrange back in Paris to fill *L'Auto*'s pages and make sure they were the ones delivering the important news first, but also assess the running of the opening stage and where changes might need to be made for the second. The most pressing issue was to guarantee that the stage-winner in Marseille arrived as close to the scheduled time of 4.10pm as possible, which would ensure the largest audience and, crucially, given the finale in Lyon, the chance for chief correspondent and race director Lefèvre to witness it. As there was good reason to think that the fastest riders would again run well ahead of schedule, the start, set to take place outside the Café de la Paix in Lyon's iconic Place Bellecour, was pushed back an hour.

Their other priority was to remind the racers and their supporters, whether official or not, of the rules. *L'Auto* picked out four in particular, articles five to eight in their regulations. These stressed that only muscle-powered bicycles could be used, that pace-makers and other on-course assistance were prohibited, that any indication of a rider riding behind a motor vehicle would result in disqualification, and, finally, that bike changes were permitted, with riders allowed to use any bike offered up by a spectator if required due to mechanical breakdown. Once again, the paper highlighted the presence of secret controllers along the course, underlining that their task would be simplified by the stage mostly taking place during daylight.

Almost 100 kilometres shorter than the first leg, the stage to Marseille followed the Rhône valley after initially heading south-west to Saint-Étienne. This flatter terrain, where the mistral would nudge the riders along if it started to gust from the north, was a far less daunting test, especially once the riders had negotiated hills between Saint-Étienne and Annonay, where the principal difficulties were the ascent of the Col de la République, often a key climb in editions of Paris–Nice in subsequent years, and 'the famous descent from Bourg-Argental with its terrible hairpins'. Even though there would be officials with warning lights here, *L'Auto* still stressed, 'attention, attention!'

There were fixed control points at Saint-Étienne, Valence, Avignon and Aix-en-Provence, with 'flying' controls at Tournon-sur-Rhône, Montélimar and Lambesc.

There was almost unanimous agreement that Garin was the man to beat. 'He's an excellent roadman, has extraordinary qualities in terms of endurance and, just like all winners the day after a great victory, his qualities are even clearer and more definite. I can't really see anyone beating him,' wrote Jacques Miral in *L'Auto*. The consensus was that riders such as Aucouturier and Wattelier who had pulled out of the first stage may have saved some energy but had not demonstrated the endurance to trouble Garin. Moreover, they had been soundly beaten, and it would require something very special to bounce back from such a drubbing. 'I really fear that once again Garin's ferocious power will see off all their valiant efforts,' wrote *Le Vélo's* Léopold Alibert.

STAGE 2, LYON–MARSEILLE, 374KM, 4–5 JULY 1903

There are still two hours before registration opens at midnight at the Café de la Paix, but the area around it is already packed with eager spectators. Race director Géo Lefèvre can't believe the scene in front of him. Yet, enthusiasm is not universal. 'We would never have imagined that so many people in Lyon would have been capable of showing interest in something cycling-related,' the correspondent from L'Express de Lyon *reports very sniffily.*

By the time a firework is set off at midnight to announce the opening of the control point, the crowd is pressing in on all sides. Riders have to struggle to make their way to the table where Fernard Mercier, Georges Abran and Lefèvre are waiting to secure their signature and hand over a numbered armband to the new racers:

100. Élie Monge from Pierrelatte
101. Garrot from Romans-sur-Isère
103. Paul Armbruster from Paris

Eight riders who abandoned the first stage are set to join them to contest the spoils in Marseille, including Aucouturier, Wattelier and Trippier.

Cries of 'Vive Garin! Vive Pagie! Vive L'Auto!' resound continuously from the enthusiastic throng, where well-dressed bourgeois couples, workers in overalls and cyclists in woollen jerseys, plus fours and stockings rub shoulders, all social barriers forgotten.

The riders are infected by the crowd's fervour. Sheer delight has replaced the nerves they felt prior to the opening stage. Garin, Pagie, Kerff, Augereau and Jean Fischer beam with pleasure, the latter looking particularly happy as he has received positive news from Paris and will be allowed to continue. 'If one day I meet that little bird who made a false report about me, you can be certain that he will get a grilling from me,' he tells a friend.

The blacksmith Dargassies, the sturdiest of racers with legs the size and strength of young oaks, has the gallery roaring with laughter when he jokes that the Tour de France is nothing more than a stroll in the park and that he plans to do it three times in a row to make it a true test. Aucouturier and

Wattelier look more focused than most of their rivals, their determination to avenge the misfortune that beset them on the road to Lyon completely apparent.

When the bell at the Chapelle de la Charité sounds at one in the morning, the immaculate and rather formidable figure of Georges Abran makes his way to the organisers' car. He stands up on the running board and calls the racers together to form the cortège that will parade through the streets of Lyon to the official start point. He orders the spectators back, imploring them to allow the riders some room.

Abran's vehicle sets off, 48 riders following in its wake, with cyclists and motor vehicles, their joyful din drowning out everything else, tracking them in turn. It could be chaotic, but the cortège's progress through Lyon's lamp-lit streets is quite serene, the whole contingent easing quite languidly and steadily southwards like the waters of the nearby Rhône.

At the Route de Saint-Genis-Laval, Abran signals for the parade to halt. He calls the riders together and briskly waves them off, the peloton speeding away into the darkness, 'burying themselves in the night like a colony of bats,' writes Lefèvre, all four dozen riders bent over their handlebars, the noise of whirring chains disappearing with them.

Wattelier is the first to surge to the front, his pace suggesting that he's riding one lap of a track rather than the thick end of 400 kilometres. He's closely tailed by Aucouturier, the pair of them immediately making clear their intention to unsettle the hitherto little troubled Garin and Pagie. Jean Fischer, his small frame and protruding ears making him easy to pick out, is another racer with something to prove, and he quickly bridges up to join them.

Only four kilometres have passed and Aucouturier and Fischer are already beginning to open a gap on the pack, where frantic attempts are being made to close this deficit. As the riders jostle, the darkness cloaking almost everything around them, the stage claims its first victim as Lucien Barroy goes cartwheeling over the bars of his Herstal bike. It's not the former acrobat's first fall, but even his tumbling ability can't prevent this being a damaging one. He staggers up, alone and injured, in the blackness. Initial reports suggest he has abandoned the race.

Up at the front, Fischer maintains his ferocious pace, pulling away from Aucouturier, who's unconcerned. He drops back to the chasing group and watches Garin and Pagie out of the corner of his eye. The former, dressed as usual in his trademark white jersey and not wearing anything that denotes he is the race leader, is swaying on his bike, which is possibly a sign of fatigue. The latter is pedalling on his heels rather than his toes, suggesting the youngster may also be paying for his efforts on the stage to Lyon. 'Things are looking good. I'll probably get both of them,' Aucouturier thinks.

Soon after three, the leaders burst out of the darkness on the edge of Rive-de-Gier and into the little town, hundreds of fans cheering and applauding as they pass. It's difficult to pick them out in the gloom. Fischer, very evident in his white jersey, is still up at the front, together with Rodolfo Muller and the local rider Garrot. Three minutes pass before Pagie and Garin roll into view, the first-stage revelation leading his mentor and team leader, who has punctured. Garin jumps from his bike, manages to find another that's just about the right size and speeds off on it, the crowd urging him on.

Aucouturier senses this might be his moment. He sets a crazy pace on the descents in the rolling terrain. 'Despite the switch-backs, I go barrelling down them at 50 kilometres per hour. I crash once and get back on my feet,' he recounts. Aucouturier continues to harry the La Française pair, dropping them on a climb near Saint-Chamond, only to see Pagie respond and lead Garin back up to his rival's wheel.

A minute before four in the morning, there is a fanfare for the first rider to reach Saint-Étienne. It's 'The Climber', Jean Fischer, who signs his name, grabs a few provisions and offers a grunted reply to journalists' questions about the current state of the race. He accelerates away towards terrain where the appropriateness of his nickname will be tested. Regional rider Garrot receives a huge ovation when he's the next to sign, followed soon after by a large group comprising most of the favourites as well as the surprising figure of Eugène Brange, who was the last recorded finisher in Lyon.

At approximately the same time that Fischer was leading the merry dance towards Saint-Étienne, Madame Duffé, a widow who worked as a cashier at the Café de la Paix where the second stage had started, had just met a brutal end in her Lyon home at 25 rue Gasparin. The owner of the cafe, a

Monsieur Crozet, told *Le Petit Journal*'s reporter that he had closed up at around three o'clock that morning and sent Mme Duffé home carrying about 200 francs in takings, which she was due to return with the next morning.

'To my great surprise, I didn't see her come back in at the usual time,' he explained. 'At eleven in the morning, I took it upon myself, together with some of her neighbours, to force open her door and we discovered the corpse of the unfortunate woman, who had had her throat cut.' The paper surmised that the assailant had watched the Tour depart and then followed Mme Duffé home, killed her and then disappeared with the money.

Suspicion fell on a dishwasher who had previously worked at the cafe. However, after being quickly tracked down, he was able to provide a solid alibi. Yet it wasn't long before the true identity of the murderer became apparent.

Little more than 24 hours on from the murder, a body was pulled from the waters of the Saône. It was a waiter from the cafe, Jean Longueville. He had waded waist-deep into the river and shot himself in the head. An autopsy carried out on Longueville revealed bruises and scratches on his face and hands, while hair taken from underneath Mme Duffé's fingernails was the same colour as the waiter's moustache. Longueville had been among the suspects interviewed by the police in Lyon following the murder. He had been asked to return for further questioning but had failed to appear.

Before deciding to take his own life, Longueville had written a letter to Monsieur Crozet implicating another waiter, a certain Hansenne, as the perpetrator. Monsieur Hansenne had walked Mme Duffé home that night and was, it initially appeared, the last person to see her alive. However, it was revealed that Hansenne, thanks to an alibi, could not have carried out the murder and that Longueville had long held a grudge against him.

Police closed the case, allowing Mme Duffé's body to be taken to Panissières, 50 kilometres west of Lyon, for burial – unfortunately becoming the first and very unwitting victim of the race's success.

The brief pause at the control point outside the Café du XXe Siècle in Saint-Étienne's Place Fourneyron, where the surrounding businesses have been open all night to take advantage of the huge gathering awaiting the riders, allows Garin to swap to a bike La Française manager Delattre has waiting. Day is breaking as Garin's group remount and speed away in pursuit of Fischer and Garrot, the heat already building and thunder rumbling ominously around the Auvergne hills surrounding the industrial city.

The race leader's composure is upset again soon after the group leaves behind Saint-Étienne's brightly lit streets for the unlit road that leads on to the Col de la République, a 17-kilometre ascent that will transport the riders to 1,161 metres, the race's highest point. He tangles with Léon Habets aboard his Humber bike and the pair tumble to the road. Once again, fortune favours Garin as he picks himself up and quickly assesses that he and his bike have avoided any serious damage.

Not so Habets, however. He has dislocated a shoulder. Racked with pain, he manages to get back aboard his bike and uses the gradient to carry him back towards Saint-Étienne. At this very early hour, with nothing yet open, he has to continue all the way back to the control point in the city to find assistance in the form of a doctor who can pop the joint back into place. After further treatment and an hour-and-a-half delay, Habets gets back underway, his race surely unlikely to continue much further.

Hearing the sound of a crash and seeing that the white-jerseyed Garin is lying on the road, Aucouturier has an opportunity. The riders do compete according to an unwritten code of accepted behaviour, but attacking the race leader when he's down is fair game when racing in such treacherous and unpredictable conditions. Aucouturier pushes hard on the pedals. 'All's fair in war,' he says later.

The rider in the distinctive jersey of blue and red hoops chases across to Victor Dupré, Gustave Pasquier and Brange, and leads them in pursuit of a group being powered along by the huge Belgian Marcel Kerff, which includes the early attacker Wattelier and dangerous Léon Georget. Ahead of them all still are Fischer and Garrot, who is accompanied on the climb by several local cyclists, urging him on with shouts of encouragement.

Having covered the opening 60 kilometres at an average of close to 40 kilometres per hour in his determination to re-establish his reputation, Fischer begins to wilt on the tree-lined upper slopes of the République. He has set a suicidal pace and pays for it before the summit, which Aucouturier crosses first, just ahead of Wattelier, Muller, Henri Gauban and Garrot, who appears to be having few problems following the pace of these renowned racers.

The early morning heat, and it is not yet quarter to six, is intense enough for Aucouturier to plunge his head into a bucket of water when the quintet drop off the summit and into Annonay. They have a good lead on Dupré, Georget, Kerff and Pasquier, with Fischer now floundering on a punctured tyre seven minutes in arrears. Garin, with Pagie in support, is almost quarter of an hour behind. Riders trail through for the next two hours, their hopes of a lucrative payday already gone. Élie Monge and Georges Borot arrive at breakfast time, and take it at a table on a terrace with fans crowding around, asking if they know whether the Tour will return next year.

When Garin and Pagie, the two riders at the top of the general classification, get moving again, Aucouturier's group is already climbing through horse chestnut woods and stands of pine in the rugged hills of the Argental. So far what had been billed as the easier of the two opening stages has been anything but. After just 100 kilometres, there are more than seven hours between the leaders and the last man on the road, Lucien Barroy, who has not abandoned as initially thought. Arriving at Annonay at half past two in the afternoon, he informs Fernard Mercier that he had been forced to stop to repair a broken frame but is determined to finish and remain in the contest for the overall title.

The final destination of that title is looking increasingly

difficult to predict when Aucouturier's group regains the edge of the Rhône at Tournon. The members of the Cyclophile Tournonnais club that have volunteered their assistance at the flying control located at the Café Serret are not finding it easy to keep the massed ranks off the road. The spectators cheer loudly as Aucouturier leads in a group of six that now features Georget, Kerff, Wattelier, Dupré and Gauban.

The local man, Garrot, arrives two minutes behind them and immediately abandons in order to return to his home in neighbouring Romans-sur-Isère. 'I'm satisfied with my performance,' he declares. 'I wasn't troubled by the pace set by the Parisians, and if I had wanted to I could have outstripped them all before Marseille.' With that he swans off east rather than south to the Med.

Ten minutes after Aucouturier's group has crossed the Rhône from Tournon to Tain-Le-Hermitage via France's oldest suspension bridge, Garin yells his name and darts away towards the east bank of the river with Brange, Fischer and François Beaugendre for company, while Samson halts for a couple of minutes to take on food and drink. Half an hour passes before Pagie appears and swaps his bike for a new one. Can he regain the ground he has lost on the flat, riverside run south into Marseille?

The pace rises as the racers trace the passage of the Rhône. When the leaders arrive at the fixed control in Valence at the Café Frasseau at half past seven, they are welcomed by an immense crowd, most of them carrying copies of L'Auto, members of Valence Vélo battling to hold the multitude back. The six riders rush like savages for the one pen on the table, Georget grabbing it first, then Dupré, Gauban, Aucouturier, Kerff, Wattelier. Their signatures are barely legible.

'They should get rid of the sheets of paper on which we have to search for our names and sign and put out blank pages with pens and pencils so that riders arriving in groups don't lose any time,' Aucouturier finds time to complain. Garin later reveals a more immediate solution to this issue – dipping his forefinger into the ink and signing with that.

While his companions swig broth and stuff their leather food bags with meat and fruit, 19-year-old La Française rider Dupré is coughing and wheezing. The thick dust has overwhelmed his airways. He becomes so racked by coughing he can't continue. Wattelier is laid low too, although only temporarily, as his bike breaks almost immediately after restarting. He trots back to the control to get a new one, leaving just four men at the front.

A dozen minutes pass before Garin's eight-strong group arrives and makes the same mad dash for the control point pen. They restock and are off again, although the eternally relaxed Muller pauses to point out a magnificent statue to Jean Fischer. 'Hang on, I must read what it says beneath it,' Fischer calls out. He circles the monument slowly, so slowly that by the time he's completed the loop the other seven riders have sped away and he has to ask spectators for the route towards Marseille. Always quick to anger, Fischer is furious.

Pagie arrives in Valence three-quarters of an hour behind the leaders, his hopes of retaining second place completely gone. His morale is failing too. At Loriol, halfway to the next control at Montélimar, an official finds him with bike and spirit totally wrecked. This previously unheralded talent abandons the race and heads to the station to catch the train south.

It doesn't take him long to reach Montélimar and find the control at the Café de Paris, where Delattre is waiting. The La Française manager wheels out a new bike and urges him to continue. The officials confirm he can, but only once he has completed the section of the route he's missed. So, he sets off with an official in tow against the steady flow of riders to Loriol, then retraces to Montélimar, which he departs with a deficit of four hours on the quartet of leaders.

Their advantage is now 15 minutes over Garin's seven-strong group, which Fischer hasn't managed to bridge back up to. Boiling with rage, Fischer sits down in a Montélimar cafe, cursing Muller, who he insists has duped him and has been attempting to do so since Paris. The crowd roar with laughter when 'The Climber' proclaims, 'Happily, he's no longer with me, as otherwise I think I would have tossed him into the Rhône. He just keeps on talking claptrap to me.' Revived by a late breakfast and the guffaws of the crowd, Fischer remounts with a shout of 'Vive Loubet!' in honour of the Montélimar-born French president, receiving a huge ovation as he gets under way once again.

The sun bakes the riders and the landscape around them. They are all complaining of thirst and hunger, of the excessive heat, la canicule. On a gentle rise south of Montélimar, the conditions exact a toll on Kerff and Gauban. The lead group splits, Aucouturier pulling Georget clear with him. Their lead is 20 minutes at Orange, enabling Aucouturier to swap his punctured bike with a bystander, whom he instructs to take the stricken machine to Avignon on the train. The gear on the borrowed bike is huge, more than 8.0m, far bigger than the 6.10m set-up he is used to, but he has a temporary ally in Georget, who is happy to collaborate.

In spite of the elevated temperature, the dusty streets around the Avignon control at the Café des Sports are jam-packed, the route lined with L'Auto-wielding spectators, the paper itself enthusing about ladies in pretty dresses adding a touch of style and gaiety to 'the vast brouhaha'. On the stroke of midday, growing cheers signal the arrival of the leaders. They bound into the cafe, Aucouturier beating Georget to the pen by a hand. They replenish themselves and pocket some provisions, the customers seated on the cafe's terrace applauding as they return to their bikes.

Twenty-five minutes pass before Garin's group arrives. He's with La Française-equipped Muller, Pothier and Brange, plus Kerff. Garin encourages the first three to share the food and water that's been readied for him, but refuses to allow Kerff to partake. The hulking Belgian is beside himself with rage and, more importantly, gasping with thirst. He looks around, spies the bucket that the riders have washed in, hauls it up to his lips and gulps the soapy water down.

Kerff fills the bottles fixed in cages to his bars. Unlike most of his rivals, he doesn't carry bottles in the front of his jersey, a legacy of his brother's fatal crash in Marseille–Paris the *previous autumn. Kerff's twin metal bottles are fitted with long rubber tubes so that he can suck from them on the move, his preferred mix being a combination of beaten eggs, coffee, kola and water.*

The wind is beginning to gust from the south as these five continue towards Marseille. The gaps behind them are vast – 15 minutes, 20 minutes, and even more. Samson bounces into Avignon on a peasant's bike fitted with solid rubber tyres. René Salais needs treatment on his calf after a collision with a motor vehicle. The heat, hills and headwind are turning this easy stage hellish.

The two leaders are finding it just as tough as the rest. When Georget punctures, there is no question of Aucouturier battling on alone into the wind. He waits for his companion to fit a new tube, which only costs them a couple of minutes off their lead. At Aix, where members of VC Aixois cycling club can only maintain a narrow corridor between the ranks of fans, the pair have managed to regain that loss. With just 31 kilometres to Marseille, they can begin to consider their tactics for the finale. Still pursuing them, Garin and his La Française cohort have shaken off Kerff by Aix, but it's the Belgian who receives the warmest welcome into the university town, the locals well remembering his brother's death close by.

Sanremo, a journalist from the local paper La Provence Sportif *has made the canny decision to await the leaders a few kilometres short of the finish, which, in order to avoid the tramlines, cobbles and other potential hazards in Marseille, is located in the village of Saint-Antoine on the edge of the port* city. A cyclist of some ability who has previously ridden with Aucouturier, Sanremo latches on to the leading pair, noting how Georget takes a water-soaked handkerchief and wipes the dust and sweat from his eyes, which are fixed at all times on his rival.

Unsure of the exact location of the finish, the pair start to sprint, only to hear the journalist shout out that they are still three kilometres out from the line. Five hundred metres out, a flag flapping furiously in the onshore breeze readies them again. Their pace rises, their eyes locked on each other. The journalist, losing all sense of impartiality, yells at Aucouturier, 'Go now and stick to the left to avoid the tram tracks, you're only three hundred metres out!'

Both riders respond. There's nothing between them over the next 150 metres, but Aucouturier has proven again and again that he can sustain an all-out sprint longer than anyone. He edges a length clear, two, three, and is still increasing the gap when he crosses the line, in front of another multitude that has travelled out on trams and in cars from the city despite the oppressive conditions.

They engulf the dust-encrusted and almost unrecognisable 'Hercules of Commentry', who stands on his pedals, raises his arms high in the air and bellows, 'I've won! I've won! I've beaten Garin!' before glugging down the contents of a bottle and wiping the grime from his face.

Close by, Georget dunks his head repeatedly in a bucket of water, then, an exemplar of the claim that 'Alcohol is food, not a poison!' shouted by wine-sellers, seizes his traditional bottle of

Bordeaux and swigs half of that down in between munching on biscuits. He lost, but he's also ecstatic. 'I've got the better of Garin. Now we'll see who's going to win the Tour de France!' The two of them sign their names, have their photos taken, then remount their bikes to continue on to the Parc Borély velodrome, where the Marseille public has massed to greet them.

Twenty-six minutes have passed and they are well on their way to the Borély when Eugène Brange clinches the sprint for third place ahead of Garin, Muller and Pothier. Garin has saved his lead, even extended it thanks to Pagie's misfortunes and loss of morale, but Georget has cut the deficit between them to less than nine minutes.

'I fell, lost contact, I ended up with men who weren't as fast as Georget and Aucouturier,' Garin tells Lefèvre, also admitting that he made a mistake by stopping in Villefranche to buy ice, which he stuffed under his hat to cool him down, but actually ended up draining his strength. 'I didn't want to tire myself out by setting a fast pace to catch up with Aucouturier, who's no longer my rival. I'm racing for the Tour de France and am only looking towards the biggest prize. And that will still not evade me.'

STAGE 2 RESULT

1. Hippolyte Aucouturier (Fra) 374km in 14-28-53 (average speed 25.826km/h)*
2. Léon Georget (Fra) same time

3. Eugène Brange (Fra) at 26-06
4. Maurice Garin (Fra) at 26-07 *
5. Rodolfo Muller (Ita) same time
6. Lucien Pothier (Fra) at 26-09
7. Marcel Kerff (Bel) at 39-37
8. Fernand Augereau (Fra) 57-17
9. Gustave Pasquier (Fra) at 1-32-10
10. François Beaugendre (Fra) same time
11. Jean Fischer (Fra) at 2-11-37
12. Henri Ellinamour (Fra) at 2-15-27
13. Charles Laeser (Swi) same time
14. Anton Jaeck (Swi) at 2-19-10
15. 'Samson' (Bel) same time
16. Josef Fischer (Ger) same time
17. Ferdinand Payan (Fra) at 2-39-37
18. Jean Dargassies (Fra) same time
19. Marcel Lequatre (Swi) at 2-57-37
20. Isidore Lechartier (Fra) at 4-38-19
21. Alexandre Foureaux (Fra) at 4-51-19
22. François Monachon (Fra) same time
23. Paul Mercier (Swi) at 5-41-47*
24. Léon Habets (Fra) at 5-50-27
25. René Salais (Fra) same time
26. Julien Girbe (Fra) at 6-05-14
27. Aloïs Catteau (Bel) same time
28. Léon Pernette (Fra) at 8-46-57
29. Pierre Desvages (Fra) at 9-35-07
30. Lucien Barroy (Fra) at 12-36-34

31. Émile Moulin (Fra) at 12-44-52
32. Philippe De Balade (Fra) at 13-09-57
33. Ernest Pivin (Fra) at 15-01-22
34. Georges Borot (Fra) same time
35. Arsène Millochau (Fra) same time

* Registered for the second stage only

Overall classification

1. Maurice Garin (Fra) 32-40-13
2. Léon Georget (Fra) at 8-52
3. Fernand Augereau (Fra) at 1-34-00
4. Marcel Kerff (Bel) at 1-56-26
5. Jean Fischer (Fra) at 2-50-25
6. Rodolfo Muller (Ita) at 2-58-00
7. Lucien Pothier (Fra) at 2-58-02
8. François Beaugendre (Fra) at 3-14-30
9. Gustave Pasquier (Fra) at 4-04-03
10. Anton Jaeck (Swi) at 4-51-03
11. Marcel Lequatre (Swi) at 5-29-30
12. Charles Laeser (Swi) at 5-52-27
13. 'Samson' (Bel) at 5-58-56
14. Josef Fischer (Ger) at 6-15-55
15. Aloïs Catteau (Bel) at 7-28-04
16. Léon Habets (Fra) at 7-32-36
17. Jean Dargassies (Fra) at 8-30-37
18. Isidore Lechartier (Fra) at 10-16-19

19. Henri Ellinamour (Fra) at 10-23-27
20. Ferdinand Payan (Fra) at 11-14-31
21. René Salais (Fra) at 11-21-37
22. Alexandre Foureaux (Fra) at 12-47-19
23. François Monachon (Fra) at 12-48-11
24. Julien Girbe (Fra) at 13-36-04
25. Ernest Pivin (Fra) at 16-25-04
26. Léon Pernette (Fra) at 18-04-24
27. Georges Borot (Fra) at 20-32-42
28. Eugène Brange (Fra) at 20-55-48
29. Philippe De Balade (Fra) at 21-06-49
30. Lucien Barroy (Fra) at 21-54-01
31. Pierre Desvages (Fra) at 22-37-57
32. Émile Moulin (Fra) at 22-44-42
33. Arsène Millochau (Fra) at 24-27-27

CHAPTER 9

'ARE THE ORGANISERS BEGINNERS OR JUST INCAPABLE?'

If any doubts had remained about the huge impact the Tour was having on the French population, they were totally eradicated during the Tour's second stage. There were hordes of spectators at every point on the route, from its middle-of-the-night start in Lyon to its late-afternoon finish on the outskirts of Marseille.

Hippolyte Aucouturier and Rodolfo Muller had suggested following their reconnaissance of the route that the race would excite huge interest among the population in the provinces, and particularly in *La France profonde*, where nothing of note tended to happen and still rarely does. However, no one had expected anything like the frenzy that engulfed the nation during those opening days and would continue to do so right to the finish, when even Parisian sangfroid was vanquished by the new race.

Described by Richard Holt as 'a sporting by-product of fin-de-siècle fanaticism', the Tour certainly drew on the combination of vibrancy and hope for a new beginning that typified that period, when there was a very strong sense that change was coming politically, socially and culturally, and particularly so in France. More vitally and very unexpectedly, though, the race tapped into what in hindsight was a latent desire among swathes of the French people, who responded to an event that offered a more optimistic and unifying perspective of the nation, and especially so when it served up an unparalleled spectacle on the very streets where they lived.

To a large degree, the clamour unleashed during those three weeks in July 1903 can be compared with the race's 2014 Grand Départ in the British county of Yorkshire. There, too, there was uncertainty until the very day itself about the response of the local population, which turned out to be way beyond anyone's expectations, with the population captivated and completely won over, roadsides besieged, enthusiasm for the race complete. 'All this for just a bike race,' many exclaimed that weekend, unaware, just as the French had been in 1903, that the Tour was and would be so much more than that. Over those two days, the Tour de France placed Yorkshire firmly on the world map, marketing the county to an extent that no amount of advertising could ever achieve.

The 1903 race offered the first proof that the race would become a triumph of marketing. It promoted the paper

backing it as well as its rival titles, the companies that manufactured the bikes and other kit, the riders who mostly
began the race as nobodies but would end it as household
names, and France itself. In that period long before mass
tourism would become so important to France, the Tour
didn't need images from helicopters and spectacular set-
tings. It simply needed to exist, to reassert the idea of French
nationhood and vigour, to bring the population together
when so many issues were pushing them apart. With Henri
Desgrange as its figurehead, the Tour could not have been
better placed to achieve this.

As a fervent nationalist, Desgrange saw the Tour as an
opportunity to display France's new vitality and to suppress
concerns about military failure and weakness, social instabil-
ity and demographic decline. Although he couldn't have
known it during the months, weeks and days of uncertainty
leading up to the start of the Tour, Desgrange's sporting and
professional life had been building towards this moment.
The race offered him the ideal platform from which to
espouse his views and impose his beliefs, while at the same
time solidifying the foundations and popularity of his publication. Initially, though, it was all about delivering a
particular perspective of France to the people who lived
within its borders.

With these goals very much in mind, Desgrange and his
staff emphasised the flavour and diversity of the regions
the Tour passed through, of the spectators who turned out
to watch it, and of the riders performing in front of them.

They also highlighted monuments, sights and natural wonders along the race route.

In a country where the capital has always dominated affairs and is still widely resented for doing so, Desgrange and his editorial team went out of their way to overstate riders' connections with other regions. Maurice Garin was often described as 'the man from the north' or 'the rider from Lens', while his protégé Émile Pagie was almost always 'The Prince of Mines', that industry indelibly associated with France's north-east. Géo Lefèvre's obsession with Grisolles' Jean Dargassies has already been noted, and could also be seen on the second stage through the attention given to the regional rider Garrot, who didn't even reach Marseille. Indeed, it's surprising that the young man's final quip about not being discomforted by the pace set by 'the Parisians' appears not in *L'Auto* but in *Le Vélo*. This dismissal of all the riders who've come down from the north as being from the capital would have fitted well with both Desgrange's desire to promote regionalism and the view of many in Isère, Garrot's home department.

Among the 11 riders who signed up to compete only on the second stage, Garrot exemplified what Desgrange was attempting to achieve with this new initative. While a handful of those who took advantage of it, most obviously Marseille victor Aucouturier, had lined up in Paris and abandoned on route to Lyon, the clear intention was to encourage regional riders to sign up and test themselves against the sport's most renowned names. Most were keen amateurs who couldn't afford to make the journey to Paris and certainly couldn't contemplate the financial outlay required for food, spare equipment and hotels. This rule offered them an opportunity to compete. Naturally, their presence also boosted interest within local newspapers, which in turn meant more publicity for *L'Auto* and its race.

Desgrange also made a great deal out of the fact that the Tour was venturing into regions that had hitherto been neglected by top-class sport of every kind, including cycling. 'Towns that are dead to sport are waking up, are demanding information, are showing concern, are asking when these giants of the road whose ardour is never-ending are going to arrive,' he wrote in his editorial a day on from the finish in Marseille.

What came next underlined to what extent Desgrange was aware of the groundbreaking impact his race was having in the regions and the commercial opportunities that this presented. 'We now come to the Marseille–Toulouse stage, which is certainly the most interesting from this perspective. It was particularly with this part of the country in mind that I decided to organise the Tour de France. It was for these brave souls in the Midi that *L'Auto* wanted to do something greater than anything ever done before,' he proclaimed in what would become Desgrange's recognisably bombastic fashion.

It is evident that *L'Auto*'s editor-in-chief had already realised that the original reason for the Tour's founding, the salvation of his newspaper, has been achieved, and that he wanted to create a new, more noble and altruistic motive for the race. Positioning himself as a sporting missionary, Desgrange was now offering enlightenment to the neglected folk in the provinces. It's an astonishing leap to have taken, yet it does tally very well with his long-established conviction that exercise and competitive sport were the answer to individual and the nation's ills.

This almost messianic belief in the benefit of sporting practice can be clearly seen in *La Tête et Les Jambes*, Desgrange's self-addressed manual designed to encourage the reader towards a fully-committed focus on achieving their full potential as a cyclist. He permits no leeway or distraction during this quest. Indeed, he warns against those that might be offered by friends, girlfriends and even work.

Nurtured by his already outstanding accomplishments as an athlete, journalist and businessman, Desgrange's self-belief and self-righteousness were without limit. When he set his mind on an objective, he almost always achieved it, no matter the criticism tossed his way. His founding of the Parc des Princes track in 1897 is an obvious example of this. At 666.66 metres, it was, most experts agreed, far too big to accommodate top-level track-racing, but Desgrange had it built and quickly made it pay.

It is hardly surprising that those who were close to Desgrange described him as being blessed with phenomenal drive. Writing in his autobiography, Jacques Goddet, Victor's son who would become Desgrange's successor as the Tour boss, reminded that Desgrange had an often forgotten twin brother, Georges, who worked for many years as an archivist at *L'Auto*, and described him as, 'a nice man devoid of all ambition, unsophisticated, to the point where it appeared that Henri, so gifted, had taken everything from Georges.' The combination of that great energy with Desgrange's huge self-belief made for a potent mix of conviction and ambition. It is no wonder that many recalled this often made him an extremely difficult man to work for.

No doubt buoyed by the news that *L'Auto*'s second special edition – these were produced in addition to the daily paper and printed as soon as initial stage results could be sent by telegraph from the finish cities to Paris – had sold 96,200 copies and that sales of the daily were soaring to record levels, Desgrange was able to turn more of his attention towards shaping the Tour into his vision of a pure sporting contest.

It has often been said, based entirely on a comment made in a book by French cycling journalist Roger Bastide in the late 1940s, that Desgrange's ideal Tour would be a race where just a single rider finished. While this chimes with the perception of 'HD' favouring a challenge that pushed racers to their physical and psychological limits with the goal of delivering the outstanding rider as the champion, it doesn't square in the slightest with his desire to ensure the Tour offered an equal chance of victory to all of its participants and, therefore, present a contest that would boost *L'Auto*'s audience as much as possible. Rather than a sole survivor, Desgrange wanted a battle between individuals dependent on their own resources who were very well matched, and he consistently endeavoured to do all he could to bring this about.

To this end, on 7 July, *L'Auto* announced the list of riders due to contest the third stage between Marseille and Toulouse. Just as they had been prior to the previous stage, the names were split into two categories: the 33 riders still eligible for the overall classification and the 14 qualified for just the third stage. Above the first group of riders was the instruction: 'Depart from Marseille on 8 July at 10.30 in the evening.' Above the second was another: 'Depart at 11.30 in the evening from Marseille.' No further details on this splitting of the two groups was given.

There had been no consultation with the riders, or at the very least not with Marseille winner Hippolyte Aucouturier, who regarded this change as penalising him directly because he would be racing alongside fewer and, mostly, less capable riders than those in the first group. His first reaction was to quit the race complaining of a stitch-up in Garin's favour. 'I won't be at the start of the third stage, I don't want to take part in a handicap,' he moaned.

For his part, the race leader was all in favour of the move, pointing out that his principal rival for the general classification, Léon Georget, had benefited substantially from his collaboration during the second half of the stage into Marseille with Aucouturier, who was not eligible for the GC battle. 'If Aucouturier starts with me in the first group, I'll abandon,' Garin affirmed.

L'Auto's rivals piled into the debate, ridiculing the race organisation, *Le Monde Sportif* pointing out that they had had six months since running Marseille–Paris to get the rules right and asking, 'Are the organisers beginners or just incapable?' *Le Vélo* was kinder, but suggested that it was unfair on riders like Aucouturier to find themselves cast in 'the midst of riders from the second level', thereby removing all hope of a stage victory.

Desgrange responded extensively in his editorial the next morning, admitting that he could understand why some riders were unhappy with the change and others supported it. Before explaining his reasoning, though, he made one point very clearly: that it was the race organisation's right to make this change and indeed any other that might be needed in what was an unprecedented event featuring successive stages. 'We believe this right extends to being able to suppress the use of pace-makers on the final stage if we judge this suppression as being useful to the interests of the race,' Desgrange stated, laying the ground for another change that he was already contemplating and would later enact.

He added that the organisers had been thinking about splitting the two groups even before the start of the Tour, but had decided to see how the second stage unfolded before doing so. Desgrange said they hadn't liked what they had seen, describing how, 'one rider from Lyon was manifestly in the pay of a rider from Paris and two riders from Paris who had only completed a small part of the first stage were also at the start simply in order to fish in troubled waters.' The crime all three had committed, and would continue to do so if given the chance according to Desgrange, was pace-making.

Further defending the decision by pointing out that Aucouturier would still be racing with some very strong and fresh riders in the second group and by acknowledging that the rules could be changed again, Desgrange concluded by asserting that, 'next year, with a few minor readjustments, we will make the second Tour de France into the perfect race'. In this, he couldn't have been more wrong. The second Tour was a disaster, beset by cheating, assaults on riders and, eventually, the disqualification of the first four riders in the general classification. Demoralised by what he described as 'blind passions', Desgrange declared the second Tour would be the last, only to change his mind when his old rival Pierre Giffard, who was by then back in the editor's seat at *Le Vélo*, intimated that his paper was ready to stage the event in 1905.

From that point, and for the next three decades, Desgrange ran the Tour in the way that he wanted. It was his fiefdom and he tinkered constantly in order to make it a contest that would engage the biggest audience and prevent any one team from establishing a stranglehold on the race. In came the high mountains of the Pyrenees in 1910, to the riders' initial disgust, the Alps in 1911, Tours where multiple stages were run as team time trials and, to the outrage of manufacturers, even a Tour in which *L'Auto* and its partners supplied the riders with bikes and kit. Sometimes

Desgrange's experiments proved miserable failures, with the latter, for instance, blamed for the death in 1935 of Francisco Cepeda due to a crash when descending off the Col du Galibier that was allegedly caused by faulty equipment. But Desgrange never left off in his attempts to improve the Tour as a spectacle.

Desgrange's articles in the days in between the second and third stages of the inaugural Tour make it clear he was very aware that as well as lifting road above track in the racing hierarchy, the sudden and wholly unexpected success of the Tour would also bring about a fundamental change in cycle sport's audience. Very much an urban phenomenon up to that point, and almost entirely so on the competitive side, cycling very rapidly became France's sport. Requiring no facilities beyond a section of road, no matter how rough that might be, it became hugely popular in France's thousands of villages and immense expanses of countryside, where the value of the bicycle in everyday life as a mode of transport was already apparent.

'Between Marseille and Toulouse on the one hand and Toulouse and Bordeaux on the other, there is no sporting link with cycling, but it is however within this region that the societies are most numerous,' Desgrange wrote prior to these two stages, adding that it would be *L'Auto*'s happy task to bring all of the elements together that would ensure this popularity grew. As a result, as Christopher Thompson points out, 'The paper turned the race's itinerary into an annual lesson in French geography, featuring maps, topographical profiles, and detailed schedules of the racers' expected times of arrival in communities along the itinerary.' *L'Auto* also played up the touristical aspect, exposing the French people to their nation's cultural diversity and beauty.

As the number of bicycles in France continued to spiral upwards, cycle races became an increasingly regular feature in local festivals and feast days. Gradually, and most obviously in Brittany, as adherence to Catholicism began to wane, the bike races became a primary focus of these festivals, enabling the most talented riders to compete against each other regularly, which led, in turn, to some of these riders becoming professionals. Consequently, while the early Tours were dominated by riders from or based in Paris, by the interwar years the majority of French racers hailed from small towns, villages and the countryside, where other spectator and competitive sports took far longer to make inroads.

In among all this finessing of race rules and offended riders, Desgrange also tirelessly found the time to take on the task of predicting how the race might unfold on the run across the Midi to Toulouse. He divided the 33 riders still contesting the general classification into three categories. The first, comprising the riders who had taken between 45 and 57 hours to complete the opening two stages, numbering 12 in all between Alexandre Foureaux in 22nd place and Arsène Millochau in last, he described as wanting to 'complete a glorious performance that they will always have good reason to be proud of'. In other words, they had no hope of contending for top honours, or at least not this year.

The second group featured those riders who had taken between 34 and 45 hours to reach Marseille, which meant everyone between Fernand Augereau in third place and René Salais in 21st. From these, he said, contenders for the overall crown could still emerge, as some of them had been hit by bad luck on one or both stages, while others such as Jean Fischer, Josef Fischer, Marcel Kerff and Rodolfo Muller appeared to be racing within themselves in order to hold something back for later. 'Will their reason triumph over the brio of a Garin or a Georget?' he wondered.

Looking finally at the two leaders, Desgrange confessed he had no better idea than anyone else about which one of them would be in first place in Toulouse. All he could say, in characteristically hyperbolic style, was that, 'This will be a magnificent and terrible duel such as the history of cycle sport has never perhaps previously witnessed.' He suggested, though, that ten years of racing experience perhaps gave Garin the edge.

Starting at Saint-Antoine, where Aucouturier had outsprinted Georget three days earlier, and extending to 423 kilometres, the stage would pass through Salon-de-Provence (fixed control), Arles (flying control), Nîmes (fixed), Montpellier (flying), Béziers (fixed), Narbonne (flying), Carcassonne (fixed) and Castelnaudary (flying).

As was the case following the second stage to Marseille when the riders had continued on to the Parc Borély velodrome to be acclaimed by a packed crowd and complete a timed lap with the fastest taking additional prize money, a good-quality track meeting was scheduled at Toulouse's Bazacle track, where the arrival of the Tour riders would be the highlight. Before that, though, they faced what was sure to be a brutal test.

As the racers relaxed in Marseille, refuelling in the evenings with, *L'Auto* reported, large helpings of bouillabaisse, they sought out Rodolfo Muller to enquire what he had learned about the south's rough and dusty roads during the course of their route reconnaissance. The Italian tried to play down their fears by describing the Midi's rugged beauty, with vines stretching into the distance on all sides under a huge sky. But he had to admit that the roads were rougher than any seen up to this point and that the heat and especially the wind were sure to complicate the challenge. And as for the dust . . .

CHAPTER 10

'EVERYONE WHO FINISHED THIS STAGE IS A MARVELLOUS RIDER'

The three days that the Tour spent in Marseille enabled the whole race entourage to rest and recharge for a stage into what was largely the unknown. Thanks to Marseille–Paris and Bordeaux–Paris, most of the Tour's leading lights knew the terrain between the French capital and those two cities quite well. But the roads between Marseille and Toulouse and then on to Bordeaux were new to all but a few. Everyone was aware, though, that the mistral could have a savagely sapping effect for 48 hours and more if it began to whistle down the Rhône valley.

On the eve of the third stage, with high pressure sitting out in the Bay of Biscay and low pressure over the Gulf of Genoa, the flow of air between these weather systems began to draw a current of cold air down from the north, accelerating as it sped south, reaching high into the atmosphere to pummel the summit of Provence's northern sentinel, Mont Ventoux, and sweeping south, west and east as it emerged from the narrow funnel of the Rhône valley into the flat, marshy lands of the Camargue and Crau where there was no shelter from its blast.

Whether making a pilgrimage to Notre-Dame de la Garde to take in the panorama over Marseille or lapping the Borély track to keep their legs supple, the Tour riders knew, just as they do now, that tackling the mistral was likely to be as fierce a battle as any climb. Yet, unlike their modern-day successors who have ample experience of riding in the wind from racing in Belgium, Holland or on Spain's central plateau, the racers of 1903 were relative novices in conditions of this kind. As the wind continued its relentless assault, they anxiously discussed whether it would even be possible to reach Nîmes, little more than 100 kilometres to the north-west.

Géo Lefèvre, who revealed to *L'Auto*'s readers that he had struggled to remain on his feet during a walk along Marseille's Corniche, such was the ferocity of the wind, was otherwise upbeat as he looked ahead. He reported that La Française boss Delattre was delighted with the management of the race, describing it as the first where everything had been done correctly and that its organisation was perfect, confirmed that Aucouturier had come to terms with the peloton's split into two groups and was sure to start, and that excitement was already at fever pitch in Toulouse, where office and shop workers and bank staff were demanding an afternoon off in order to see the stage finish. He also revealed that 26 amateur riders had signed up to compete in a race of their own on the stage 4 route between Toulouse and Bordeaux. It appeared there was no end to the spread of Tour fever.

L'Auto correspondent J. Amy couldn't resist offering a reminder of the example the riders in the Tour peloton were setting. 'These 30 or 40 men are giving an admirable lesson in willpower to the youth of France,' Amy proclaimed. After going on to compare them to the troubadours of the Middle Ages who used to tour the chateaux of France sharing their love of poetry, he suggested that, rather than popularising verse, the Tour's riders were 'introducing a bit of modern vitality into the somnolence that affects very old things just as it affects very old people. Their struggle and progress offers a message to everyone: you have to fight to live, you have to battle to win . . . these valiant men are an example of perseverance and modesty.'

The words could have come straight from the pen of Henri Desgrange, and perhaps they did, given his liking for a nom de plume. There's the obvious comparison between soldiers campaigning on the battlefield and the racers fighting for victory at the Tour, highlighting the qualities required to succeed in both fields of action. Once again, the riders are presented as models for French youth and indeed the whole population to follow. In addition, there's a subliminal message to those in the privileged classes concerned by the clamour for rights from those further down the social scale, who, it is suggested, can be extremely productive members of society if encouraged in the right direction. Amy affirms that the Tour is nothing less than a manifesto for social and political change.

STAGE 3, MARSEILLE–TOULOUSE, 423KM, 8–9 JULY 1903

With Géo Lefèvre already heading up the route to assess how the riders are coping with the challenge of riding into the fearsome mistral, responsibility for procedures at the start and for delivering the first report on the third stage fall to Georges Abran, later described by Lefèvre as, 'that magnificent and truculent personality, who was also perfectly useless . . . whose role was to wave an immense yellow flag at the start and finish and, with his hat tilted at an angle, his moustache bristling, his face reddened, parked himself down in front of a well-topped up Pernod at the control point cafe at quiet times during stages.'

There is little time yet, however, for a Pernod to take the edge off the heat still stifling Marseille as dusk begins to fall at the end of another broiling Midi day. As he makes his way to the control point for the start on the grand avenue of La Canebière at the Café Riche, which fulfilled the same role prior to Marseille–Paris, Abran is already reflecting on how bereft he will feel when the Tour reaches its conclusion in Paris on 19 July. 'It's a nomad's life for me, and this existence built around the fever at starts, the impatience of waiting for finishes, the anxiety for news, and this bustle at stage towns all provides me with endless delight,' he writes.

Spectators swarm around the cafe, chatting and, says Abran of Marseille's distinctive nasal twang, 'joking with a terrible accent'. When the riders begin to appear from 8.30, the crowd becomes a rabble. The forces of order and L'Auto's volunteers have to push them back as Garin, Fischer, Muller and the rest, all deeply tanned after their stay by the Mediterranean, enter the cafe to sign in and collect their armbands. When they venture back out on to La Canebière, spectators compare their number with the list in L'Auto. 'C'est Garaing, c'est Georgetti, c'est Gaubnannn!' they exclaim in the Provençal burr that, according to Abran, makes it sound as if 'they are always in the process of eating bouillabaisse'.

At 9.30, the sign-in control closes for the riders, who form up in a space in the road cleared by the police to begin the slow parade to Saint-Antoine for the official start. A lady waving a scarf shouts with all her might, 'See you next year, gents!' as the cortège, escorted by 20 bike-riding gendarmes and another 60 on foot, sets off. It is 37-strong following the decision of Swiss rider Marcel Lequatre not to start and the addition of the riders in the second group, Aucouturier, Pagie, who had ultimately failed to finish the second stage, Guillarme and two new faces:

110. Colonna from Marseille
111. Marcel 'Valpic' Vallée-Picaud from Paris

Once arrived at the Café du Mûrier in Saint-Antoine, Abran takes a rollcall to check that none of the riders has sneaked off into the darkness to get a head start. At half past ten, Abran unrolls his yellow flag and waves the first group of 32 riders away. Despite the wind drilling into their faces, they are as keen to get going as they were on the first two stages. Within a few seconds, and despite the full moon, the night has consumed them.

There's an incident almost immediately as Ernest Pivin punctures, a victim of tacks scattered on the road. L'Auto offers no mention of the incident, Le Vélo just a brief one in passing. Was it mindless vandalism or a deliberate attempt to scupper the hopes of a favourite?

It is impossible to escape the incessant force of the mistral. It takes the leaders 45 minutes to cover the opening 23 kilometres to Vitrolles, where the spectators must be applauded for staying out to cheer them on in such conditions. The two general classification favourites, Garin and Georget, watch each other closely, staying near the front of the group but trying not to sit out in the wind for too long.

At least they don't have to worry about Aucouturier, who has made it known that he's only planning to ride the early part of the stage with a view to saving himself for the easier ones to come later in the race. They aren't to know yet that this is nothing more than a ruse, that the stage-2 victor is attempting to bluff them into riding a little slower. He's even fitted a smaller gear than usual in order to let his legs spin more and take some of the sting out of the mistral's sapping blast.

Almost two hours pass before the lead group of 16 riders reaches the control in Salon's Café de l'Avenir after 49 kilometres. Following unseemly scenes between riders and crowding by fans at the same establishment during Marseille–Paris, barriers have been placed at the entrance, but it's inside where the problems occur. Already fatigued, hungry and mightily thirsty, more than a dozen pairs of hands make a grab for the two pens and the sheets of paper on the officials' table.

Ink gets spilled and glasses knocked over and smashed as the sweaty, dust-coated riders are close to fighting for the chance to sign, then to grab food and drink. Every few moments another one or two appear and add to the deafening chaos. Someone yells out that Garin has disappeared, with La Française riders Anton Jaeck and Jean Fischer on his heels, and there's a stampede for the door. Peace returns to the cafe.

There's far less clamour 50 minutes later with the arrival of Aucouturier, Pagie and Valpic, as Marcel Vallée-Picaud is commonly known. The latter has been signed up as a correspondent by La Provence Sportive and offers a rider's-eye view of the battle against the mistral. 'At one moment, a gust came so strongly from the side as I was leading the line that I was carried right across the road and almost ended up in the ditch on the far side. Aucouturier bellowed with laughter,' he says. 'I was forced to put my 47 kilos behind Aucouturier's bulk in order to continue.'

There's no let-up in the wind as the riders continue on to Arles. Garin is among the leading quartet that passes the flying control at the Café Puech. It also comprises Dargassies, René Salais, the man from Angers racing on his self-made bike, and Swiss Charles Laeser. They are six minutes ahead of the next group, where Georget is either riding within himself or wilting *in the gale. Forty-seven minutes after Garin's passage, Aucou-turier, Pagie and Valpic sweep by having picked up Barroy, another three minutes knocked off their deficit. Parisian Henri Ellinamour becomes the first rider to abandon this stage due to injuries sustained in a crash.*

Having travelled by train from Marseille to Arles and had a tour of the city's Roman artefacts courtesy of L'Auto's corres-pondent Monsieur Crouanson – 'the ancient theatre with its broken columns and its amphitheatre with its arched arcades through which the silver disc of the moon shines above' – Géo Lefèvre has ridden out in the night north of Arles with Le Monde Sportif's Léopold Alibert. Even without the wind, the desolate, stony landscape of the Crau that lies between here and Nîmes would be a formidable test.

The two journalists see four phantoms closing in on them.

— What are your names? Lefèvre asks.
— Who are you? The voice is clearly Garin's.

Lefèvre identifies himself.

— OK, Monsieur Géo. Bonjour, or rather, bonsoir. I've dropped Georget. I've got him this time.

Dargassies identifies himself, and Lefèvre can't believe it's him, the blacksmith who had no idea who Garin was just a few days ago. Now they are riding together, following the infernal pace set by Laeser, which quickly becomes too much for the journalists.

— *Goodbye, Monsieur Géo.*
— *Goodbye, Garin.*

Lefèvre and Alibert tool along for a few minutes, then hear shouts from behind. 'On the right! On the right!'

Lefèvre recognises Muller's nasal voice. 'Well, well, the sur-veillance is being very assiduously carried out.' There are eight others with the Italian, including Georget. Their pace is not as fast and slows even more when they reach a level crossing. Beyond it, the road splits. Muller, recalling the fork from his reconnaissance, directs the group to the right. Kerff accelerates to the front, the rest crouch over their bars and charge after the powerful Belgian.

Once again the two journalists are left in the dark for a few minutes until another group approaches. Lefèvre is surprised to recognise Garin's white jacket and almost as quickly detects his anger. Lefèvre tells the race leader that ten riders have passed.

'This is devastating,' mutters the race leader. 'I took the wrong road at the level crossing and these lot all came with me.'

His complaint is cut short by Dargassies. 'Let's get going! We'll catch them!' With that, he's off, Garin and the other two on his wheel, the four of them having lost a quarter of an hour. They are now pursuing the group that was pursuing them, and that group is still chasing, believing it is behind the race leader. Will it cost Garin the stage win or even victory in the Tour?

Lefèvre and Alibert ride on, Jean Fischer, Léon Habets and

Julien Girbe passing them just before Nîmes. Moments later, they come across Habets and Girbe at the roadside, picking themselves up after a terrible crash. Girbe's frame is bent, but both men get back under way again, heading for Nîmes.

The Roman city is 'all lit up, Nîmes in festival mood, the control point streaming with lights that blind us after all that time in the dark'. Arriving at the Grand Café on the Boulevard de l'Esplanade, within sight of his second Roman amphitheatre of the night, Lefèvre receives the news that Garin's group caught the leaders right at the control just as Georget, Muller and Samson were signing in, resulting in another frantic free-for-all for pen and paper. These riders are still milling about. Garin chomps down a bar of chocolate, downs his favourite broth from a milk can, takes a new bike from the La Française agent and leads his rivals away from the brightness and back into the moonlit night.

Thirty-seven minutes later, Aucouturier arrives. Having dropped Pagie, who soon abandons, and Valpic as a result of punctures, he is riding alone. He notices La Provence Sportive's Alphonse Benoît and acknowledges him. 'You were right to make me change my gear in order to deal with the mistral – this 5.50m is splendid. I'll soon have them riding in this armchair,' he says, the anger at being isolated by the organisers still firing him on.

Turning south-west towards Lunel and then Montpellier, the riders finally receive the advantage of the mistral pushing them along. Beyond Lunel, Benoît manages to catch up with the front group on a shockingly potholed road where his driver often has to swerve into vineyards at the roadside to avoid mechanical disaster. He can see Georget and Muller setting a fierce pace. Suddenly, Garin and Pothier fall back. They stop, swap bikes, remount and charge after the group ahead. Then Pothier stops again, swaps bikes with an official wearing a blue armband, and rejoins the group. The 'official' then spends the next few minutes ferrying drinks up to the La Française riders, much to Kerff's consternation, who waves his empty bottle desperately, but gets nothing in return. This is as far as the objections to this blatant breaking of the rules goes. Garin's rivals ride on, ignoring the cheating.

At Montpellier, where L'Auto's correspondent thanks the paper for creating 'sporting excitement to which we've unfortunately not been accustomed because the region isn't blessed with sporting events,' nine riders arrive at the control point at quarter past five in the morning and sign in like 'madmen', ink cascading everywhere. They are Georget, Brange, Garin, Samson, Muller, François Beaugendre, Kerff, Pothier and Kerff's fellow Belgian Aloïs Catteau. The gap in the levels of support they are receiving becomes apparent. Most have to find their own food and drink and make any repairs, while Garin has several soigneurs ready to help. One has a new bike ready, another slots bottles of milk and Vichy water into his bottle cages, a third has oranges pre-peeled ready for him to stuff into his leather food bag. They don't object when Garin relieves himself as they're doing this, his urine splashing them.

La Française's star wants the stage win, but isn't yet aware that Aucouturier is now just 32 minutes behind and, therefore,

28 ahead on the stage. Soon after departing Montpellier's Place de la Comédie with its magnificent fountain of the Three Graces, Garin is distracted from thoughts about Aucouturier when Georget punctures. More than anything, he wants the overall victory and his rival's misfortune offers 'The White Bulldog' the chance to take a grip on the biggest prize. Unlike Garin, Georget has no teammates or soigneurs to help him. He has to rely on his own skills as a mechanic, as the race rules demand.

Garin and the rest of the lead group have disappeared into the early morning heat haze on the Hérault plain by the time Georget fits a new tyre and gets underway again. He's resolved one issue but now contemplates two more. His stomach is churning, the result perhaps of eating something past its best earlier in the morning or the cockles he ate the previous night in Marseille. The wind is getting up again too. After battling the mistral, the racers now have to deal with the Tramontane, blowing from the north-west down the wide corridor between the Pyrenees and the Montagne Noire and out on to the coastal flatlands.

Over the 70 kilometres between Montpellier and Béziers, Georget falls more than half an hour behind Garin's group. Weakened by illness, he is unable to follow the pace of Aucouturier, Jean Fischer and Fernand Augereau when they pass him on the approach to Béziers, and Georget continues to lose time on the flat ride to Narbonne, another 28 kilometres into the stage, where the route turns west towards Carcassonne and into the teeth of the wind.

Georget is not the only one toiling in the face of this unremitting force. Swiss duo Jaeck and Laeser abandon in Narbonne, as does Barroy, the three of them trailing away to the railway station to await the Sète-Bordeaux train that will be their route into Toulouse. Pagie, Valpic and journalists Lefèvre and Alibert already have seats on it. Approaching Narbonne, the line and the road run parallel, and the passengers cheer as they ride alongside Augereau, Fischer and Aucouturier, the latter offering a bow of gratitude from the saddle.

The 60 or so kilometres between Narbonne and Carcassonne are among the most demanding of the race so far. Rodolfo Muller had warned during his reconnaissance about the road's poor condition and constantly billowing dust, but he hadn't had to deal with the Tramontane, which is now whipping up grit that peppers the riders. With slow-moving carts, motor vehicles kicking up dust and curious spectators also to contend with in the road, the lead group now comprising just Garin, Pothier, Brange and Julien 'Samson' Lootens takes more than three hours to reach Carcassonne, where Samson, discovering there are no supplies waiting for him, breaks down in tears at the control. Spectators crowd in on all sides, many shouting for the riders to be given space, to be shown respect, but others pressing in regardless, desperate to get a view of these heroes on two wheels.

On they go towards Castelnaudary, the wind reaching storm force. Thankfully for Samson, when they pause in the home of cassoulet, there is cool lemonade waiting for the riders. They gulp it gratefully and take a few moments to wipe the dust from their faces. Yet they've barely got started on the final few dozen kilometres into Toulouse before their dusty masks are set in place again.

Forty minutes pass before the next riders arrive. The crowd cheer with delight when they realise that the huge, dust-caked figure before them is Aucouturier, with Beaugendre on his wheel. They, too, stop for a drink. When they set off again, Valpic joins them, having repaired his bike on the train and got off at Castelnaudary in order to encourage the irrepressible Aucouturier over the final stretch into the finish.

'It's been a real struggle because of this mistral, particularly around Narbonne,' Aucouturier tells Valpic, who conducts an impromptu interview. 'I've surprised myself by having ridden like this, especially after the high speeds early on. I thought I would weaken and when I saw that I was still going OK my confidence increased and I feel very fresh now.'

Valpic drops in behind Aucouturier and notes the presence of an official on a motorbike just adrift of them. He looks around again. It's not an official, at all. It's Delattre, who is watching for the least misdemeanour on Aucouturier's part. The La Française manager is leaving absolutely nothing to chance.

There is, however, no reason for Delattre and his team leader Garin to be concerned. The wind and roads have scattered every one of the Tour leader's rivals. Georget is now more than an hour behind, waylaid by more punctures and diarrhoea. Third-placed Augereau has suffered repeated punctures and breakdowns and is trailing even further back. Fourth-placed

Kerff, whose morale and energy have been eroded by lack of support, is lagging too.

The only thing able to temporarily halt Garin's progress towards a huge overall lead in Toulouse is a herd of cattle blocking the course at Villefranche-de-Lauragais. The four leaders pick their way carefully through the nervy livestock, before Brange, the red and black of his jersey just about visible through the white mantle of Occitan dust, accelerates and the four men regain racing pace.

At the finish, located on the edge of Toulouse at the Café Saint-Michel, a crowd perhaps 10,000-strong eagerly awaits the finale. Among those watching is Henri Desgrange, newly arrived from Paris and determined to quell riders' concerns about the splitting of the peloton and, more vitally, to investigate reports of cheating. He wants nothing to detract from the success of the Tour and his first impressions in Toulouse suggest nothing will.

The setting couldn't be any more splendid, the sun starting to sink in the cloudless late-afternoon sky, the pink stone of Toulouse's grand buildings beginning to glow as the sun yields a little of its intensity. It's 'a pleasure to the eyes, a sweet symphony of turquoise blue and soft pink' according to Géo Lefèvre. L'Auto banners clack in the wind, which has lost most of its bite and has switched around to the south-west so that it's finally favouring the racers. There are faces in every window. The corridor of spectators stretches four kilometres out from the line, with thousands more waiting at the Bazacle velodrome for the post-stage meet that will include the Tour riders completing a timed kilometre with 50 francs on offer to the quickest man.

The first indication that the leaders are approaching comes when La Revue Sportive reporter Ouzou arrives in his car, closely followed by chief judge Léon Collet. The riders are 20 kilometres away, they say. Le Vélo's Alphonse Baugé arrives at the control point, but is barred from entering by Édouard Pons, president of Cycle Sud Toulousain, who is overseeing it. Baugé protests, with Desgrange looking on, but Pons won't yield and asks two gendarmes to escort him away. The irate scribe, who volunteered to assist the officials at the hectic finish in Marseille and reminds all those within earshot of that fact, reluctantly moves away but manages to find a perch in a corner close to the table at the control point where the riders will sign in.

At three minutes to five, a growing crescendo of noise announces the arrival of the lead group. A whirlwind of energy and noise, they come charging up the finishing straight, hunched over their bars, pressing furiously on the pedals, elbows out, bikes swinging frenetically from side to side beneath them as they wring every last piece of energy from their weary bodies. Eugène Brange and Samson are the quickest, the ecstatic Frenchman edging out the Belgian by a tyre's width, with Garin three lengths back in third and Pothier fourth. Even a collision with a lady who has wandered into the road beyond the line that sends him tumbling to the ground can't dent Brange's delight. Second to last in Lyon, he's first into Toulouse, despite Samson's protests that it was in fact he who won the sprint.

But Brange is not the quickest to reach Toulouse. The gendarmes and volunteers have just managed to clear spectators off the road following a melee of excitement in the aftermath of the sprint finish when Aucouturier and Beaugendre fly into view. Beaugendre just takes their two-up gallop to claim fifth, which almost instantly becomes sixth. Having started an hour behind the first group, Aucouturier has completed the stage 32 minutes faster than anyone. It has been an outstanding performance, undoubtedly underpinned by his wise selection of a smaller gear in the unrelenting wind.

Jean Fischer, Muller, Catteau and Kerff finish together, a little over an hour after Brange, with the ill-fated Georget, fatigued and coughing, next home almost two hours behind, and the unlucky Augereau a few minutes behind him, a place ahead of Dargassies, who receives a tremendous ovation from 40 of his friends who have travelled the 30 kilometres in from his hometown of Grisolles.

No sooner do they arrive, sign in and get a wipe down than they're off again, this time escorted by dozens of cyclists to the Bazacle, where Muller makes his legendary endurance count, clocking a time of 1 minute 36 seconds for the kilometre, a tad quicker than Catteau and Jean Fischer. Garin records a time more than a minute slower for the two-and-a-half laps on what is nothing less than a ceremonial parade in front of an enthusiastic audience.

'All those who have finished or will finish this stage are marvellous riders,' Rodolfo Muller tells Henri Desgrange, who describes the Toulouse finish as 'certainly the most beautiful I've ever seen'.

Desgrange has already received the news that L'Auto's special edition, which had been print-ready and required the addition of just the first stage results before going on to the presses, was on sale in Paris just half an hour after the finish, and is just as delighted with that, even though Le Monde Sportif *was available even sooner. The reason Desgrange is in such a good mood soon becomes clear, as his paper reports of the rival edition, 'It wasn't very complete, that's true. It wasn't very precise, that's also true. But it did appear. This is the news alert it featured: "Toulouse: 1st. Garin."'* L'Auto *asks the public to make up its mind on how useful this was.*

Just after midnight Gustave Guillarme trots in having completed the final three kilometres on foot due to mechanical breakdown. He is the only rider apart from Aucouturier to finish from the second group. Two hours later, three more shattered riders roll in out of the darkness. René Salais, Ernest Pivin and Arsène Millochau. Forty minutes behind them is the final recorded finisher, Pierre Desvages, who is riding a Champion, an apt name considering his courageous performance.

Late that evening, with a large number of fans still awaiting the arrival of the final racers, Desgrange takes up his pen to write his editorial for the next morning's paper. He describes his astonishment at the achievements of the Tour riders, then turns to the fuss that erupted following his decision to split the peloton into two groups for the Marseille–Toulouse stage.

'If you believe some, Aucouturier, who wasn't actually

eligible for the complete Tour de France any longer, had literally been deprived of any chance of victory on the individual stages as a result of his exclusion from the lead group. It's Aucouturier himself who has delivered the response to that argument by winning the third stage of the Tour de France superbly . . . If I had listened to the demands of Aucouturier's friends, I would quite simply have prevented him from accomplishing the marvellous thing that he managed to achieve,' he writes, adding that he does harbour a regret about Aucouturier's performance, as he is still disappointed that a rider of his stature did not finish the opening stage and by failing to do so lost all hope of contending for overall victory. Save for a catastrophic crash or debilitating illness, that prize now seems destined without question for Garin.

At half past nine the next morning, Fernand Mercier closes the control point in line with the time required to complete the course at an average speed of 12 kilometres per hour. A matter of minutes later, Lucien Barroy arrives, his progress hampered severely by a broken bike. Mercier has to inform the distraught racer that he is no longer eligible for the overall competition. Barroy's fate encapsulates the merciless test endured by all of those who have reached Toulouse.

STAGE 3 RESULT

1. Hippolyte Aucouturier (Fra) 423km in 17-55-04
   (average speed 23.607km/h) *

2. Eugène Brange (Fra) at 32-22
3. 'Samson' (Bel) same time
4. Maurice Garin (Fra) same time
5. Lucien Pothier (Fra) same time
6. François Beaugendre (Fra) at 1-00-00
7. Jean Fischer (Fra) at 1-35-18
8. Rodolfo Muller (Ita) at 1-35-19
9. Aloïs Catteau (Bel) at 1-35-20
10. Marcel Kerff (Bel) same time
11. Léon Georget (Fra) at 2-22-24
12. Fernand Augereau (Fra) at 2-43-05
13. Jean Dargassies (Fra) at 2-46-59
14. Gustave Pasquier (Fra) at 3-18-04
15. Ferdinand Payan (Fra) at 3-32-06
16. Isidore Lechartier (Fra) at 3-58-08
17. Julien Girbe (Fra) at 4-37-36
18. Georges Borot (Fra) at 4-38-33
19. Philippe De Balade (Fra) at 5-21-47
20. Josef Fischer (Ger) at 6-48-56
21. Alexandre Foureaux (Fra) same time
22. Gustave Guillarme (Fra) at 6-49-11 *
23. Emile Moulin (Fra) at 6-53-36
24. René Salais (Fra) at 9-56-11
25. Ernest Pivin (Fra) same time
26. Arsène Millochau (Fra) same time
27. Pierre Desvages (Fra) at 10-34-14

* Registered for the third stage only

Overall classification

1. Maurice Garin (Fra) at 51-07-40
2. Léon Georget (Fra) at 1-58-53
3. Lucien Pothier (Fra) at 2-58-02
4. Marcel Kerff (Bel) at 2-59-23
5. François Beaugendre (Fra) at 3-42-08
6. Fernand Augereau (Fra) at 3-44-42
7. Jean Fischer (Fra) at 3-52-21
8. Rodolfo Muller (Ita) at 4-00-57
9. 'Samson' (Bel) at 5-58-56
10. Gustave Pasquier (Fra) at 6-50-45
11. Aloïs Catteau (Bel) at 8-31-02
12. Jean Dargassies (Fra) at 10-45-14
13. Josef Fischer (Ger) at 12-32-29
14. Isidore Lechartier (Fra) at 13-42-05
15. Ferdinand Payan (Fra) at 14-04-15
16. Julien Girbe (Fra) at 17-41-18
17. Alexandre Foureaux (Fra) at 19-03-53
18. René Salais (Fra) at 20-45-36
19. Eugène Brange (Fra) at 20-55-48
20. Georges Borot (Fra) at 24-38-53
21. Ernest Pivin (Fra) at 25-48-53
22. Philippe De Balade (Fra) at 25-56-14
23. Émile Moulin (Fra) at 29-05-56
24. Pierre Desvages (Fra) at 32-39-49
25. Arsène Millochau (Fra) at 33-51-16

Top left: The first page of the 1 July 1903 edition of *L'Auto*, with a route map and Henri Desgrange's iconic editorial 'La Semence'.

Top right: Desgrange set numerous records on the track in the early 1890s, including marks for the trike.

Bottom: Géo Lefèvre, who first suggested the Tour and was the race director and *L'Auto*'s chief correspondent during the first edition.

Some of the cyclists *L'Auto* highlighted to watch (clockwise from top left): a rare picture of Maurice Garin smiling; blacksmith Jean Dargassies (right, in black) with gentlemen's clothing buyer Pierre Desvages (left, in white); the unmistakeable Hippolyte Aucouturier with his trademark handlebar moustache; Swiss cyclist Charles Laeser.

1re Année · N° 102   10 CENTIMES   Dimanche 12 Juillet 1903

L'ACTUALITÉ

DIRECTION : 7, rue Blanche, Paris   FRANÇAISE, ÉTRANGÈRE, ARTISTIQUE & LITTÉRAIRE ILLUSTRÉE   ABONNEMENTS
ADMINISTRATION :   UNION POSTALE : Six mois, 4 fr. ; Un an, 8 fr.
6, Chaussée d'Antin, Paris   REVUE DE LA FAMILLE   FRANCE : Six Mois, 2 fr. 25 ; Un an, 6 fr.

Pasquier   Aucouturier   Garin   Fischer
LE TOUR DE FRANCE. — Le départ à Villeneuve-Saint-Georges.

Garin (in white half obscured) with Josef Fischer to his left lead the peloton down the road from the Auberge au Réveil-Matin to the new start of the opening stage.

Charles Laeser (left with armband) on his way to victory in Bordeaux.

Top: Léon Georget signs in at a stage start under the watchful eye of race official Alphonse Steinès.

Bottom: Hippolyte Aucouturier sprints down a corridor of spectators ahead of Léon Georget to win the second stage into Marseille.

Top: A gendarme (in white trousers) keeps an eye on spectators lining the roadside on the Toulouse–Bordeaux stage.

Middle: Géo Lefèvre (left) offers Maurice Garin a glass of wine after the finish of the stage into Nantes.

Bottom: Jean Dargassies gets instructions from a race official during the fifth stage between Bordeaux and Nantes.

Top: Géo Lefèvre points the way onto the Nantes track for Maurice Garin, who leads fellow La Française riders Georges Pasquier and Lucien Pothier.

Bottom left: Encrusted with dirt, Garin smiles at a stage finish, while rival Léon Georget (left) appears completely spent.

Bottom right: The Ville d'Avray control point in Paris, the final one of the Tour.

Ville-d'Avray. — Arrivée de Courses

D.W.D.

Top: Eager spectators pack the finish area outside Père Auto's restaurant at Ville d'Avray.

Bottom: Maurice Garin poses with his victory garlands and one of his sponsors at the Parc des Princes in Paris.

Top: Maurice Garin, complete with victory sash and post-stage cigarette, poses with his race-winning bike and young son while receiving attention from renowned masseur Brillouet.

Bottom: Tour boss Henri Desgrange pictured at a running race in his later years.

CHAPTER 11

'YOUR BICYCLE IS YOUR SALVATION'

The Tour's third stage, 'incontestably the hardest of all' according to Henri Desgrange, may have cemented the event's status as a popular success, but it also underlined dilemmas that would dog the race for years to come and still continue to do so.

Examine any sporting contest, and it's clear that athletes will aim to benefit from any kind of competitive advantage permitted by the rules. It is equally evident that there are almost always some athletes who are prepared to go beyond regulatory boundaries, either in the knowledge or the hope that their misdemeanours won't be uncovered. Although the lack of penalties handed down by race officials may have suggested otherwise, there were plenty who fell into this second category during the inaugural Tour.

When Desgrange travelled to Toulouse to watch the finale

of the third stage, his primary objective was to ensure that the riders competed within the rules. Yet, from the beginning, Desgrange, Géo Lefèvre and their assistants on the race were outmanoeuvred and hoodwinked. Disqualifying Jean Fischer on stage 1 may have prevented this – but almost certainly wouldn't have. However, by giving 'The Climber' the benefit of the doubt, largely based on the word of two of Fischer's fellow competitors, and allowing him to continue, ignoring the evidence of two officials who had witnessed him being towed – apparently via a cork clenched between his teeth into which a wire had been fixed and connected to the vehicle ahead – the Tour organisers made it clear that their overriding goal was not to ensure the race was a fair contest, but a competitive one.

Desgrange and Lefèvre weren't the first and would be far from the last to opt for the status quo. Cycle races, both on the track and road, were almost habitually fixed or beset by cheating. Indeed, the general use of pace-makers in road events pretty much guaranteed this, as the big and therefore well-backed names could always hire the fastest pacers. Yet, Desgrange and Lefèvre had to balance their desire for a clean race with the need to ensure that their newspaper extracted as much commercial value as possible from the Tour. Inevitably, given the precarious financial state *L'Auto* was in, they leaned towards the second option, and in doing so set the race on a path that almost led to its destruction the following year, when cheating was endemic.

Of course, the nature of the Tour and other cycle races

during that period almost guaranteed that cheating would occur, and go unseen and unpunished. When Liège–Bastogne–Liège, the oldest race on the modern international calendar, was first run in 1892, the organisers chose Bastogne as the destination for their out-and-back route because it was a stop on the express train south from Liège. At that time, when motor vehicles were all but unknown, the organisers could only watch the riders set off from Liège, take the train to the checkpoint at Bastogne to check that the riders passed through, then return north to check them in at the finish. They had to depend almost entirely on the racers themselves for details on what happened in between.

A decade on from the foundation of Liège, organisers were able to take advantage of the increased availability, reliability and speed of motorcars and motorbikes, although their provision was often dependent on the goodwill of well-to-do fans in some cases, or manufacturers and sponsors in most others. Consequently, race reports in the sporting papers often included mention of such beneficence. Following the stage into Toulouse, for instance, the reporter from one of the local papers, *L'Express du Midi*, was gushing in his gratitude to director of the local Renault agency, M. Bonneville, relating how the Renault Type E they had at their disposal ran much better than the Darracq L being used by *La Provence Sportive* and detailing how, 'Our car seems to glide over the road. At 60km/h, there are no irregularities, no noise, the driver accelerates and slows the speed easily.'

Oddly, given its main backer was a major motor vehicle manufacturer and several others also featured among its shareholders, *L'Auto* didn't use motorcars to anything like the same extent as some of their rivals, Lefèvre declining the offer of a vehicle from which to follow the race because trains were more reliable. In fact, just one reporter, *La Revue Sportive*'s Émile Ouzou followed the whole race in a little Cottereau that he had been loaned. As a result of the clouds of dust thrown up by the riders and passing vehicles, Ouzou was often the last to know what was happening in the race and missed most of the details that *L'Auto*, thanks to its extensive network of correspondents and eager volunteers, was able to report.

The only motorcar that *L'Auto* did use throughout was the vehicle that carried Georges Abran and Fernard Mercier from the stage starts to the finishes. Although they would have got a fleeting glimpse of every rider as they made their way up the course, their job was not to report on the action but to ensure that the race began and ended in the proper fashion. Otherwise, Desgrange and his staff relied very much on France's already very extensive and efficient railway network for getting around. On those occasions Lefèvre did make use of an alternative mode of transport, he generally opted for his own bike as this enabled him to get very close to the riders and obtain a far better idea of the challenge they faced.

For surveillance of the riders and implementation of the rules, Desgrange and Lefèvre depended on chief controller/

official Léon Collet. Travelling on a motorbike, he was better placed than anyone to see what riders were getting up to. Reports in the various papers suggest that he had at least one or two assistants moving around the race in a similar fashion. Yet, as *L'Auto* made very clear before the Tour started, its main deterrent when it came to preventing rules being broken was the secret controllers.

In theory, their introduction was a good idea. The suggestion that they might be waiting absolutely anywhere along the route was clearly intended to make riders desist from cheating. In practice, and especially after Fischer was cleared to continue after being caught in flagrante by two officials lying in wait on stage 1, they appear to have been little more than window dressing, highlighted in every stage preview, but effectively doing no more than persuading everyone looking on that *L'Auto* was doing all it could to ensure a fair contest.

This assessment is supported by the fact that Desgrange and his staff undoubtedly knew that cheating was taking place, even if they didn't witness specific transgressions. *La Provence Sportive* reported in detail on the bike-swapping incident its correspondent had witnessed between Nîmes and Montpellier involving Garin, Lucien Pothier and the soigneur blatantly working for La Française during the Toulouse stage, but no sanction was imposed. Indeed, *L'Auto* didn't even refer to it.

The obvious question of why they didn't react and why Garin's rivals also remained silent can be answered in two

words: La Française. Alone among the major bike manufacturers of that era in prioritising the Tour de France, the
company that supplied bikes to a dozen starters, including
Garin, Pothier and Émile Pagie, effectively had the race won
from the start. Their 12 riders were either very experienced
professionals or very promising youngsters. Although they
did have some very strong opposition: riders such as Aucouturier, Georget, Kerff and Brange rode for a range of
manufacturers and only collaborated when best able and
positioned to do so – on the stage into Marseille, for example,
where the former pair combined forces to distance Garin.

In addition to numbers and talent on the road, La Française spared nothing when it came to support off it. This
was less marginal gains and more overwhelming spending
power. Delattre had a team of soigneurs and mechanics to
ensure his riders, and particularly Garin, had everything
that they required when they reached any control point. *La
Provence Sportive*'s article makes clear that, despite this
being in breach of the race rules, they were also offering that
backing in between the controls. Why did no other rider
object? The only answer to that is that they must have been
paid off, either with a cash payment or with an assurance
that they would be able to share the prize money that lay
ahead at the finish. They had little choice but to agree to
these terms, as would be demonstrated by Garin's ruthless
response to a rival's attempt to break free of his shackles
later in the race.

It is fair to say that *L'Auto* too was paid off. A quick scan through their July 1903 editions reveals advert after advert proclaiming, 'Garin 1st, still leading the general classification on his La Française bicycle (Diamant version)'. It made no commercial sense to challenge La Française or unmask Garin as a rogue. The first would have resulted in the loss of advertising revenue, the second in the Tour being exposed as flawed, which would likely have cut sales. Hence, when it came to cheating, almost everyone at the 1903, whether racing or officiating, had dust in their eyes.

. They were perhaps still trying to rub it out following that horrifically severe Toulouse stage when, in *L'Auto*'s next edition, an ad was placed by the American Bicycle Company. 'Aucouturier, winner of Paris–Roubaix and Bordeaux–Paris, riding the Tour de France without any back-up and having been poisoned during the first stage, wins again after Lyon–Marseille: Marseille–Toulouse on his Crescent', it proclaimed. Garin's biggest rival had been nobbled. By whom, no one could say. It may have been coincidence that the next rival to Garin's hopes, Léon Georget, suffered a similar debilitating sickness to Aucouturier. After all, water was often far from pure and food would have gone off quickly in the withering heat. There again, it may not have been.

In defence of those racing in the Tour de France who might have been in the pay of rival riders, the financial rewards for competing were fairly meagre unless you had a good chance of finishing well up on most of the stages or in the general classification. When the race reached Toulouse, Aucouturier's victory edged him ahead of Garin in earnings with total winnings of 1,800 francs as against his rival's 1,725. Both amounts were well in excess of a year's pay for the average male worker.

Behind this pair, though, the rewards tailed off quickly. Émile Pagie and Léon Georget had earned around 700 francs each, Eugène Brange 600. Then there was a big drop to Fernand Augereau on 250, Samson on 200, before another half a dozen or so riders who had netted between 50 and 150 francs. There were other prizes on offer at intermediate points on most stages, put up by benevolent individuals and organisations, but most of these were snaffled by the big guns as well, as were the main prizes on offer at the end-of-stage track meets. More than 80 per cent of the riders who had lined up in at least one stage hadn't won anything at all. They were pinning their hopes on being eligible for the *L'Auto*'s five-franc daily stipend, approximately equal to the average male worker's daily wage, which had to cover accommodation, food and repairs.

As a result, you could hardly blame a rider who hadn't won anything and almost certainly wouldn't for agreeing to pace a big name or ignore blatant cheating in exchange for a small payment that made the extreme brutality of the test they were enduring a little easier to bear. Desgrange and Lefèvre regularly depict these riders as heroic, as competing in order to be able to say in future that they had done it, that they had ridden against the great Garin. Yet, drawing on the vocabulary of war to which *L'Auto* was so attached, they were no more than cannon fodder. Given this, their achievements are just as deserving of admiration as Garin's or Aucouturier's.

Sadly, in most cases, all that we know about them are their names, hometown, occupation and the bike and gear they rode. The exploits of a few, notably Jean Dargassies, were recorded in some detail, but most raced in near-anonymity. Beyond their name and finishing position, they are barely remembered at all. Take Georges Borot, for instance. By the halfway point of the race, apart from being listed in dispatches from controls that gave the times riders passed by and the final results, he hadn't earned a single mention anywhere in the sporting press. A rider of some experience, the Parisian had finished 73rd in the 1901 edition of Paris–Brest–Paris, which had been won by Garin, and would go on to complete all six stages of the Tour, finishing 19th in Paris. For this outstanding feat, he earned 95 francs.

There were plenty more Borots within the rest of the field, men who fully deserve being described as the original *baroudeurs*, to borrow the modern-day term describing 'adventurers' that has long been used to describe breakaway specialists who relish nothing more than an early attack off the front of the peloton that leads into a long escapade almost certain to end in failure. Borot may not have led the Tour at any point in any stage and been chased down by Garin and the other big names, but he was assuredly an adventurer – doughty, determined and undaunted by any obstacles in his way. *Chapeau* to Georges and the rest who filled out the Tour's start list and made the race viable, then added a little to its legend.

While cheating was ignored and many of the competitors were forgotten, *L'Auto* did include regular mentions of women in its coverage of the Tour. There were, of course, none competing. Instead, women featured as fascinated onlookers, tearful wives or concerned mothers. They add a little colour, but remain on the sidelines. Indeed, their occasional appearances in the organising newspaper and other papers would barely merit a mention if it weren't for the fact that this situation didn't change within cycle sport for many decades. Could Desgrange's Tour be to blame for this?

In 1896, American social reformer and women's rights advocate Susan B. Anthony proclaimed, 'Let me tell you what I think of bicycling. I think it has done more to emancipate women than anything else in the world. I stand and rejoice every time I see a woman ride by on a wheel . . . the picture of free, untrammeled womanhood.' Anthony was far from alone in that opinion. That same year, an article in *Munsey's Magazine*, which then sold more than 700,000 copies a month, declared that, 'To men, the bicycle in the beginning was merely a new toy, another machine added to the long list of devices they knew in their work and play. To women, it was a steed upon which they rode into a new world.'

In France, that new world took decades to take shape. As in North America, women, primarily from the moneyed middle classes, followed fathers, brothers and husbands in taking up cycling, which was a liberating experience in all kinds of ways. The bike offered a limited degree of independence, enabled them to swap constricting corsets and heavy skirts and petticoats for lighter dresses or even trousers, and allowed young people to socialise with each other without being chaperoned. However, political and social rights were very slow in arriving.

The Third Republic did see the introduction of the right for women to initiate divorce proceedings. However, universal suffrage wasn't introduced until 1944, which meant it wasn't until October 1945 that women voted for the first time in French parliamentary elections, just prior to the establishment of the Fourth Republic.

During the belle époque, increasing calls for the emancipation of women conflicted with widely voiced concerns about the future of the French nation. Between 1870 and 1914, the birth rate in France fell by 27 per cent as the population grew by 10 per cent. At the same time, the population of Germany, France's great rival, more than doubled. Aware and very troubled by their neighbour's military build-up, and particularly of its navy, politicians and commentators in France were extremely critical of anything that might distract French women from performing their reproductive duty, and this included cycling.

Baron Pierre de Coubertin, the French founder of the modern Olympic movement and a peer of Henri Desgrange's in the sporting world, spoke for many when he affirmed that, 'Woman's glory rightfully came through the number and quality of children she produced,' and that where sports were concerned, 'her greatest accomplishment was to encourage her sons to excel rather than to seek records for herself.' For good measure, he said of women's competitions that they were 'impractical, uninteresting, ungainly, and, I do not hesitate to add, improper.'

This concern about the threat to the vitality and even the existence of the French nation, which had been stirred up by that shattering defeat at the hands of the Prussian forces, also tied with increasing alarm about women's sexual feelings and, as Christopher Thompson puts it, 'the perceived threat such feelings posed to the bourgeois order'.

During the final three decades of the nineteenth century and into the early years of the twentieth, when sport was increasingly presented as a means for France to regain its vitality and for Frenchmen to reassert their virility, cycling played a very significant role. Even before the establishment of the Tour de France, commentators highlighted the extreme difficulty and dirtiness of road cycling and the tribulations endured by those who competed. The racers, who were always men, were evoked as heroic and unflinching in their suffering. At the same time, it was made quite clear that no one would appreciate seeing women suffering in the same way, that this would be nothing less than exploitation of 'the weaker sex'. Women participating in competitive sport, and especially one as tough as cycling, simply didn't fit with their habitual depiction as maternal and domestic.

While Henri Desgrange regularly declared his belief that

sport could revitalise France, and particularly when he was writing about cycling, he was very much in the camp of the traditionalists and nationalists who regarded France's survival as being completely dependent on the reassertion of the nation's manhood. He was as concerned as De Coubertin and many others by France's stagnating birth rate and the threat posed by its bristling neighbour, and to them his newspaper offered a comforting and very traditional perspective on gender identities. This was evident in *L'Auto's* pages before, during and subsequent to the first Tour. Yet, well before that race was founded, Desgrange had already offered an illuminating insight into his attitude towards women in his training manual, *La Tête et Les Jambes*.

The book regularly touches on the distraction that girls are likely to present to a fit and healthy young man who is devoted to his vocation as a cyclist. His advice? Resist all temptation to be drawn in by them as this is sure to impact on your focus on training. 'Don't give these nice young girls the least bit of yourself, of your spirit, of your intelligence, of your soul . . . avoid the childlike temptation of giving them a present,' Desgrange implores early on in the book.

When the youngster he's advising develops into a professional track racer, Desgrange reminds him to beware. 'Among the delicate, gloved hands that are loudly applauding you, a good number belong to pretty little lecherous souls who would be delighted to experiment on you, that same night even, in order to assess whether your qualities as a man in bed are as remarkable as your qualities as a racer on the track. You've not been training for that, have you?' he affirms, adding that he's seen many a young man's racing career go off the rails due to the influence of a young lady. Later on, he insists that, 'Your bicycle . . . is your salvation. It will lead you to marriage, healthy, strong, vigorous, and honest. Only then will you leave it.'

All of this advice is based on Desgrange's own racing experience. He married Marie Lucienne Dulaurens in December 1896, some months after his competitive career had ended and he had become well established in his new career. Their only child, Denise, was born exactly a month before the inaugural Tour kicked off, when Desgrange was 38. He was devoted, but apparently to *L'Auto* and the Tour de France, rather than to his wife and daughter. Desgrange and Denise weren't close, especially once he began a relationship with avant-garde artist Jeanne Deley during the First World War that resulted in separation from his wife.

During the first Tour, Desgrange and *L'Auto*'s position on the role of women within cycle sport is unmistakeable. They are presented as simpering but supportive wives, girlfriends and mothers, ready to offer a hug and a kiss at a stage start or finish, then happy to disappear into the background. The paper's suggestion during the opening stage that Édouard Wattelier's puncture-enforced abandon had been the result of a woman's unthinking discard of a hat pin set the tone.

In many other places, ladies are described as offering grace, beauty and colour amid dusty and chaotic scenes, their dresses providing an obvious counterpoint to the grubby attire of 'the giants of the road', who battle relentless on, stoical and heroic. Occasionally, the descriptions hark back to warnings in Desgrange's training manual. At the start in Marseille, Georges Abran details how, 'The faces of the ladies are lit up with curiosity just as those of their Greek forebears must have been when gazing at the marvellous athletes who were competing in the arena. They push and jostle each other, edging forwards; I think that some of them would like to feel the steely muscles to check that there's not a motor hidden within them.' Reading Abran's words, you can almost picture the ladies giggling nervously, fanning themselves frantically, perhaps on the verge of coming over a little funny given the proximity of these virile physical specimens, who are taking on a challenge from which they are naturally excluded.

At the finish in Paris, *L'Auto* records Jean Dargassies receiving a telegraph from his tearful wife, summoning him home to south-west France, the analogy with the war hero returning to his sweetheart at the end of a campaign too obvious to miss. Underpinning these descriptions is the women's acceptance of their position as onlookers, appreciative of their gallant men's deeds, occasionally giving care or comfort, but too fragile to contemplate such deeds themselves.

For decades, the most obvious role for women within the sport was as the supportive wife or doting mother. Indeed, such representations became very much part of the narrative for *L'Équipe*, which focused quite deliberately on Jean Robic's proud mother hugging her son after his Tour win in

1947, on Fausto Coppi's scandalous affair with Giulia Occhini, dubbed 'the woman in white', during the 1950s and many other women who filled almost any role except a competitive one.

Even the tradition for racers to ride on ahead of the peloton when in their home region to greet their family belongs to this narrative – the hero returns home, plants a kiss on his wife's cheek, then rides off into the distance again in the search for more adventure – as does the Tour's ongoing use of tottering podium girls at race finishes to hand over the spoils of victory to Garin and Aucouturier's Lycra-clad heirs. This throwback fits perfectly with Baron de Coubertin's belief that the primary role of women in sport was to crown the victors.

Some might dismiss these as outdated foibles that have little significance now. However, the paucity of attention and investment in women's cycling that continues into the twenty-first century highlights the damage caused by such deep-set and long-standing attitudes. As Christopher Thompson maintains, 'By asserting the timeless nature of conventional gender roles, heroic Tour narratives have continually offered a conservative counterpoint to fears that increasingly emancipated and empowered women were blurring fundamental sexual differences and undermining social stability as they gained new rights and opportunities. Not surprisingly, defining Tour heroism as exclusively male has had a debilitating impact on competitive female cycling in France.'

There was never any likelihood of Desgrange and *L'Auto* taking a lead in demanding change to this situation. In 1909, a reader's call for a Tour de France Féminin was dismissed with the suggestion that this would require the bulldozing of the country's mountains. Three years later, the French federation decided that it wouldn't sanction women's races. Other papers were equally dismissive, *Le Vélo* declaring in an editorial during the 1903 Tour that, when compared to men, women 'rarely have the physical aptitude and especially the moral aptitude' for cycling.

Eight decades passed before the Tour finally acknowledged that women should have a place in the race beyond flanking the day's winner on the victory podium. In 1984, at the instigation of co-director Félix Lévitan, the Tour Féminin took place for the first time. 'Women do not occupy the position they deserve in society,' Lévitan said of the long-overdue event, adding that he wanted to organise 'something greater than anything that had been done to this point in cycling for athletic women.'

The event, which ran ahead of the men's race on a much shorter course, survived for six editions, the final three of them won by Jeannie Longo. The Frenchwoman was arguably the greatest female rider in cycling history, but obtained just a fraction of the coverage devoted to male compatriots Bernard Hinault and Laurent Fignon, who commented in Desgrange-like fashion after sharing the Tour podium with inaugural Tour Féminin winner Michelle Martin in 1984, 'I like women, but I prefer to see them doing something else.'

Although it ran for several more years under different names and organisers, the Tour Féminin disappeared from the calendar after 2009. It is worth noting, though, that several leading men's races that were on the verge of suffering the same fate during that period were saved by Tour organisers ASO, including Paris–Nice, Liège–Bastogne–Liège, Flèche Wallonne and the Dauphiné Libéré.

Thankfully, there are signs that women's cycling will soon have a more extensive and high-profile calendar. ASO has been increasing its investment in this side of the sport, albeit very slowly, new races are appearing and media attention is also growing. The sexist, dismissive attitude towards women's racing, cemented in large part by Desgrange and *L'Auto* during the early years of the twentieth century and sustained long after that, is finally dissipating. At long last, the sport's fans, event organisers and the media are, to use Susan B. Anthony's words, standing and rejoicing every time they see a woman racing by on a wheel.

CHAPTER 12

'ROAD CYCLING HAS BEEN DEMOCRATISED'

Arriving in Toulouse meant three days' rest for the Tour's diminished and very drained peloton. Dropping from their bikes in the infield of the Bazacle velodrome, almost every one delivered a tale of personal calvary. Naturally, *L'Auto* and its rivals lapped these up with relish. François Beaugendre revealed that he hadn't eaten or drunk anything over the last three-quarters of the stage. Philippe de Balade hobbled around on a swollen knee caused by a crash near Montpellier that had reduced him to pushing the pedals around with one leg for the remainder of the stage. Josef Fischer had been waylaid by no fewer than eight punctures. Meanwhile, the ailing Léon Georget hurried to his hotel bed, unsure and, for the moment, unwilling to continue on towards Paris. The consolation for the 25 left standing and any others who might decide to join them on the next leg to

Bordeaux was that it was shortest and most straightforward of the race.

While the riders recuperated and tried to raise their sunken spirits, the press and manufacturers were relentless in squeezing everything they could from the Tour, with *L'Auto* leading the way. Its stage 3 special edition had been its first to sell more than 100,000 copies, which provided good reason to crow in its one thousandth edition on the morning of 11 July – 'We don't have sumptuous lodgings or the vanity to dominate everything; what we do have is our love of sport and our desire to spread that love around. That's enough for us.' – and to be bullish, as Desgrange swatted away criticisms of the race organisation made by *Le Monde Sportif*'s Jean Lafitte, pointing out once again that Lafitte's paper had got the stage 3 result completely wrong. To Lafitte and his colleague Frantz Reichel's complaint that this mistake was the result of deliberate misinformation on *L'Auto*'s part, Desgrange responded tartly. 'It's almost as if the telephone line between Toulouse and Paris was our accomplice,' he commented, pointing out that the line had been under repair.

There was magnanimity, too, as Desgrange hinted that the five-franc daily stipend paid out to any rider in the general classification who averaged a speed of at least 20 kilometres per hour would be extended to those who hadn't achieved that rate. A mere 13 riders of the remaining 25 had covered the first three stages at above this pace, so

Desgrange's suggestion of a relaxation in the rule gave hope to a dozen more.

Desgrange's benevolence also extended to agreeing to a significant change to the fifth stage between Bordeaux and Nantes. Fear at seeing racers charging at high speed through La Rochelle's streets when most locals would be out celebrating Bastille Day had encouraged the town's mayor to introduce a bylaw preventing cyclists from riding any faster than walking pace through its streets. Generally, this would have been sufficient to produce a volcanic reaction from the Tour boss, perhaps even the suggestion of a boycott of the town and its businesses, as had been the case when Saint-Germain slapped a ban on cars. However, on this occasion he announced that the control would be moved to the outskirts of the town and that the race would be neutralised for half an hour after that point to allow the competitors time to walk into the centre and pick up the supplies they needed to continue onwards to Nantes.

In between long periods of rest at the Hôtel du Sanglier – 'which offered the riders an extraordinary welcome, looking after them in all kinds of ways including lending clothes to those who hadn't yet received theirs,' noted Géo Lefèvre – the riders returned to the Bazacle to keep their legs supple. The prospect of the short – only 268 kilometres! – and relatively flat run to Bordeaux lifted the morale of most. It was, many said, going to be 'an easy stage, like a rest day'.

STAGE 4, TOULOUSE–BORDEAUX, 268KM, 12–13 JULY 1903

The Toulousains have clearly decided to make a night of it. The first group of riders isn't due to start the fourth stage to Bordeaux until five in the morning, but the streets around the control point at the start are packed more than three hours beforehand. The night is balmy, a gentle breeze is blowing from the south that will encourage the riders along. The air is filled with the music being played by the orchestra that Café Sion proprietor Monsieur Auberdiac has hired. It mixes with the bustle, chat and laughter of spectators, eagerly awaiting the arrival of the first riders when the control opens at three o'clock, and the shouts of newspaper vendors and hawkers touting refreshments to the throng.

Ovations resound as the riders start to appear at the Café Sion, the most nervous appearing first as they've not been able to sleep. They sign their names, take the green armbands that denote their now quite elite status as general classification riders and move away to check their bikes and fill the bags hanging from their bars. Close by, an impromptu outdoor cinema is showing pictures of the finish in Toulouse to goggle-eyed fans.

The crowd continues to build, enthusiastic but not beyond control thanks to the substantial presence of the local police and gendarmes. There are cheers as Maurice Garin arrives, followed by most of his main challengers for the title. He looks shy in the midst of such wholehearted adulation, saying nothing after losing his voice bellowing at his rivals in the roar of the mistral, doffing the peak of his flat cap to acknowledge the warm reception before entering the Sion.

Henri Gauban, who hails from Muret just to the south of Toulouse, and Jean Dargassies from just to the north are greeted with some of the loudest cheers. The crowd is equally vociferous when Hippolyte Aucouturier appears, shaking hand after hand as he makes his way towards the cafe to sign in and pick up the yellow armband he will wear as a member of the second group on the road. He's confident of repeating his stage-winning performances in Marseille and Toulouse, insisting he's the strongest and fastest man in the race. There are 17 new faces too, amateurs, mostly young and from Bordeaux, laughing nervously as they admire the famous names around them, entering the Sion almost apologetically in search of the sign-in sheet and white armbands that they will wear on the road north.

At four o'clock, Georges Abran signals that the control is closed and orders the peloton together. The riders gather in behind him as he sets off on foot for the Café St-Roch in the Toulouse suburb of Minimes, a thousand or more cyclists tracking the racers through the city's streets beneath a cloudless sky that heralds another sun-baked day. It takes half an hour for this immense parade to meander to the official start. At twenty to five, Abran calls the first group forward. The road ahead is black with spectators, police officers lined out in front of them to keep the route open.

The riders make their final checks, take a swig from a

bottle, bite down a last morsel of food. It is five o'clock on the dot when Abran raises his starting pistol and fires off a shot, triggering a sprint away from the start line. This is headed by the first man to reach Toulouse, Eugène Brange, who is the first out of the city, with Garin and Samson also prominent until the speeding 25-man gaggle disappears into the cloud of dust they've kicked up in their wake.

Forty-five minutes later, Abran goes through the same procedure with the second set of riders. Comprising 20 professionals and 17 amateurs, this group is much larger than the first, which has fuelled expectations that Aucouturier will once again prove too strong for his peers in the lead peloton. Although the amateurs are unlikely to be of much help to him in maintaining a fast pace, the likes of Gauban, Pagie, Jaeck and Laeser have already shown their ability during this race. They are well aware that if they can stay with the great Aucouturier, a lucrative payday may be their reward. Henri Desgrange is pleased to see that alongside them are mainly locals, hopefuls from Pamiers, La Réole, Sérignac and Peyrehorade, eager to test themselves against the big guns.

At six sharp, Abran's pistol sounds again and the second group accelerates away. The pace in both groups is red-hot from the off. The leaders are aware that Aucouturier will take advantage of even the slightest easing of their momentum. The chasers are just as determined to make up any ground.

The first place of note is the broom-making town Grisolles, where the whole population has turned out to cheer local hero Dargassies, who has revealed in the papers that one of his *favourite mid-race snacks is a piece of bread seasoned with beetroot snatched from a roadside field. There is no time yet, though, to indulge himself in this manner. Aboard the Gladiator bike he bought just a few months earlier from the brand's representative in Agen, he's set on giving his friends and neighbours an unforgettable show. He leads the way, the sight of his huge frame and blond goatee setting off an indescribable roar, which travels with the riders from the Toulouse end of Grisolles to the Montauban road on its northern edge. On his wheel are just a dozen riders, the infernal pace already too wicked for half of the peloton. Acknowledging the acclaim with a wave and shouts of 'Adieu! Adieu!', Dargassies, smiling, powers on towards Montauban.*

Reporting for La Petite Gironde, *veteran cycling journalist Maurice Martin, who was behind the founding of Bordeaux–Paris more than a decade before and knows these roads extremely well, can't believe the speed being set. His Panhard-Levassor 6CV hasn't the speed to get past them. 'They are travelling at 35km/h,' he reports. 'Others pass by us with that same supple speed on the pedals, that beautiful style . . . that shows the mastery of the great athlete.'*

On the road between Grisolles and Montauban, Dargassies' bravura showing rebounds on him as he falls off the pace of the leaders and drops back to the second group on the road, three minutes behind the 12 leaders. By Montauban – 'Does it need to be added that everyone has L'Auto *in their hands?' – the heat is extremely intense even before seven o'clock, but that doesn't appear to have persuaded many to remain indoors. The streets are packed as the leaders reach the control having covered the opening 60 kilometres in less than 90 minutes, averaging more than 40 kilometres per hour. Garin is the first to sign and get under way again, the rest racing to get on to his back wheel. Incredibly, Aucouturier's group are moving even faster and are four minutes up when they sign in at the same control, the amateurs contributing their share of pace-setting according to Charles Laeser.*

The searing pace of the lead group continues through Castelsarrasin, where they are 40 minutes ahead of schedule. Soon after, every member of the group apart from Garin and Georget crash when a dog runs into the road. Initially, there appears to be no serious damage apart from to the air from the curses yelled by Jean Fischer. But as persistently unfortunate Fernand Augereau struggles to his feet, blood running from a wound in his face, he realises his bike is almost unusable. He eventually manages to persuade a spectator to lend him his machine, but by then his rivals have long gone.

This brief delay results in a further loss of time to Aucouturier's pack of chasers, who, astonishingly, fly through Castelsarrasin with an amateur on the front. However, halfway between Castelsarrasin and Agen, close to the small town of Lamagistère on the north bank of the Garonne, the impetus of Aucouturier's little band of professionals and amateurs is shattered when another dog wanders into the road. One rider – an amateur, Aucouturier later complains – drifts too close to the double-stage-winner's front wheel and catches his pedal in it. The whole group tumbles, resulting in what Laeser describes as a 'salade terrible' when 15 riders, their bikes and provisions end up strewn across the road.

'The Hercules of Commentry' hits the ground hard, his knee taking most of the impact. He remounts, rides for a couple of kilometres, stops again, has his knee bandaged in a pharmacy, then announces he is going to abandon. His route to Bordeaux will be on the midday train. Laeser, meanwhile, remounts and rides, head bowed, until his senses return fully. When he looks around, he realises he's alone. He begins to chase, but has no idea who he's pursuing.

The eight leaders – Garin, Kerff, Georget, Brange, Fischer, Samson, Muller, Pothier – rampage into the fixed control in Agen's Café Russe. They tussle with each other in order to sign first, Garin swearing, Kerff shouting for a drink, the desperate Samson yelling for a pump having ridden for the last few kilometres on a flat rear tyre and then noticed his front one is leaking air too. Signatures scribbled, the group rides on, leaving Samson to spend a dozen minutes fitting two new tubes a mechanic from an adjacent shop has generously donated to him. They are not yet aware of Aucouturier's abandon and are still giving all they have to keep him at a distance.

Back at the control, Dargassies and Catteau are next through 11 minutes later. Soon after, there's a huge ovation for local rider Philippe de Balade's arrival. He signs in, then announces his intention to abandon having reached his hometown. A Monsieur Georges Thomas, who is assisting at the control, encourages him to continue, promising him a work of art for the best rider from the south-west if he agrees to *continue. Swayed by this and urged on by the crowds, de Balade rides on.*

The heat, which has reached 39 degrees in the shade, and speed are taking a heavy toll on the amateurs, who are dropping out at regular intervals, the group of riders in yellow and white armbands now scattered. The only member of this second group still showing good form is Laeser, who is going like a bullet according to Maurice Martin, but is all alone. Exactly an hour behind the leaders when he reaches the Agen control, his hopes of a high finish are remote given he's just one man duelling with seven, but once again he is showing his class.

At the Café du Progrés in Marmande, 86 kilometres from Bordeaux, where, it almost goes without saying, another horde awaits, the lead group is just five-strong, Brange and Catteau having lost ground. An hour later, Laeser, still riding alone, signs his name. The man from Geneva presses on, knowing he has a chance, albeit a slight one. Seeing the unmistakeably large figure of Marcel Kerff sat disconsolately at the roadside trying to repair a damaged tyre as he doesn't have a spare, Laeser tosses the Belgian one of the pair he has wrapped around his shoulders, his act of charity barely costing him a second.

'One hundred metres further on, I punctured too. That resulted in me having a companion to ride with all the way into Bordeaux,' he later explains. As he starts to fit his spare tyre, Kerff pulls up alongside him. 'Kerff thanked me by helping me to set a frightening pace,' says the Swiss. As far as

Laeser's hopes are concerned, there is arguably no better wheel to follow than that of the strapping and indefatigable Belgian, who now has the chance to avenge the slights that he believes Garin to be guilty of towards him.

Like Kerff, his compatriot Samson is also giving everything that he has with the objective of thwarting Garin after fitting those two new tyres in Agen. 'Like a madman, I started out again, not even feeling the sun, even closing my eyes at some points as I was giving every little resource that I had,' he says. He catches Dargassies, Catteau and Brange, three good men to chase with. At a level crossing, one of them spies a water butt that's full and shouts out. Each of the quartet leap from their bikes and dunk their heads. They're away again in a few instants.

After Marmande, Samson drops Dargassies and Catteau, and Brange punctures after already crashing twice. Samson doesn't wait. Finally, on the sharp climb at La Réole, 66 kilometres from Bordeaux, he bridges up to the five leaders. 'Someone's come back from the dead,' quips Muller, surprised to see the Belgian reappear.

The six riders fly through Langon, one of them noticing Aucouturier's manager, Titus Postma, and shouting out to him that his rider has quit. On they go, the wind caressing their backs, propelling them towards the finish, which is now less than 50 kilometres distant. Their collaboration has one primary objective: preventing the 'stage-only' riders from outshining them once again.

Ahead in Bordeaux, crowds are only just starting to gather at the end at the Pont de la Maye, where the finish will take place. Georges Abran arrives to supervise, closely followed by Géo Lefèvre, who's travelled north by train and then onwards to the final control at the Café du Petit-Trianon in a Darracq that has been put his disposal and driven by Joseph Jiel-Laval, runner-up to the legendary Charles Terront in the inaugural Paris–Brest–Paris of 1891.

Receiving news by telegraph that the riders are now little more than 20 kilometres away, Abran instructs one of his assistants to hurriedly draw a line across the road with a piece of coal. He then places a young man brandishing a flag on either end of the line. They have only been in position for a few minutes when a cloud of dust begins to build 500 metres away down the bumpy road.

It's ten to two. The crowd, which has only started to gather in the last few minutes in the expectation that the riders will finish at three and is only a few hundred strong, hears the clamour and spectators surge to the roadsides as figures emerge from the whirlwind, bent over their bars. In the centre is the large shape of Samson, who opens up a two-length gap on Muller and maintains it to the black finish line that's already disappearing under the dust. Georget is third, Garin fourth, Jean Fischer fifth and Pothier sixth. Three minutes later, Brange beats Catteau for seventh, having managed to rejoin the leaders on the road into Bordeaux only to puncture again two kilometres from the line.

'I accelerated when I saw the flags and I won,' the rider from Brussels tells Lefèvre, before heading with the others to the

Vélodrome de Parc for a victory parade and a kilometre time trial. Typically, Garin has waited for no one and is already there. Even though he's not won, as overall leader he's quite happy to collect the victory bouquet and stand on the podium as a band plays La Marseillaise. *Arriving in the midst of this, Samson is very disgruntled at having his thunder stolen, and his mood doesn't improve when the band reveals they don't know the Belgian national anthem. If that's bad, worse is about to come . . .*

A few kilometres away at the Pont de la Maye, Samson's compatriot Kerff barrels over the line with Laeser glued to his wheel. Laeser has completed the stage 4 minutes and 3 seconds faster than Samson, earning him 700 francs and making the 23-year-old mechanic from Geneva the first foreigner to win a stage of the Tour de France.

Despite the disappointment of fans still arriving at the Pont de la Maye in the hope of seeing the finish, the stage has been another huge success. Every one of the general classification riders has completed it and is set to start the fifth stage to Nantes at 11 o'clock the next evening. Once again they have been upstaged by a startling performance from a rider in the second group.

Although only five of the 17 amateurs completed the course, they have also distinguished themselves, the pick of them proving to be Maisonneuve, who was 23rd fastest to Bordeaux, quicker than seven of the professionals. There's also finally reason for Fernand Augereau to smile too as he claims the 100 francs for the fastest kilometre on the track.

The loss of Aucouturier is a setback for fans and organisers, but barely dents the all-consuming enthusiasm for the event, as witnessed by sales of L'Auto's special edition, which reach a new record of 117,000 copies. Géo Lefèvre proclaims that, 'These riders are more than men. They surprised everyone at Bordeaux, they literally flew along the road at a speed of 30km/h under a sun that could have blanched even the most tanned of skins and made them suffer like martyrs.'

He suggests that Laeser's victory proves the success of the decision not to allow the use of pace-makers. 'Three months ago, there was absolutely no way for a new man to break through without having previously completed a series of fearsomely hard races where he would always be beaten by a crack rider receiving very potent support from pace-makers and soigneurs. Now the likes of Brange, Samson, Laeser not only have the ability to produce magnificent performances, but even to win when they're up against the cracks,' he writes in his gushing post-stage report.

Almost inevitably, he weaves mention of Jean Dargassies into his argument, insisting that the likes of the blacksmith from Grisolles wouldn't even have lined up under the usual format that penalised them so heavily. 'He was the first to understand that road cycling had just been democratised and that those who took charge could now be anyone who decided it was finally time to quit their village,' he enthuses.

Henri Desgrange is elated too, but can't resist another tweak to his new formula. Having seen the confusion caused once again by a rider from the second group winning the stage, with spectators witnessing one rider triumphing only to be told an hour later that another has in fact taken the honours, he points out that, 'At Nantes the race will be simplified, as it will be unburdened of that eternal second group that it has been dragging along since Marseille,' adding, 'it will not be dragging it along next year.'

As has long been planned, there will only be one group competing on the final stage between Nantes and Paris. It will comprise only the riders still eligible for the general classification, who will, as the rules currently stand, be able to take advantage of pace-makers. Defending his decision to change a regulation that was heavily criticised in the first place, Desgrange first points to its partial success, underlining that those that were in the second group were not only competitive but even provided the winner of the two most recent stages. He adds that it is still too soon to draw any solid conclusions about the race as it is still ongoing, but admits, 'We won't make the ridiculous mistake of telling ourselves that we've put together a perfect event.'

STAGE 4 RESULT

1. Charles Laeser (Swi) 268km in 8-46-00 (average speed 30.570km/h) *
2. 'Samson' (Bel) at 4-03
3. Rodolfo Muller (Ita) same time
4. Léon Georget (Fra) same time

5. Maurice Garin (Fra) same time
6. Jean Fischer (Fra) same time
7. Lucien Pothier (Fra) same time
8. Eugène Brange (Fra) at 7-41
9. Aloïs Catteau (Bel) same time
10. Jean Dargassies (Fra) at 26-00
11. Jean-Baptiste Dortignacq (Fra) at 27-45 *
12. Fernand Augereau (Fra) at 38-00
13. Pujol (Fra) at 40-16 *
14. Ferdinand Payan (Fra) at 51-00
15. Isidore Lechartier (Fra) same time
16. Marcel Kerff (Bel) at 1-00-00
17. François Beaugendre (Fra) at 1-30-40
18. Paul Émile (Fra) at 1-31-40 *
19. Gustave Pasquier (Fra) at 1-47-07
20. Alexandre Foureaux (Fra) same time
21. Josef Fischer (Ger) same time
22. Julien Girbe (Fra) at 2-14-52
23. Philippe De Balade (Fra) at 2-44-50
24. Pierre Desvages (Fra) at 2-53-09
25. Émile Moulin (Fra) at 3-41-49
26. Ernest Pivin (Fra) at 4-13-23
27. Léon Durandeau (Fra) at 4-23-33 *
28. René Salais (Fra) at 5-15-11
29. Arsène Millochau (Fra) at 5-15-12
30. Georges Borot (Fra) same time

* Registered for the fourth stage only

Overall classification

1. Maurice Garin (Fra) at 59-57-43
2. Léon Georget (Fra) at 1-58-53
3. Lucien Pothier (Fra) at 2-58-02
4. Jean Fischer (Fra) at 3-52-21
5. Marcel Kerff (Bel) at 3-55-20
6. Rodolfo Muller (Ita) at 4-00-57
7. Fernand Augereau (Fra) at 4-18-39
8. François Beaugendre (Fra) at 5-08-45
9. 'Samson' (Bel) at 5-58-56
10. Gustave Pasquier (Fra) at 8-33-49
11. Aloïs Catteau (Bel) at 8-34-40
12. Jean Dargassies (Fra) at 11-07-11
13. Josef Fischer (Ger) at 14-15-33
14. Isidore Lechartier (Fra) at 14-29-02
15. Ferdinand Payan (Fra) at 14-51-12
16. Julien Girbe (Fra) at 19-52-07
17. Alexandre Foureaux (Fra) at 20-46-57
18. Eugène Brange (Fra) at 20-59-26
19. René Salais (Fra) at 25-56-44
20. Philippe De Balade (Fra) at 28-37-01
21. Georges Borot (Fra) at 29-50-02
22. Ernest Pivin (Fra) at 29-58-13
23. Émile Moulin (Fra) at 32-43-42
24. Pierre Desvages (Fra) at 35-28-55
25. Arsène Millochau (Fra) at 39-02-25

CHAPTER 13

'COLOSSAL, GIGANTIC AND MONSTROUS'

One unchanging feature for riders at the Tour de France is their focus on doing as little as possible when they aren't competing. The long-standing adage for professional racers has it that, 'You should not move if you can stand still, don't stand if you can sit, and don't sit if you can lie down.' With just a single night to recuperate in Bordeaux before gathering for the start of the fifth stage in the wine-growing centre sitting astride a huge bend in the Garonne, the riders only stirred from their beds for meals at the Hotel Lacassagne, where rooms were available at a reduced rate of five francs – the same amount that some were earning for their daily stipend from the Tour organisers.

By this point, grumbles about the cost of racing the Tour were becoming increasingly hard for the organisers to ignore. While Henri Desgrange and Géo Lefèvre were right to underline the success of the format they had introduced that had allowed lesser names not only to compete with the well-established competitors, but even to beat them, there were plenty of riders whose efforts hadn't yielded any reward.

Consequently, while the performances of a rider like Jean Dargassies were hugely impressive and fully deserved the praise they received, the gushing reaction of Lefèvre in particular gave a very false impression of racers' motives, playing up the amateur ethos of competition simply for the love of it. Whereas, these were professionals or want-to-be professionals, drawn in primarily by *L'Auto*'s pre-race lure that suggested they could, 'Pay a few francs and you could win thousands.'

Clearly, many of them hadn't read the small print – and the font used in the organising paper was extremely small – detailing how this prize fund would be divided. They had, it should be remembered, no experience at all of participating in a stage race, where their finishing position would be decided over a period of several days. Usually, they raced and, if they did well, they got paid. Now they were racing and receiving nothing at all, or at least hadn't yet. For these riders, the only ready guarantee of payment was to sign a contract to be a pace-maker for one of the general-classification leaders on the final stage into Paris, and several had quit the Tour to do so.

Yet the race organisers weren't intending to edge them towards some kind of British-style competition in which amateur ethos and status were essential requirements, where, as Britain's Bicycle Union advocated, prize money and expenses should never be paid. While often conservative in his attitude, Desgrange was essentially progressive. His aim wasn't to exploit the Tour's competitors, but to raise them up with the sport as a whole, and not only financially. He wanted them to be and be seen as role models or, more accurately, as model workers.

Although he had competed as an amateur, and at a high level too, Desgrange made it clear in *La Tête et Les Jambes* that any successful amateur rider had to take the step up to professionalism, viewing this as the only way for an athlete to devote himself entirely to their chosen discipline without the distraction of requiring another career to make ends meet. Therefore, Desgrange did what he could to ensure that riders received a fair return for their labour, tinkering throughout the Tour with the provision of prize money.

As he made these adjustments, he was also more conscious than anyone of the complete change of mindset that the Tour demanded of everyone involved in cycle racing, a change it was by now apparent that no one had fully foreseen and most were completely unprepared for. As Desgrange pointed out in his editorial during the halt in Bordeaux, he and his staff needed time to reflect on events at the Tour and consider future changes that might be needed to improve its organisation. Riders, manufacturers and spectators would also need to take stock. The Tour had provided a totally new perspective on what professional sport could be.

For those drawn out to watch 'the giants of the road', the

democratising effect of the race must have been very evident. Unlike almost every other entertainment on offer to the general public in that era, the Tour did not divide classes according to the price of the seats they could afford. Rich and poor mingled at every point on the route, literally rubbing shoulders at starts, finishes and the busiest towns along the route, pressed together in a way that they never would never contemplate when going about their everyday business.

Although the role of the bicycle and the Tour de France in breaking down social barriers might not have been hugely significant, both the bike and what had already become its biggest race did have an impact in changing established attitudes. These could be clearly seen in French journalist Baudry de Saunier's series of best-selling books about cycling, written in the 1890s and to which Pierre Giffard contributed. As well as enthusiastic musings on the wonders that bicycles and cycling opened up, they also included sections on how to behave and dress on the bike in order to maintain your social status. Sitting upright was especially important, particularly for ladies, as leaning forwards over the bars in order to attempt to increase your speed was regarded as lacking self-control and respectability.

Over that decade, as the number of bikes sold in France spiralled upwards and bike clubs and societies flourished in all parts, most were characterised by social homogeneity. There were clubs for bankers and races for lawyers, for example, while those in the working classes tended to set up their own organisations precisely because they didn't want to feel out of place. If they didn't gravitate towards fellow professionals, many in the bourgeoisie opted to join organisations like the Touring Club de France, which was based on Britain's Cyclists' Touring Club and catered to those who were more interested in cycling as a leisure or tourist activity.

Inevitably, conflict arose between these different groups. By 1900, policemen were patrolling Paris's Bois de Boulogne on bikes in order to monitor and ensure good behaviour between the many cyclists from all sections of society who gathered there. Bans were imposed on cycling in some towns and certain parts of Paris because of concerns about riders' speed and unruliness.

Very occasionally this conflict took on physical shape, with tacks or nails scattered on a road to scupper a ride or race. Generally, though, it was more ordered, although still extremely unpleasant. For example, the April 1903 edition of *La Revue du Touring Club*, the Touring Club de France's monthly magazine, features a letter in which the correspondent complains: 'The bicycle is charming but there are too many cyclists . . . it breaks my heart to see this treasure wasted, available to everyone. It should be reserved for the intelligent who alone know how to enjoy what it offers . . . For goodness sake, leave nature to the true tourist, and do not transport people out of their normal sphere. In the end they will be happier that way.'

The Tour, though, challenged ignorance and patronising attitudes of this type. It opened France up to the whole population, thanks to the reports carried not only in the sporting press, but also in the high-circulation dailies such as *Le Petit Journal* and *Le Petit Parisien*, which devoted more and more space to the Tour as it progressed during that first July and very quickly became a popular sensation. In the former, the nation's biggest paper with a million copies sold each day, coverage of the Tour broke away from the small section devoted to sport and featured in the main news section alongside updates on the deteriorating health of Pope Leo XIII, that month's signing of a new Entente Cordiale between France and Great Britain, and the closely followed trial and execution by hanging of Samuel Herbert Dougal, a serial fraudster renowned as the biggest scoundrel in Victorian England who had been found guilty of the murder of his common-law wife Cecile Holland.

The Tour reports in the mainstream press didn't carry much detail, their dryness revealing that they were clearly supplied by a wire service such as Havas rather than an on-the-spot reporter. However, in a period still long before the emergence of radio, the French people received everything they knew about their country and the rest of the world from these papers, which meant they certainly knew all about the exploits of Garin, Aucouturier and their peers. As shown by *Le Petit Journal*'s founding and continued backing of Paris–Brest–Paris, although these papers didn't devote extensive coverage to sport, they were aware of the sales and marketing lift that could be achieved with the organisation of events that catered to the public's growing craving for entertainment and leisure diversions. The development of and fascination with air travel, for example, would encourage *Le Matin* to organise aeroplane races and a cross-Channel dirigible contest.

The daily updates from the race also complemented the serial novels that were a hugely important part of the editorial in these mass circulation papers, slotting in neatly alongside Louis Letang's *Les Amours de Jacqueline* or Maxime Villemer's *Les Détresses de la Vie* (*The Distresses of Life*), which both ran for several days in the July 1903 editions of *Le Petit Journal*. As Lefèvre had presciently predicted beforehand, the Tour became, 'A great athletic drama whose magnitude will captivate [the public's] attention during almost three weeks . . . as the giants of the road offer us six consecutive tragedies, [each] with its particular ups and downs, its dénouement.' The race was nothing less than *Les Détresses de la Vie on Two Wheels*.

The democratising aspect of the Tour also derived from its importance as a commercial lever. Drawing hundreds of thousands of people and maybe more out to watch bike racing presented an unprecedented opportunity for marketing all kinds of products, and especially bicycles and related equipment. In this respect, *L'Auto*'s claim that the Tour racers were 'unconscious messengers of progress' is undeniable. Desgrange, Lefèvre and cycling writers on other titles maintained that numbers of bikes were sure to rise. Within a decade they had tripled.

It was of vital importance for Desgrange and his staff,

though, to stress that higher bike sales and, therefore, greater mobility for the working classes would be of benefit to France. This was done by not only stressing the boost it would provide to national vitality and virility, but also by celebrating the working-class roots of the racers and suggesting that by following the rules laid down by the Tour organisation they were being transformed into responsible citizens, who would bolster rather than threaten the status quo.

While their uncouthness, rudeness and, for some at least, rapidly gained wealth may have aroused concern in some quarters, Desgrange persistently attempted to allay such fears by offering up an image of the race being an instrument of civilisation and social advancement. He also made it clear that its organisation and the riders, who were presented as model workers – according to Christopher Thompson 'the first unskilled labourers to turn their physical capital (strength and endurance) into socioeconomic success (fame and fortune)' – as being very much under his control.

Rather than playing down their working-class backgrounds, L'Auto and other papers highlighted them. For instance, in its report on the stage into Bordeaux, Le Vélo details the 'winner' Samson's life as a painter in his native Belgium, revealing how he worked from eight in the morning until seven in the evening and fitted a 50-kilometre ride in around his working hours every day. A similar perspective was offered on Parisian carpenter Alexandre Foureaux, describing how he had gained his strength and fitness by riding around the capital's streets with a six-foot-long workbench strapped to his back.

The butchers, clowns, miners and blacksmiths hoping for an escape from poverty did, in a very few cases, achieve that. However, with only one major manufacturer committed to the race initially, most remained dependent on Desgrange's daily stipend, if they were consistent and fortunate enough to be eligible for it, and his goodwill. They had merely swapped one boss for another, and there's absolutely no doubt that Desgrange saw them as his employees, as he decided what to pay them and changed the race rules if he felt they weren't performing in the way that he wanted. In later years he extended this control by introducing fines for what he regarded as bad behaviour.

The counterpoint to this was the praise lavished on those who were seen to have behaved in the right manner. Jean Dargassies was a most obvious example of this, receiving regular eulogies for taking on the established names – of whom he knew none, *L'Auto* had been delighted to report before the race – and doing so in the right spirit. He never complained, showed huge perseverance and courage, and was always quick to smile and joke.

The paper also made particular mention of those riders who showed courtesy towards their rivals, such as Charles Laeser tossing a spare tube to Marcel Kerff, or racers who delivered a particularly elegant signature on the sheet at control points, *L'Auto* picking out Julien Girbe, Fernand Augereau, Rodolfo Muller and Maurice Garin for producing 'among some of the most beautiful signatures on the control sheet'. Highlighting such niceties made for good copy, but was also designed to soothe *L'Auto*'s middle-class readership by stressing indications of social redemption and conformity.

Indeed, such was Desgrange's belief in his race's ability to civilise and turn the riders into responsible citizens that it appeared to blind him to those who refused to conform. The stand-out example is Maurice Garin. In many ways, 'The Little Sweep' was the Lance Armstrong of his era. The Tour's outstanding rider with his desire and determination reinforced by the hardships he had endured during his childhood and early adult life, Garin toed Desgrange's line to an extent, but always let go of it when there was a chance of his dominance being threatened.

The only thing that did bother Garin was the prospect of losing. His supreme ability meant that he had become unaccustomed to defeat in those races that really mattered to him, and none mattered more than the inaugural Tour de France. He started as favourite and cemented that position in any way that he could. 'No gifts,' Armstrong growled after sweeping to yet another stage win in a crushing domination of his rivals in 2004. The quote could just as easily have come from Garin.

On the opening stage, he made the most of Émile Pagie's

unexpectedly strong showing, the pair collaborating, as the rules permitted, in order to put as much distance between them and their rivals. Beyond that point, Garin didn't much care for the race regulations and the norms of cycling etiquette. Following his loss of time to Léon Georget and of the stage win to Hippolyte Aucouturier on stage 2, he blackmailed the organisers prior to stage 3, insisting he wouldn't continue unless Aucouturier started in the second group. During that stage, he was seen to be cheating by *La Provence Sportive*'s reporter. This was surely not a one-off. Fellow racers accused him of roughhousing at control points so that he could sign in and leave first, refusing to share food and drink with rivals, and reneging on agreements to halt to take on supplies. As will be seen, he was also prepared to resort to violence when his rivals refused to comply with his idea of how the race should unfold.

While Desgrange and Lefèvre held the power within the Tour, Garin held it within the race. To a large extent, between the points when Georges Abran waved his flag at the start and the finish, Garin was effectively the Tour director, deciding how it should unfold, what riders could and couldn't do, and who should win.

Desgrange and his *L'Auto* staff may have built him up as 'a giant of the road' based on his racing ability, but instances of him being presented as a model worker in the same way as Jean Dargassies or Lucien Pothier are far harder to find. Garin, more than any other Tour rider, rejected the idealised working-class identity that *L'Auto* sought to portray. Unfortunately for Desgrange and the Tour, Garin's conniving and cheating established a quite different model for his peers to follow. Having witnessed him getting away with rule-breaking and riding off with the greatest share of the spoils, many of his peers opted to take the same path in the 1904 race, which 'The Little Sweep' won on the road, but ultimately lost thanks to the sport's officials.

Garin's response to losing his Tour title and receiving a two-year ban more than a century before Americans Floyd Landis and Armstrong became the second and third Tour champions to be stripped of their titles? Rather than appeal, he quit racing altogether to run a garage in Lens with his brothers. Yet his legend and example lived on. Like training and nutrition, cheating has subsequently been worked on and refined and almost every generation of cycling administrators and fans has had its scandal to deal with.

One thing that is very evident from contemporary reports is Garin's high standing among fans at the roadside during the first Tour. Lauded by the press for his exploits, 'The White Bulldog', as he was also known, received a tremendous reception wherever he appeared. Instantly recognisable in his white jersey, with the number one displayed on the large square of red cloth tied between the top-tube and seat-tube of his La Française Diamant, his bushy moustache failing to hide his cocksure expression, Garin was, just like Armstrong a century or so later, the one rider everyone wanted to see. Many, and particularly so during and after stages when he was caked with dust and dirt, must have seen something of themselves in him, very much a working-class man, albeit one on the up.

Indeed, nothing separated the racers from Desgrange's idealised model of what the working-class man could be than the state of their clothes combined with the nature of the event they were participating in. After only a few kilometres of racing, all of the riders would have looked less like professional athletes and more like farm labourers, miners, quarrymen or sweeps. In a country that had perhaps the least regulated labour market and the longest working hours of any industrialised nation, the challenge set before the Tour riders may not have been extraordinary but was undoubtedly exploitative.

Even very early in the race, Desgrange, his staff and correspondents described the racers' deeds and trials using terminology that was essentially Stakhanovite. They may not have been digging coal in the prodigious quantities produced by Stalin's model miner of the mid-1930s, but the challenge and working conditions they faced were equally inhuman. As the difficulty of the first stage was exceeded by that of the second and then again by the third, *L'Auto*, and all of its rivals, presented the riders not only as heroic, but also persistent and dogged, putting particular emphasis on moments when they prevailed despite the odds being stacked very heavily against them. The reporting of Aucouturier's success from the second group on the stage to Toulouse is a clear example of this, as are any number of stories about riders sustaining bad injuries or suffering repeated mechanical breakdowns only to continue on.

Three weeks prior to the Tour, the deputy mayor in Sens bemoaned 'that the necessities of existence reduce men to such excesses' in a critique of the Tour that also included a call for the authorities to impose regulations that 'prevent human beings from going beyond the limits of their normal strength except in the event of an urgent obligation'. Viewing the race as regressive rather than progressive, he followed that up with a municipal bylaw that restricted the speed of racers to 10km/h and required them to proceed on foot on busy roads. Naturally, and not only because Sens featured on the route of the opening stage, Desgrange was apoplectic. In response, he served up an editorial entitled 'A Mayor Who is Ten Years Behind the Times' that suggested that Sens would lose out because races would avoid the town. He also derided the mayor's contention that road races had resulted in fatalities among participants.

Yet at the same time Desgrange and his paper made huge play out of the almost inhuman nature of the challenge the race presented and reported in detail on the suffering the racers endured. It was a contradiction that he struggled to reconcile, just as his successors as race director have done. From the very first stage, the classic Tour themes of suffering and survival emerged, seasoned with tales of courage, camaraderie and endurance. It was nothing less than entertainment through exploitation. In this, it chimed with other popular sports and events in that era – six-day races that were precisely that, dance marathons where couples were quickly doing no more than propping each other up, walkathons and events where contestants vied to spend as much time as possible up a flagpole.

Given such physical excesses, it is therefore no wonder that races became beset by cheating and drug-taking. It was evident in the 1920s when the Pélissier brothers revealed the details of what they were taking to get through the Tour to journalist Albert Londres, resulting in his renowned 'Prisoners of the Road' article in *Le Petit Parisien* that blew the lid on the conditions at Desgrange's race. It became tragically apparent again when Tom Simpson died on the slopes of Mont Ventoux in 1967, amphetamines, alcohol, heat and his phenomenal persistence resulting in a fatal mix, and it is still very evident now. Described by *L'Auto* as 'colossal', 'gigantic' and 'monstrous', the Tour still is all of these things, and it is these elements that continue to make it a challenge without compare in which the first objective for most is simply to reach Paris and be able to say, 'I made it.'

CHAPTER 14

'SICKENED BY THE BEHAVIOUR OF MY RIVALS'

The question of how many riders would make it to Paris was likely to be answered on the fifth stage between Bordeaux and Nantes. At 425 kilometres, it was significantly longer than the previous leg, which meant a late-evening start in order to ensure the front group reached the Breton capital in the early afternoon of Bastille Day, when the winner would receive a specially minted gold medal to commemorate their success on France's national day.

The riders spent all of the daylight hours leading up to the late-evening start sleeping and recuperating in their hotel beds. Scanning the 13 July edition of *L'Auto* for the final details on tweaks to the route – the main one being an instruction that anyone arriving at the flying control in Saintes between the hours of eight and ten on Bastille Day morning would have to dismount and walk for a 100 metres because of a military parade and inspection – they would no doubt have smiled wryly at the news from elsewhere in the cycling world.

A report on the Lyon–Tarare–Lyon amateur race revealed that 'vandals had once again scattered nails on the route . . . Will they ever catch these savages who throw nails down every time a road race takes place in our region?' Alongside it, an extensive report on 'the Italian Bordeaux–Paris', a 600-kilometre race organised by *La Gazzetta dello Sport* that started and finished in Milan, included the news that Giovannis 'Gerbi and Rossignoli had been caught in flagrant breach of the rules relating to pacing behind a motor vehicle.' The pair were the biggest names in Italian racing at that point.

While the riders gathered their resources, Bordeaux had become the latest city to come down with Tour fever. A delay in the delivery of the 10,000 copies of *L'Auto* dispatched from Paris encouraged some to seek out information from the best-placed source. Holed up in his room at the Hotel Lacassagne, churning out copy required for the next special edition, Géo Lefèvre heard a knock on his door, then another, then another . . . 'That morning and afternoon I had more than two hundred visitors, and had to answer all of their questions, which was enjoyable but rather time-consuming,' he wrote. When the papers finally reached Bordeaux at five in the afternoon, they were snapped up in no time.

They informed the Bordelais that, as on the previous two stages, the riders were to be split into two groups, the general classification riders setting off an hour before their

stage-only rivals. The papers had covered Hippolyte Aucouturier's departure extensively, noting that 'The Hercules of
Commentry' would be in Paris for the finish of the final
stage. Oddly, though, there's not a single explanation of Bordeaux victor Charles Laeser's absence from the second
group. Had he injured himself on the way to success? Had
he run out of tyres and departed happy with the 700 francs
he had won? There was no word at all. Yet, even though he
didn't start in Bordeaux, Laeser would still end up playing a
significant role on the outcome of the stage to Nantes.

There was, though, one very familiar name in that second group: Garin. Not Maurice, but his younger brother
Ambroise. Would he become the latest rider to upset the
favourites and confuse watching fans by finishing quicker
than anyone in the first group?

STAGE 5, BORDEAUX–NANTES, 425KM, 13–14 JULY 1903

*At five o'clock, four hours before it is due to open, the control
point close to Saint-André Cathedral is already attracting large
crowds. By eight it is surrounded by a multitude more than
2,000-strong. There's a degree of elegant chaos, the oompah of
military bands preparing for France's national day and the buzz
of spectators in a carnival mood resounding around Bordeaux's
grand eighteenth-century buildings that were the inspiration for
Baron Haussmann's nineteenth-century revitalisation of Paris.*

*The orchestra performing at the Café Français earns gener-
ous applause for its harmonious playing until, at nine, the
attention of spectators switches with the arrival of the riders to
sign in. First to the control point desk is the Parisian Magdelin,
no doubt impatient to get started on what will be his debut in
the race. Soon after, the now well-known and much-loved figure of Jean Dargassies enters the cafe, shaking hands, smiling,
cracking jokes. You would think he is about to ride out into
surrounding winelands for a Sunday afternoon picnic rather
than spend the night racing furiously over diabolical roads in
what is likely to be a vain pursuit of a few francs.*

*The rest of the racers are not long behind him. Jean Fischer
believes that his travails are now behind him and says that he
could ride around France for another month. Rodolfo Muller
is just as bullish having gained several places in the general
classification. Belgian duo Marcel Kerff and Samson arrive
together, confident that their brutish strength will keep them
in the thick of the action on roads that so many of the starters
know well from Bordeaux–Paris.*

*As the riders gather, Géo Lefèvre watches them collect their
armbands, chatting with one or two, thanking the officials who
have been responsible for another well-disciplined start. 'In
each town it is really heart-breaking to have these hurried
starts, these sudden goodbyes, this separation of friends who
only knew each other before via correspondence and for whom,
within a few hours, one can feel a solid affection building,' he
will write soon after the start, already on the train north
towards Nantes.*

When the control closes at ten, Georges Abran and his assistant for the evening, Monsieur Amigues, ask the riders to line up. Each competitor earns great applause as he comes forward. Maurice Garin, who hasn't been as talkative as at previous stage starts, nerves perhaps getting to him at last, receives a huge cheer as he takes his place in the pack. Once Abran has confirmed they are all present, the cortège moves away through Place Pey Berland and out over the Garonne towards the Place du Quatre Pavilions, Bordeaux–Paris's traditional start, finding their way between a corridor of spectators through the hot, windless streets, the hint of a storm in the air.

At the lantern-lit start point where L'Auto banners are barely rippling in the stillness, the first group of riders are called together, the crowd falling silent in anticipation of the frantic flurry to come. At 11 o'clock, Abran points his pistol to the clear night sky, where the moon only four nights past full will provide the racers with some assistance in the darkness. With a shot, they are off.

Overcome with anticipation, L'Auto's local correspondent, a certain Dhermet, decides to follow the riders in his motorcar as far as Libourne, 25 kilometres into the stage. 'Oh, what savages! There they are ahead of me, in the majestic calm of the night, a gaggle of demons who've set off at a hellish pace, battling from the very first metres as if they were fighting on the course of Paris–Versailles; but they've got 425 kilometres ahead of them,' he reports, stunned by what he is seeing.

Jean Fischer leads the initial charge, Garin on his wheel, followed by Georget, Kerff, Samson and Pothier. Moulin and

Borot are hanging on desperately at the back of the pack, knowing that losing contact will mean a long, lonely night. Millochau and Desvages have already resigned themselves to this fate. Georget delivers the next acceleration, which sees Moulin and Borot drop back into the darkness with just each other for company.

Suddenly, swearing fills the air, the shouted curses warning of an unlit dray on the left-hand side of the road, the riders just managing to swerve right to avoid it. Garin, canny as ever, takes advantage of the disorder and gets a few metres clear, until Fischer and Kerff respond quickly to chase him down.

L'Auto's correspondent in Libourne describes the fervour in the town as being way in excess of what is normally seen when Bordeaux–Paris passes through. Not long after, the first group of riders have all passed this point, back at the Quatre Pavilions Georges Abran fires his start pistol a second time for the eight riders who form the second group. The chase is on. Fifty-six minutes have passed when the first three members of the second group, Ambroise Garin, H. Lesur and Daniel Roques emerge from darkness at Libourne, already four minutes up.

Mechanical breakdowns cost Jean Fischer and Samson their place in the lead group as it speeds through Montguyon with 62 kilometres covered, reports Fernand Mercier, his presence noted by several of the riders. They call out to him to praise the quality of the organisation's surveillance.

The front group has been reduced to around ten riders when it reaches Barbezieux at quarter past two in the morning, another 30 kilometres nearer to Nantes. Garin and Georget *are setting the pace, which Julien Girbe drops off in order to get some refreshment. He sets off again with Josef Fischer and Salais when they pass through ten minutes later. Little more than half an hour afterwards, Ambroise Garin and Lesur steam through, their advantage on the leaders now a very healthy 13 minutes. Reaching the same point, Daniel Roques, who started with this pair, is the first to abandon. Running almost last, it's a doubly wise move as this is his hometown.*

Travelling on the northbound express, Géo Lefèvre has taken advantage of rapid progress, the most superb night and an accommodating train timetable to jump on his faithful bike and cast his eye over some of the route that will soon be the battlefield for the giants of the road. 'I saw Rochefort beneath the moon. I discovered La Rochelle, its old towers and thick walls protecting the tranquil port where fishing boats slept with their pink and white sails lit up by the sun that is already rising over the smooth mirror of the Atlantic. And that night and morning were so deliciously fresh that I almost envied those devourers of kilometres whom I was going to beat to Nantes thanks to the railway,' he writes.

But, as Lefèvre saunters through Rochefort and La Rochelle, these towns are still hours away for most of his giants of the road. The first fixed control is at Cognac, where the locals have put up a 50-franc prize for the first rider, who is expected at around ten to five in the morning. Half an hour beforehand, the spectators massed along the road leading up to the control are surprised by the arrival of a motorcyclist who says the leaders are right on his tail.

A few minutes later, a ten-strong group charges in the brightness, all crouched over their bars. Fernand Augereau claims the prime by a length, Garin, Pasquier, Kerff, Georget, Muller, Pothier, Payan, Catteau and Dargassies signing in that order. The reporter on the local La Constitution des Charentes *describes them as nothing more than 'sacks of dust, their eyes the only discernible feature on their faces' as they fight to get served first at the bar.*

'Ah, that prime!*' Garin recalls later. 'They fought for it like savages. It was a four-kilometre sprint. In the end, Augereau took it by a length from Pasquier, but after that the effects of that effort were bound to be felt.' Having already seen Samson and Georget drop back when Kerff upped the pace and only return to the front group when its pace dropped, Garin senses that an opportunity beckons.*

While the leaders fly on towards Saintes, the rocky, rutted road is taking a toll on those behind. Samson complains of several punctures. Josef Fischer has blood running from a wound in his face after a crash. Eugène Brange quits at the control after being waylaid by a string of mechanical failures. The sun is well up when Millochau weaves in to the control with wounds to almost every part of his body. He spends half an hour getting medical attention while the local mechanic, Monsieur Tacher, tends to his bike.

In between the leaders and the stragglers, Ambroise Garin remains the fastest man on the course, the flowers placed in his buttonhole before the start still neatly in place, although rather dusty. Receiving dispatches via telegraph back in L'Auto's *offices in Paris, Henri Desgrange cannot resist the chance to take another swipe at his critics. 'The question of the second group is being asked once again. What is it going to do between Bordeaux and Nantes? Will it repeat Aucouturier's exploit between Marseille and Toulouse and Laeser's between Toulouse and Bordeaux? Is starting an hour after the first group, which many critics considered a very weighty handicap, actually an advantage, as the first group becomes a motivational pace-maker for the second?' he asks. He doesn't mention that Ambroise Garin has freshness on his side as well.*

Up ahead, his elder brother pushes up the speed on the front of the first group, causing it to splinter. Approaching the control at Saintes, little more than 25 kilometres on from Cognac, Garin has just five riders for company: Pasquier, Pothier, Augereau, Muller and Kerff, until the latter two get waylaid by punctures just before the town, where the streets are packed with spectators, and police and volunteers are having a difficult task keeping the route clear for the riders.

Dropped but close to the lead group, second-placed Léon Georget also punctures, two kilometres outside Saintes. A 'kind-hearted sportsman', the English phrase often used to describe those who show proper sporting spirit, lends the stricken rider his bike. Georget shoulders his own and continues on to the control, where he spends 11 valuable minutes carrying out a repair. Similarly affected, Muller reaches the control moments later, throws down his La Française bike and leaps aboard a new one that his team manager has waiting. His puncture has barely cost him 11 seconds.

Ambroise Garin's lead is still a healthy 11 minutes at Saintes, where the early morning sun is already causing many to flag. Several riders stop to recuperate, others to carry out repairs. Local man Magdelin receives an enthusiastic reception when he arrives. An hour later, Pierre Desvages' arrival coincides with the Bastille Day parade and inspection of the sixth infantry regiment. As they march by, Desvages has to dismount and walk the final 200 metres to the control point.

Ernest Pivin, who started in the front group, and Léon Durandeau, who was in the second, are the last to pass, reaching Saintes at ten past two, Pivin already seven hours behind Garin's lead group after 178 kilometres of racing and averaging less than 12 kilometres per hour, not even half of the speed of the frontrunners. Pivin abandons soon after, leaving Durandeau to battle on alone.

Up at the head of the race, the only change at the fixed control in Rochefort is Ferdinand Payan's unexpected presence in Garin's group. Sitting just outside the top ten in the general classification, the 33-year-old professional from Arles who is backed by Marseille's renowned Cycles Payan shop has a good reputation on the road, but this is undoubtedly one of his very best days. At the Café À Ma Campagne, he engages eagerly in the contest for the ink and pen along with Garin, Pothier, Augereau and Pasquier, all four of whom can count on La Française's backing. They've barely departed when Georget, Dargassies and Kerff have a similar battle.

Behind this trio, almost every rider is on his own. Muller, Jean Fischer, Samson, Catteau pass. Next through is Ambroise

Garin. Although he's overtaken half of the first group, his advantage over the quintet containing his brother has been sliced to six minutes and he's only halfway to Nantes. Can he hang on to his lead over another 200 kilometres?

That will become clearer at La Rochelle. Approaching it, the leading group once again numbers just the four La Française riders, Payan having succumbed to the persistently fierce pace, when Augereau punctures. With no spare tube and unable to swap his bike for a new one before the control where Delattre has them waiting, he bumps along on the rim, riders passing him, until he comes across stage 4 victor Charles Laeser spectating at the roadside. 'Seeing me in distress, he offered to lend me his machine,' Augereau recounts in Le Vélo. 'I accepted and, pushing hard, managed to catch up with the fugitives [at the front].'

Thanks to the mayor's edict banning bicycles from travelling at any more than walking pace through La Rochelle's streets on Bastille Day, a decision that is being heavily debated by the locals, Garin and his cohorts arrive at an intermediate checkpoint at the Tasdon crossroads on the edge of the town. From there, they have half an hour when the race will be neutralised to make their way to the fixed control at the town centre Café Française, then return to the Tasdon crossroads and continue towards Nantes.

When the quartet begin to make their way through La Rochelle's streets, it is clear that L'Auto's bleating about the mayor's edict is unjustified. The town is rammed to overflowing thanks to Bastille Day military review and festivities, combined with the Tour's arrival. 'There could have been serious accidents,' the local paper asserts in the mayor's defence. At the control, a mechanic, Monsieur Perreaud, and two assistants are waiting to help the riders, but Garin, Pasquier, Pothier and Augereau have no need of them, thanks to Delattre's unparalleled logistical support. Bikes, food and drink await the quartet. No doubt they receive orders too.

Muller and Payan are 20 minutes in arrears. Kerff, Jean Fischer, Dargassies and Georget are more than 30. 'They are all in excellent shape,' notes L'Auto's correspondent Monsieur Gendre. However, that most experienced of cycling writers, Maurice Martin, is not so sure. 'I saw Georget sign in at La Rochelle, and he seemed unwell and very tired to me,' he reports in La Petite Gironde. He's far from the only one to be feeling the pace. Long-time leader Ambroise Garin has now slipped behind the four leaders in the hard-to-follow contest for the stage win. His deficit is a mere minute, but it's growing steadily.

There is no sign of the leaders relenting, either. Riding on roads bordered by ash, poplar and weeping willow that cut through the low-lying Marais, with its salt flats and intricate network of canals and dykes that keep out the Atlantic, they reach Marans and enter the final third of the stage, their lead now 25 minutes over solitary pursuer Muller. They swap positions regularly, each taking a turn on the front to set the pace, before dropping to the rear of the line to recuperate and ready themselves for their next stint in the wind.

It takes them only a little more than two hours to complete

the next 60 kilometres to the final fixed control point at the Café Dion in La Roche-sur-Yon, where they are welcomed with tumultuous cheers and applause. Muller is next to arrive, holding his deficit despite being on his own, still smiling despite the ceaseless effort this demands. The Italian chomps two eggs and downs a glass of Vichy water. Twenty minutes later, Kerff and Jean Fischer arrive, the latter shouting out that the La Française riders are being too well looked after, his complaint eliciting much laughter in the crowd.

The trickle of riders continues. Dargassies on his own, Payan too. Then Catteau and Ambroise Garin, who is now 20 minutes behind his brother's pace having very evidently gone off too fast in the first third of the stage. There is, however, no sign of Léon Georget. Le Vélo reports a rumour that he has been caught being paced by a car by race officials along with Ernest Pivin. However, this seems unlikely as Pivin abandoned several hours earlier. So where is the Tour's second-placed rider?

The answer comes from Julien Girbe, who tells Lefèvre, 'I had just left the control at La Rochelle and was coasting along on a deliciously flat road when, suddenly, I saw a machine abandoned at the side of the road and, under a tree, a rider who was sleeping. It was Georget. I woke him and he jumped up. "Quickly, let's get going!" We set off together and he told me that, demoralised by two successive punctures, he had sat down for a moment and slept for an hour. We were travelling at quite a slow speed, but Georget got terribly tired. Clearly, the man had reached the limit of his resources. Every few *moments he stopped to plunge his head into some water or to drink red wine. In the end, as he couldn't go on any longer, he told me to keep going. We were close to Luçon and I carried on there alone.'*

Exhausted, Georget is taken in and offered a bed by a spectator. He fails to finish the stage. His race is over, and a lap of honour at the famous Parc des Princes and a lucrative payday are now beyond his grasp.

There's drama at the front too. What appears to have been a happy collaboration between four riders backed by the same manufacturer has, it will soon be revealed, been anything but. Fernand Augereau, who hails from the same town of Châtellerault as Georget and is a close friend of Garin's hitherto biggest rival, has endured a roller-coaster ride since the moment he punctured just before reaching La Rochelle and was fortunate enough to benefit from Laeser's generosity. Suddenly, he finds himself caught in a wholly unexpected situation.

'At Roche-sur-Yon, Garin put the following proposal to me: "I want to win on my own, and neither you nor anyone else must beat me. I will make it worth your while if you do." I still hadn't managed to finish at the front on any stage and, believing myself to be in marvellous condition, I responded to his offer with a firm refusal,' he later tells Le Monde Sportif's Léopold Alibert. *'I implored him to go back on his decision, but in vain. He refused to. At that point Garin said to Pothier: "Ride ahead and knock him over." What he said was exactly what happened. Pothier got a few metres ahead, dismounted and threw his bike in front of mine. I tumbled over, but got*

back to my feet. Garin took my machine, stamped on it and rendered the rear wheel useless. Garin offered the few [spectating] cyclists who happened to be with us a hundred francs if they didn't offer me any assistance.'

Augereau's account of the tale in Le Vélo *differs only in his addition of the fact that Garin twice lifted up his rival's bike and threw it to the ground before stamping on the spokes. With this, Garin, Pothier and Pasquier rode off. Augereau, meanwhile, is forced to walk for a kilometre until he meets a spectator who lends him his bike. Rage and adrenalin pumping through his body, the tall, powerfully built rider who is the prototype* rouleur, *able to pound on the pedals for kilometre after kilometre on the flat roads like those to the south of Nantes, catches up with the three leaders at Montaigu, less than 60 kilometres from Nantes. No sooner has he done so than he punctures twice and loses them for good. The sprint at Nantes will be contested by three riders, although contested may not be quite the right word.*

The finish in Nantes is special in two particular ways. It's Bastille Day, which will surely guarantee a bumper crowd, and it is the first to take place on a cycling track. 'When I arrive at the Longchamp velodrome, the sun has turned fiery and roasts us to such an extent that even the smallest patches of shade are invaded by the crowd, which nevertheless maintains its enthusiasm,' says Géo Lefèvre, who notes that the expensive seats in the stands fill up before the cheap seats in the sun.

Invited by Monsieur Charles Rodde, director of the Celtic bike company, into his car to watch the three leaders cover the final kilometres, Lefèvre is astounded by the crush of fans outside the finishing arena, an army of policemen and gendarmes keeping them on the pavements. Suddenly, the three leaders appear, 'unbelievably dusty, unrecognisable'. Garin, 'that sharp operator who sees everything and allows absolutely nothing to escape him, immediately shouts out, "Bonjour, Monsieur Géo! I seem to be bumping into you absolutely everywhere."' Monsieur Rodde's car slips into the massive pack of cyclists trailing the triumphant trio, then follows the three men through the gates of the velodrome, which is now a cauldron.

In the stands and on the terraces, the spectators wave hats, handkerchiefs and canes. On the grass in the track centre, officials shout at the riders, 'Two laps to go!' The three La Française riders take the first lap very steadily, apparently sizing each other up. Then comes the bell. Garin watches, and watches, and then, on the final bend, he accelerates, hunched forward over his handlebars. 'From that moment, it's over,' reports Lefèvre. 'Pasquier sticks to his wheel. Pothier doesn't attempt to get out of third position. And the three champions from the Société La Française pass the finishing post in that order. Marseillaise, bouquets, a lap of honour.' To Garin goes the 'Marathon runner' trophy that has been created for this Bastille Day occasion.

Lefèvre hurries to the riders' enclosure in the centre of the track to get their reaction, Garin's first of course. 'The Little Sweep' offers his perspective on the stage and on Augereau. 'He seemed to go mad,' he tells the race director. 'He accused us of bearing a grudge against him. He cried on his machine, then *said he had come up with a scheme to have a track bike ready at the velodrome. In the end, he crashed 60 kilometres from the finish. As might be expected, we left him for dead. Then the velodrome, the sprint, and here I am!'*

Monosyllabic before the stage, Garin is now in full flow. 'What crowds there were on the route, it was unbelievable that so many people spent the night under the stars between Bordeaux and Nantes,' he continues. 'The controls were marvellously well organised, the enthusiasm was crazy. In short, this was the most beautiful stage in my opinion.'

Pasquier confesses that he's happy to have cast off the ill-luck that has hitherto dogged him. The young and very shy Pothier says not a word despite having all but sewn up second place in the general classification thanks to Georget's abandon. 'This kid is unbelievably fresh,' says Lefèvre. 'He is the real revelation of the race.'

From a racing point of view, Lefèvre may be right, but there are other revelations to be had and L'Auto, it is impossible to ignore, is not interested in printing them. The organising paper crows that its last special edition has shattered all sales records, reports that British sprinter Tom Linton has broken several records at the Manchester Wheelers track meeting in front of 22,000 fans, and that the UCI's annual conference will take place the following month in Copenhagen. However, there's not a word on or from Fernand Augereau, apart from mention of him recording the fastest time for the final two laps of the track.

Upon noticing Augereau's distress as he sits in his enclosure in the middle of the track, Le Vélo *and* Le Monde Sportif *don't hesitate to investigate. The former reports that the race referees have been informed of the nefarious actions alleged to have taken place and have promised an inquiry into them. 'Garin, Pasquier and Pothier are making out that Augereau was victim of an hallucination and that he was affected by a persecution complex from the start. In all honesty, he didn't seem to be that way and appeared very lucid,' says* Le Vélo.

Le Monde Sportif *goes further in its report on Augereau's allegations, publishing details that will allow the officials and organisers to corroborate the devastated rider's claims if they so wish. Augereau tells them that, 'This nasty act wasn't appreciated by one of the cyclists who was with us, Monsieur Murail, who lives at 25 Boulevard Babin-Chevaye in Nantes and offered me his machine. Having only lost a few minutes I was able to rejoin the front group. Garin, who was furious, yelled threats at me once again. Monsieur Gourbellière, a postman living at Saint-Philibert-de-Grand-Lieu, was present with an official on a motorbike.*

'I didn't reply to my rival's threats, but, plagued by bad luck, I punctured again. This time Monsieur Gourbellière gave me his machine, but it was poorly set up and the saddle was far too high. I lost several minutes repairing it and ended up losing all chance of victory. I'm crying because I've been beaten and because I'm sickened by the behaviour of my rivals.'

STAGE 5 RESULT

1. Maurice Garin 425km in 16-26-31 (average speed 25.848km/h)
2. Gustave Pasquier (Fra) same time
3. Lucien Pothier (Fra) same time
4. Fernand Augereau (Fra) at 10-35
5. Ambroise Garin (Fra) at 33-34 *
6. Rodolfo Muller (Ita) at 36-33
7. Jean Fischer (Fra) at 1-04-03
8. Marcel Kerff (Bel) same time
9. Jean Dargassies (Fra) at 1-21-09
10. Ferdinand Payan (Fra) at 1-33-24
11. Aloïs Catteau (Bel) at 2-02-42
12. 'Samson' (Bel) at 2-32-02
13. Julien Girbe (Fra) at 3-22-11
14. Isidore Lechartier (Fra) at 4-26-51
15. René Salais (Fra) at 5-22-29
16. François Beaugendre (Fra) same time
17. Eugène Jay (Fra) at 9-22-29
18. Josef Fischer (Ger) same time
19. Émile Moulin (Fra) at 10-23-40
20. Georges Borot (Fra) at 11-01-22
21. Alexandre Foureaux (Fra) at 11-01-26
22. Pierre Desvages (Fra) at 11-03-29
23. Arsène Millochau (Fra) at 15-08-29

* Registered for the fifth stage only

Overall classification

1. Maurice Garin (Fra) 76-24-14
2. Lucien Pothier (Fra) at 2-58-02
3. Fernand Augereau (Fra) at 4-29-15
4. Rodolfo Muller (Ita) at 4-37-31
5. Jean Fischer (Fra) at 4-56-24
6. Marcel Kerff (Bel) at 4-59-24
7. 'Samson' (Bel) at 8-30-58
8. Gustave Pasquier (Fra) at 8-33-49
9. François Beaugendre (Fra) at 10-31-14
10. Aloïs Catteau (Bel) at 10-37-21
11. Jean Dargassies (Fra) at 12-28-20
12. Ferdinand Payan (Fra) at 16-24-36
13. Isidore Lechartier (Fra) at 18-55-53
14. Julien Girbe (Fra) at 23-14-18
15. Josef Fischer (Ger) at 23-38-02
16. René Salais (Fra) at 31-19-13
17. Alexandre Foureaux (Fra) at 31-48-23
18. Georges Borot (Fra) at 40-51-24
19. Émile Moulin (Fra) at 43-07-22
20. Pierre Desvages (Fra) at 46-32-24
21. Arsène Millochau (Fra) at 54-10-54

CHAPTER 15

'AN OUTPOURING OF LOCAL CHAUVINISM'

The fifth stage of the Tour de France was a pivotal moment for the race organisers and *L'Auto*. Buoyed by remarkable popular support, soaring sales and huge interest in what was still a very competitive race, Henri Desgrange and his staff faced a dilemma. How should they respond to the cheating and violence that Maurice Garin, Lucien Pothier and Gustave Pasquier were almost certainly guilty of? *Le Vélo* and *Le Monde Sportif* had made it very clear that Fernand Augereau had been the victim of competitive robbery.

.The situation demanded that Desgrange and *L'Auto* take a lead. After two days of prevarication following Garin's victory in Nantes, they did, announcing a radical change to the race. However, it was not the one that many expected.

The first indication that Garin, Pothier and Pasquier's progress towards Paris would not be disturbed came in

Desgrange's editorial in *L'Auto*'s second edition on 14 July. 'Not a moment of weakness, not even the slightest one. Yesterday he started at the front; at the end of the two thousand kilometres it is still him who is leading the dance,' he wrote in praise of the Tour leader. He was, Desgrange added apparently without irony, 'A brutal force that nothing can hold back.'

A day later, having had a night to ponder events that had occurred during the final kilometres of the Nantes stage, *L'Auto* remained silent. Desgrange instead highlighted the astonishing effort produced by the 21 resolute racers remaining in the contest for the overall classification who would be the only ones tackling the final stage between Nantes and Paris. The 471-kilometre stage, four kilometres longer than the first and therefore the race's longest, 'will be nothing more than child's play' after what they had already been through, he suggested. In typically overblown style, Desgrange declared that, 'The crowds will clap their hands as they pass, just as the crowds once used to welcome Napoleon Bonaparte's old guard when they returned from Spain or Austria.' In short, Desgrange's message was for fans to get out on the roadside and support conquering heroes who were reviving memories of France's greatness.

Rather than investigation, this was distraction, and the smoke screen billowed as thickly as the dust on France's roads when, the very next morning, Desgrange made a big announcement. 'No more pace-makers' the title of his column proclaimed. 'It's done!' he affirmed. 'I have suppressed the use of pace-makers on the final stage of the Tour de France. It seemed to me that given the success of the first five stages I needed to do right by the race and not give the final one a different character.' To do so, he added, would be 'lame and unfitting . . . the Tour de France is now homogenous and there's no reason that the sixth stage won't be as worthy as the first five.'

Of the injustices suffered by Augereau, there was no further mention, not even in the pages of *L'Auto's* rivals. The race officials said nothing; no penalties were handed out. Evidently, this was no time to shoot down cycling's golden goose.

The deliberate ditching of 'the Augereau affair' as an editorial consideration was perhaps the first occasion within professional sport when cheating or similar underhand behaviour was swept under the carpet by those running a sporting event in order to ensure that its status and earning power continued to grow. The same attitude has prevailed on numerous occasions within professional cycling in the century and more since the 1903 Tour, particularly with regard to doping.

There was the amphetamine-induced collapse of Jean Malléjac on Mont Ventoux in 1956, for example, which provoked lots of hand-wringing but no action with regard to the implementation of anti-doping regulations until Tom Simpson's death on the same mountain in similar circumstances 11 years later. In 1998, the 'Festina Affair', instigated by the police's arrest of a soigneur on that elite trade team when he was caught transporting large quantities of doping products, almost resulted in the Tour being abandoned before it had reached Paris. Yet, the following year, the widely hailed 'Tour of renewal' saw Lance Armstrong take the title for the first time while, it was later revealed, doping continued unabated. More recently, it has become clear that the Tour and professional cycling were far from the only sporting events to have been compromised by a fudged response from those running them, due to financial greed and the desire to avoid damaging headlines.

Cycling was one of the first sports to feel the impact of commercialisation in this way and was definitely the first in France, where football and rugby, now the nation's two biggest sports in terms of popularity, were still very much amateur and regional. Almost from the moment Britain's amateurs swept the board at Bordeaux–Paris in 1891, French event organisers and manufacturers adopted a professional approach to road cycling, mimicking track-racing's well-established and successful model. Unlike its British counterpart, the French federation didn't put up barriers to prevent racers from earning appearance and prize money. At the same time, realising the commercial benefits of organising and participating in road events, manufacturers signed up the best talent, and their exploits provided the headlines that the newspapers depended on.

Caught between his commitment to the nobility of his sport, which comes through on almost every page of *La Tête et Les Jambes*, and the chance to encourage its popularity and of course his paper's rising reputation within it, Desgrange opted for the latter course, thereby ensuring road cycling's status as the nation's sporting entertainment of choice well into the latter part of the twentieth century.

He may have come under pressure from bike manufacturers and his newspaper's backers to choose this path, as they were determined to exploit the opportunities the Tour afforded them, but Desgrange had already demonstrated on many occasions he was prepared to stand up to anyone if he believed he was on the right path. Consequently, having built up Garin as a star in the eyes of the public, it was undoubtedly Desgrange who decided that his newspaper's fate depended to an extent on maintaining that image of 'The White Bulldog'. In this there is, once again, an obvious comparison with Armstrong, who attracted new fans, manufacturers and money into the sport during his years as the Tour's top dog. Like Garin a century earlier, Armstrong effectively wrote his own rules for racing, which were too readily accepted by organisers, the ruling body and the media.

L'Auto's continued lionisation of the little man from Lens as well as his rivals not only appeared to offer the best strategy to guarantee the commercial success of the Tour, but also complemented Desgrange's long-standing obsession with revitalising the image of French manhood and of the nation itself.

It is interesting to note, and especially so given its total lack of reaction to the 'Augereau affair', that *L'Auto*'s reporting of the Tour's fifth stage contains many more references to France's past glories, its shared national heritage, regional diversity and the beauty of its towns and countryside. Indeed, it was the first stage that was reported in a style that is familiar today when getting updates on the race from *L'Équipe* and elsewhere in the French media.

It was Géo Lefèvre rather than Desgrange that led the way in this. His recounting of the start in Bordeaux and his lengthy description of his halts in Rochefort and La Rochelle provided a clear sign that the Tour was going to be used as an instrument for the marketing of France. In this respect, the Tour's foundation could not have been more timely.

Until the middle of the nineteenth century, commercial tourism in France had been centred around spa towns and coastal resorts, and was essentially the preserve of the upper classes who had both the time and money to indulge in such leisure activities. This emphasis began to change in the late 1850s when British travel company Thomas Cook began to organise circular tours around France and other European countries, triggering a new passion for sightseeing, which was further boosted by the establishment of the Touring Club de France in 1890.

Created by a group of cycling friends with the aim of encouraging 'the development of tourism in all its forms, both by the facilities it provides to its members and the conservation of all that is picturesque or of artistic interest when travelling', the TCF had three principal objectives: the modernisation of hotels; the promotion of tourism in France;

and the protection and promotion of the nation's touristic and natural heritage.

The organisation reached out primarily to the moneyed classes – paid holidays were not written into French law until 1936 – and its membership took off rapidly. By 1903, when it established the first French school for hoteliers, the TCF numbered almost 100,000 members, almost all of them cyclists, many of them undoubtedly also regular readers of *L'Auto* and its rivals, for amid the mass of sporting news they provided were extensive details on upcoming excursions for TCF members. Initially, the TCF also produced an annual tourist guide, but abandoned this when Michelin published its first *Red Guide* for French motorists in 1900 with the intention of boosting demand for cars and therefore for the tyres the Michelin brothers' company manufactured.

Lefèvre's musings about 'the tranquil port where fishing boats slept with their pink and white sails lit up by the sun that is already rising over the smooth mirror of the Atlantic' would have resonated with many of *L'Auto*'s readers, perhaps even more so than the exploits of Garin and his dust-covered rivals. As Thompson rightly says, 'From the very first Tour, media coverage of the race was a way of imagining the nation, interpreting its history, and defining its people', and *L'Auto* led the way in this.

From its tongue-in-cheek ribbing of the accents of southerners to its wonderment at the France's natural beauty and glorification of the nation's heritage, *L'Auto* immediately turned the race into a three-week geography and history lesson. Each stage preview featured a carefully hand-drawn map detailing all of the control points and their distance along the route, together with an even more detailed timetable listing the Tour's expected arrival time in every significant place between the start and finish. For those many readers of the paper who had never travelled more than a few kilometres from their home, reading these names and plotting where the race was and how close it was getting to their own region would have been a unique thrill, the Tour's itinerary tying them to places near and far that they knew very little about, shaping the identity of France in the process, as well as promoting the nascent tourist industry.

Continued and developed over subsequent years and decades, the Tour has become intimately associated with the French landscape and culture, and to an extent well beyond that of any other sporting event in that country and perhaps any other. Every year, its route celebrates significant anniversaries, places and events. In 2016, its Grand Départ in La Manche commemorated the D-Day landings. Two years earlier, several stages in Belgium and northern France remembered the First World War.

The advent of television, live broadcasts and aerial pictures from helicopters have continued and cemented this aspect of the Tour. Indeed, when Jean-Étienne Amaury, the chief executive of Tour owners ASO, welcomed 4,000 guests and the world's media to the presentation of the 2017 route in Paris's Palais des Congrés in October 2016, his first move was to hail the race's award of Le Prix du Rayonnement Touristique for services for French tourism. Receiving the award, race director Christian Prudhomme said, 'It is the vocation of the greatest cycling race in the world, which is broadcast in 190 countries, to highlight the image and the treasures of the regions it travels through,' highlighting the Tour's unparalleled value as a marketing tool for a country that attracts almost 100 million tourists a year, the highest total of any nation in the world.

This 'annual pilgrimage into the nation's glorious, if not painful, history', as Thompson puts it, which has defined France and her people still fits quite snugly with Desgrange's conservative, traditional and even nationalistic perspective. However, while this was understandable and largely appropriate in early twentieth-century France, it is much less so now. As its population has doubled from 30 million to more than 60, France's complexion has changed with the arrival of immigrants from across the world, and particularly from North and West Africa. Yet the Tour barely reflects these communities, white faces continuing to dominate just as they have done since its inception – white, male faces, it should be added.

As a result, cycling in France has become a sport generally associated and practised by white, middle-aged men in Lycra. It is exclusive rather than inclusive. The race, which was originally associated with progress, modernity and encouraged participation by all, still aspires to these objectives, but achieves them in only a piecemeal manner. It is perhaps no coincidence that as this situation has developed, France's production of Tour champions has dried up, despite the country enjoying its most sustained period of sporting success ever, often thanks to teams drawn from multi-ethnic backgrounds, notably in football, rugby, basketball, handball and tennis.

At the same time, and not coincidentally, the Tour's portrayal of the French nation still chimes perfectly with the foreign perspective of what France embodies. Over the last 25 years, as the professional peloton has become more international and the number of countries broadcasting the Tour has soared, the number of foreigners on the roadside has risen to the point where it often surpasses the quantity of locals. Once avowedly French in perspective, it is now an international event with its anchor set firmly in the French landscape, heritage and culture.

If Henri Desgrange's intention with his announcement about the suppression of pace-makers was to distract from the 'Augereau affair', he fully achieved his aim. It was greeted with unanimous support, most rival papers pointing out that the original decision to use pacers on just the final stage could falsify the result. 'It gives the race a homogenous character, which would have been upset by this change of method,' suggested *La Vie au Grand Air*, adding that riders who weren't able to call on the support of major manufacturers would have been hampered by 'inadequate pace-makers'.

Le Vélo took the same stance. Its only criticism was that

the decision had been taken so late, and as a result would deny a number of riders who had dropped out of the Tour a big payday. 'It will dismay those riders who had already been retained as pace-makers. Among others I've seen in Nantes are Daumain, Jaeck, Laeser, Trippier, etc., who had all travelled there having been engaged as pace-makers,' commented Alphonse Baugé.

The fact that stage-4 victor Charles Laeser was among the riders who had gathered in Nantes is evidence of the amounts that pace-makers would receive for making their services available to the peloton's stars. Laeser had earned 700 francs for his win in Bordeaux and would have been a favourite for the stage to Nantes. His contract as a pace-maker for the final leg evidently made it well worth his while to pass up this chance of personal glory. In fact, stories abound of manufacturers paying pace-makers twice or even three times the total prize money on offer to a winning rider, the commercial benefits of this investment no doubt making it well worthwhile. The prospect of a bumper pace-making payday did falsify the race, by encouraging one or two riders like Laeser to abandon it for what was ultimately no reason.

With four days in Nantes and now having no need to organise a pacing team to get them to Paris, the riders unexpectedly found themselves with time to kill in the two hotels where they were lodged. Touring them, Géo Lefèvre marvelled at the freshness of most of them, reporting Rodolfo Muller's declaration that he would drop everyone if the race was two or three thousand kilometres longer.

Interestingly, the first rider Lefèvre mentioned in his account of the days in Nantes was Augereau, pointing out that, 'he arrived at the velodrome a few moments after the lead group and seemed disappointed to me at not being able to contest first place'. Lefèvre confirmed Augereau had told him why he was so upset. Yet, rather than respond to the allegations, the race director, chief judge and *L'Auto*'s special correspondent swerved the issue, commenting only that the incident 'didn't prevent him from accomplishing a superb performance', and then continuing, 'in fact, Augereau is one of those that the Tour de France has highlighted the most'.

Having added that Jean Dargassies was 'as fresh as a young rose' and had already asked to be assigned the number one in the 1904 Tour, and that Ambroise Garin was still regretting not being able to hang on to first place on the stage into Nantes, Lefèvre moved on to the race leader. Naturally, focusing on Maurice Garin's most laudable qualities, he pointed out that Garin had completed the 1,286 kilometres of the last three stages in 51 hours, 7 minutes and 40 seconds. In winning Paris–Brest–Paris with the help of pace-makers two years earlier, Garin had covered the same distance in 52 hours.

As well as emphasising Garin's competitive and physical brilliance, which Lefèvre backed up by adding that the race leader had averaged more than 25 kilometres per hour over the first five stages, this statistic made an even more convincing case for the suppression of pace-makers from all races.

They were still employed at Paris–Roubaix, for instance. Yet, within just a few seasons, all of the major events on the road cycling calendar had banned the use of pace-makers except for Bordeaux–Paris, where they remained the event's reason for being until its dissolution in 1988, when the format had become decidedly archaic.

With two days remaining until the start of the final stage, Lefèvre returned to Paris to devote himself to editorial duties, leaving colleague Fernand Mercier to describe the increasingly relaxed mood among the racers to L'Auto's readers. As is still the case now for the man in the yellow jersey, race leader Maurice Garin was the obvious focus during these rest days. Mercier records him going to the baths, having a quiet dinner and then a gentle stroll through the streets of central Nantes before heading to bed, then rising at six the next morning for 'a solid breakfast'. Many of his rivals also wandered or rode through Nantes, 'And these are men who have just completed two thousand kilometres by bike. Fantastic!' Mercier gushed.

In the Hôtel des Voyageurs, one of the two hotels where the riders were accommodated, the management set up a big table around which the riders could dine together. La Revue Sportive's Émile Ouzou took to the piano, his tunes leading to an impromptu concert where the stars of the show proved to be Émile Pagie, Julien Girbe and Rodolfo Muller, the ever-exuberant Italian then leading all those gathered in a frantic cakewalk. Another rider joked that Mercier should ring a bell before the start of the final 'lap' into Paris. 'There's no shortage of cheerfulness among the champions of the road,' Mercier reported.

Not all of the racers were quite so full of vim, though, after the exertions of the opening five stages. Belgian Aloïs Catteau passed out due to exhaustion in his bath and was only saved from drowning by his returning roommates. Arsène Millochau was still uncertain about his chances of starting the final stage having effectively ridden since the start of the fourth with just one of his legs after sustaining a serious injury to the other soon after leaving Toulouse.

Meanwhile, Fernand Augereau continued to stew, unaware for now that Desgrange had started to receive angry letters from the rider's home region of Poitou-Charentes, protesting Garin's acts and threatening revenge. Some made it very clear that they were prepared to step in where the race officials hadn't and ensure the race leader would face repercussions as a result of his actions on the road to Nantes.

At this point, Desgrange snapped. In a blazing editorial, the Tour boss decried the localism, regionalism and nationalism plaguing his race. 'I don't think any sporting event has ever unleashed such an outpouring of local chauvinism compared to what we've seen at the Tour de France. For the last fifteen years we've been trying to convince crowds that sport has no country and I'm beginning to think our efforts have all been totally in vain,' he complained, before detailing the accusations that had been made against him and his staff since the start of the race.

To begin with there had been recriminations from

Belgium, where fans believed that the organisers' focus on home riders had left Samson and Marcel Kerff in the shade. 'A sportsman from Commentry' had then alleged that the organisers had given that town's local hero, Hippolyte Aucouturier, a tainted brew of some kind. Within days, fans in Lens, home of Maurice Garin, were up in arms about Aucouturier winning two stages on the trot. Swiss fans had also been unhappy with the organisers' conduct towards Anton Jaeck and Charles Laeser, asserting that such behaviour during the Middle Ages would have resulted in defeats as bloody as those handed out to the Duke of Burgundy by the Swiss confederation in the late fifteenth century. Later, there had been some upset in Toulouse when local favourite Henri Gauban had failed to finish that stage.

Then he turned to Georget and Augereau's hometown, Châtellerault. The locals had risen in their defence to a man, Desgrange decried. Clearly at the very end of his tether and unconcerned about his stereotyping of the passionate nature of people in the south, he angrily proclaimed: 'We've received from Châtellerault, which isn't even in the Midi, letters so exuberant, so violent, so injurious, which were also anonymous. They accused us of the worst crimes.' One letter, he added, had been sent by 'a sportsman whose name you will become acquainted with through the courts' who was outraged that in cycling 'the rich rewarded the weak'. Another seething correspondent from Châtellerault insisted that if the Tour had passed through the town any rider who had been ahead of Augereau and Georget would have had their legs broken.

A year later, hooligan acts such as these would become reality as fans in all parts of France terrorised riders, attacking them with stones and clubs, threatening them with guns. Over the next one hundred years and more, the Tour has often witnessed senseless, regionalist and later nationalist chauvinism of this type. In 1937, the entire Belgian national team quit the race after being pelted with stones by French fans. Italian great Gino Bartali persuaded his teammates into quitting in 1950 after he was attacked by irate supporters of Jean Robic. More recently, Britain's Chris Froome had urine thrown in his face on his way to victory in 2015. These incidents underline that cycling, a sport that unifies fans behind all of its athletes in a way that few others manage, can still succumb to the basest of emotions.

Desgrange acknowledged that the insults and threats cast in his and his paper's direction were the result of the passion that cycling aroused, but asserted that this was no excuse for such behaviour. He beseeched the anonymous correspondents from Châtellerault to calm down, to be thankful for the fact that they boasted two such great champions, and to be patient because their time would come. However, with no penalty still imposed on Garin and his cohorts, it was doubtful that this plea for calm would prove effective.

CHAPTER 16

'VIVE GARIN! VIVE LE TOUR!'

The four-day stopover in Nantes allowed the press more than enough time to reflect on events during stage 5, Henri Desgrange's suppression of pace-makers, what stage 6 might bring and their almost final verdict on the Tour de France as a whole. *Le Vélo* described it as 'A HUGE SUCCESS', and even *Le Monde Sportif*, so often very critical, was magnanimous, confessing, 'We can only congratulate those who came up with the idea for this race and organised it all.'

Lapping this up and the hugely positive reaction from readers and new devotees of the sport, *L'Auto* was in self-congratulatory mood. It published letters and telegraphs from newly established fan clubs hailing the exploits of riders, praise for the event from competitors and even noted the reaction to the race outside *L'Héxagone*. Among the latter was the report of a notice pinned up in one of the biggest bike shops in Brussels, which instructed: 'The shop's staff are prohibited from talking about French velocipede races during work hours because these conversations hamper the proper functioning of the business.'

The organising paper also offered its own perspective on the Tour. In an over-the-top paean to Desgrange's dispatch of pace-makers – 'I simply wouldn't know how much to applaud that extremely logical and sporting decision . . .' – Géo Lefèvre proclaimed that the Tour had taken on the status of a monument that had been 'erected piece by piece on granite'. He concluded that, 'This monument will have simple, pure and homogenous lines. Consequently, it will be imperishable.' Reiterating a point he had made prior to the Tour's start, Lefèvre also noted how the decision to look backwards to road cycling's roots in the pre-pacing era had paid off by revitalising the sport.

The first publication of details for the Sunday meeting at the Parc des Princes track underscored the extent by which it had already eclipsed track-racing as the main event. L'Auto announced that the 100-kilometre race had been switched to the start of the meeting to ensure it didn't conflict with the arrival of 'the giants of the road' and that, in the event of rain, there would be no refunds as the racing would continue no matter the weather. Generally, track meets would be postponed in these conditions and spectators would get their money back, but Lefèvre explained: 'If it rains, well then it rains . . . there will be no question of reimbursement as the finish of the Tour de France is certainly the centrepiece of the day and it will go ahead even if there's deluge coming down.'

L'Auto also offered a final incentive for the 21 riders left in the race to complete the course by confirming a significant tweak to the conditions relating to the payment of the five-franc daily stipend. Rather than only being paid out to those riders who completed the whole route at an average of more than 20 kilometres per hour, it would now be paid to any rider who reached Paris and 'completed the buckle', referring to the Tour's loop, which quickly became known as *La Grande Boucle*. In addition, any rider who had earned 150 francs or less in completing the course would also be eligible for the daily stipend, taking their earnings to almost 250 francs. Any rider who had earned between 150 and 245 francs would also see their return rise to the same total.

This incentive almost certainly encouraged the ailing Millochau to start, even in conditions that were now very different to those endured during the first five stages. After weeks of *canicule*, the weather had broken. Nantes and the north of the country had been doused by heavy rain, rendering the roads east towards Paris unforgivingly muddy and heavy, and evoking memories for some of the monstrousness of Marseille–Paris nine months earlier. No wonder Rodolfo Muller, who had survived that sappingly brutal test, had pointed out to Mercier that his huge appetite was not gluttony but pre-race loading. 'We need to store up every calorie we can if we want to show some speed on "the final leg of the Tour de France",' explained the Italian.

Géo Lefèvre's preview of the final stage into Paris under-lined how the competitive landscape had changed since the race left the French capital. Then, he had picked out Garin as his favourite, but had completely dismissed the hopes of Eugène Brange, Émile Pagie, Lucien Pothier, Fernard Augereau and others, and admitted, 'that page from *L'Auto* already seems strangely faded, its yellow colour like that of last year's dead leaves'. At the same time, riders he had pre-dicted would be prominent had failed to stay the course, including Hippolyte Aucouturier, Léon Georget, Claude Chapperon and Édouard Wattelier, but most notably the rider whom he had selected as his second favourite, German Josef Fischer, 'a magnificent athlete whose mechanism seems to have been malfunctioning'.

Almost the only prediction that he had got right, Lefèvre confessed, was that 'Maurice Garin will finish as the winner in Paris, or he won't finish at all'. Extolling his qualities, Lefèvre described the squat, powerfully built Franco-Italian 'crushing the pedals in powerful and raging style, crouched over his low machine, climbing hills and then plunging down descents, harassed by successive rivals, he has been tireless, and now he is finally going to arrive at his goal hav-ing shaken them off one after another'. Drawing on his initial declaration, Lefèvre concluded, 'Maurice Garin will finish as the winner in Paris, or he won't finish at all. But he will finish.'

STAGE 6, NANTES–PARIS, 471KM, 18–19 JULY 1903

After four days of rest, the riders are eager to return to battle but, as they make their final preparations, they receive news of a delay. The organisers have put back the start by an hour due to the briskness of the westerly wind that will be encouraging the riders towards Paris, as they don't want these hardened warriors to arrive at the Parc des Princes before the spectators. Most shrug and sit. It means another hour of rest. Yet the extra 60 minutes is a bonus for Fernand Augereau, who has received a new bike just that morning to replace the one put out of service by Maurice Garin on stage 5 and is frantically fitting a mudguard to it with dark clouds looming menacingly on what has been a perfect afternoon.

It is approaching six in the early evening when the riders make their way to the Café Continental in Nantes's very appropriately named Grande Place to sign in for the final time, surveyed by 600 fans who have paid for the privilege of a seat in the salubrious establishment. Georges Abran, wearing the blue and yellow armband of controller-general, awaits them, his heart heavy as the prospect of the Tour's end makes him feel like he's 'losing a good friend or going through divorce that's come about due to an unfortunate misunderstanding.'

Once again, the crowd is substantial, newspaper vendors doing a busy trade in between bellowing the name of their title they're brandishing, men bearing sandwich boards on which the latest details of starters and times are displayed circulating amid the

287

throng. Inside the Café Continental, enthusiastic spectators climb on to chairs and tables to watch Salais, Borot, Dargassies, the revitalised Millochau and Desvages arrive to sign the start sheet.

This group of ever-hopefuls are delighted with Henri Desgrange's decision to abandon the use of pace-makers, which keeps them on something like the same footing as the headlining performers. They're also buoyed by the prospect of finishing. Dargassies, beaming broadly, declares, 'We're going to enjoy ourselves in Paris,' twirling the end of his moustache. 'But don't say that in L'Auto because they read it now in Grisolles and, as you'll understand, my wife would be worried,' he adds.

Garin surprises both by being the next to arrive and with his outfit. Although unhappy with the decision on pacers, the race leader is full of smiles and shakes hand after hand as he makes his way to Abran and Fernand Mercier's table. He looks quite different, though, clad all in black, as if trying to distance himself from his notoriety as 'The White Bulldog'. Less obvious, but of equally vital importance, he has also changed his bike's set-up, opting for a 6.1-metre gear rather than his usual slightly smaller choice, having felt the wind gaining in strength and aiming to make it his ally.

Twenty-year-old Augereau, his mudguard fitted, is talking up his hopes of taking second place from 19-year-old Pothier, who, as usual, is saying nothing, but looks calm and confident. Jean Fischer arrives in a typically ugly mood, and Alexandre 'The Flying Carpenter' Foureaux turns equally indignant when he discovers that the soup he's asked to be prepared for the start has been forgotten. Pierre Desvages, the most dandy of racers who is vice-president of Intermagazines Sports, a company that oversees sporting activities within department stores such as Bon Marché and Samaritaine, appears in an immaculate white flannel shirt, and tells the irked Foureaux off when he threatens to blemish it by brushing up against him.

At seven, Abran signals the riders together, the crowd now 10,000 strong and forming a human corridor through which the cortège will travel to the official start outside the Café Babonneau on the Route de Paris. The procession has barely moved a hundred metres, though, when Abran and Mercier's car splutters to a halt. They hastily summon a horse-drawn carriage and are away again, the spectators cheering them and the riders as they make for the outskirts of Nantes.

Another multitude awaits outside the Babonneau. As the riders halt, Fernand Augereau is the centre of attention. A member of the Racing Club Nantais comes forward and presents him with a garland in recognition of his thwarted effort on the stage into the Breton city. Moved almost to tears, Augereau hangs it carefully on the front of his bike and waves a salute of gratitude to the crowd for his ovation.

The reception for Garin is somewhat cooler. Amid shouts of 'Vive Augereau!', the race leader is the target for boos and cat-calls. There are cries of 'Down with Garin!' His assault on Augereau may have been overlooked by the officials, but the spectators aren't as ready to forget. Pressing in on all sides, there's a threat of violence in the air, the police and volunteers straining to hold the throng back. But there's also curiosity and fascination for these giants of the road with their thin, tanned faces who *have already covered 2,000 kilometres and are now set for 500 more. Gradually, the marshals ease them back, allowing Monsieur Terrien, the local correspondent overseeing the start, to step forwards and inform the riders of the principal difficulties lying ahead on the opening section of the race to Ancenis.*

At six minutes to eight, Abran fires his pistol and Mercier waves the blue and yellow flag and the riders are away into the early evening dusk. As ever, they start at close to sprinting speed as if their objective is a mere five kilometres away, not halfway across the country. They are averaging well in excess of 30 kilometres an hour when they reach the sharp ramps of the Côte de la Seilleraye, a dozen kilometres from Nantes, where the pace of the strongest only slackens a little, with the buoyant Augereau the first to open a gap, albeit just a handful of metres. On the treacherous descent, where several riders opt for caution over catastrophe, he stretches his advantage a little, forcing a reaction from Samson, Pothier, Garin and Pasquier, who bridge up to him as the road roller coasters back up again.

The incessantly high pace and this rolling terrain cause the peloton to splinter into several groups, Augereau at the front of the first, Pierre Desvages, his white flannel shirt now substantially blemished, bringing up the rear on his own, all of them soon disappearing into the darkness and leaving the journalists in their wake to return to the start. They arrive there to find it in uproar following the very late arrival of thousands of fans disappointed to have discovered that one of L'Auto's rivals has published the start time incorrectly.

At Ancenis, 38 kilometres into the stage, the peloton is

almost back together. Helped by the wind, the leaders pass the heavily fortified renaissance castle once renowned as 'the key to Nantes' at nine o'clock. In the darkness beyond the town, the line stretches again, and Garin finds himself alone at the front. Out of the night, an unknown cyclist suddenly appears beside him and asks his name. Wary of revealing his identity after being widely painted as the race's villain over recent days, Garin wisely gives the name of his one of his rivals, adding for good measure, 'Garin? We dropped him a long time ago and he must be a long way behind us!' Hearing this, the mystery rider slows, turns and heads back in search of his quarry, unaware that his target has just evaded his grasp.

Angers, at 89 kilometres, is the location of the first fixed control point and it has been mobbed by thousands of eager locals, who haven't witnessed a major race since Paris–Nantes–Caen– Rouen–Paris the previous year. For three weeks, the talk has been about nothing but the Tour de France, and there's a tremendous clamour as the 15-strong lead group barrels up to the control at the Café du Sport, their average speed now approaching 40 kilometres per hour thanks to the favourable breeze on their backs. Beaten to the pen at the sign-in desk by Julien Girbe, the favourites are all present bar Gustave Pasquier, whose chain broke in a collision with an unlit wagon before Angers, leaving him with no choice but to run with his bike for 10 kilometres and costing him an hour on the lead pack.

Girbe compounds the impertinence of signing in first by then slipping away from the control, chased by Garin and most of the rest, the exception being the unflappable Muller. Girbe is soon reeled in and is being subjected to a host of insults when someone in the group realises they've taken the wrong route. They turn back to the junction where the error occurred, then charge off in the right direction, closing up quickly on the bemused Muller, who can't understand why spectators at the roadside have been shouting out that he's leading when he was the last away from the control. Only when he hears the vitriol still being directed at Girbe as Garin's group closes back in on him does he realise what's happened. Girbe remains the target for all manner of curses for another hour until Jean Fischer attempts the first of several night-time ambushes to which his rivals are forced to react.

Carrying out secret surveillance of the racers in the dark countryside close to Angers, Géo Lefèvre startles one rider when he shines his light on him. 'I haven't got any money with me! You can search me!' he yells fearfully before the race director manages to work out who he is.

It's one in the morning when that front group reaches the celebrated wine-making town of Saumur, its old town with the tenth-century castle standing sentinel over it sandwiched between the waters of the Loire and Thouet rivers. Although hosting only a flying control, the Tour's arrival has drawn an impressively large crowd, who applaud, cheer and wave hats and canes as the 13 leaders rush past, like a flock of birds bursting out of the night and just as quickly disappearing back into it. Only moments behind them and chasing hard, Isidore Lechartier tumbles spectacularly passing the control, staggers to his feet, checks his bike is still rideable and is away again, the spectators responding with even louder shouts of encouragement. Very soon, another crash will have far more critical repercussions.

It is almost three in the morning, the moon a waning crescent that offers the racers very little assistance. Despite several attempts by Jean Fischer to break away, all of which have been nullified, the leaders are still together, perhaps glad of the security numbers provide in the darkness, when, close to the town of Luynes, there's a loud commotion in the road just behind them. Two motorcyclists, both members of the Vélo Club de Tours who are volunteering as officials, have collided. A group of their club-mates stop to give assistance to the pair, who are lying seriously injured in the road. A passing car is stopped and the driver asked to fetch a doctor.

Reaching the scene of the motorcycle crash, the doctor can see that both of the volunteer officials have severe head trauma. One, 30-year-old taxman Monsieur Neau, has also sustained damage to his spine. Lifted on to a mattress in the back of a carriage, he's taken to hospital in Tours but dies soon after, reports Le Vélo, *which offers its condolences to his wife and two children. The other injured motorcyclist, Tours bike shop owner Monsieur Cotti, is said to be in a stable condition.*

No one ahead is aware of this unfolding tragedy when the leaders reach the fixed control at the Café du Helder in Tours, where the numbers aren't as impressive as earlier on the route, no doubt a result of the very early hour and the city's regular hosting of major road races. For the riders, though, this control is the same as any other, which means a frenzied battle to sign first and get back on the road. Blows are exchanged, voices raised and, as so often, it's Garin's name that goes on the sheet first. Within a few moments, having stuffed food bags and grabbed bottles of Vichy water and whatever else they can lay their hands on, the 14 frontrunners are under way again.

At Amboise, almost halfway to Paris, where the first light of the sun is just beginning to brighten the sky at almost half past four, Samson, the strongest man in the group since leaving Nantes, is setting a pace that has slimmed down the front group, which now comprises 11 riders. Salais and Catteau pass a few minutes later. The sun is starting to rise when the next trickle of racers comes through, most on their own, including the blood-covered Pasquier, who has sustained a face wound in a collision with a spectator who was standing in the road, the incident eventually proving fatal to the unfortunate fan.

It's almost six when slightly built Émile Moulin arrives, dismounts and goes off to spend the next hour having breakfast with a friend who lives in the town. Yet even this lengthy delay doesn't relegate him to last place. He's had his fill and been back on the road for 40 minutes before the arrival of the back marker Pierre Desvages, who is no fewer than 50 kilometres behind the leaders.

Just as Moulin is sitting down with his friend for breakfast, the leaders are approaching Blois on the south bank of the Loire having tracked the river almost all of the way from Nantes. Dawn has broken to a beautiful day, which has enticed huge numbers to the streets leading to and around the Café de Blois, which looks out over the river.

Samson has dropped off the pace due to a puncture, leaving

ten in the battle for the pen at the sign-in table, which Muller
wins. These riders are all in a 'remarkably fresh state', according to L'Auto correspondent Monsieur Fournier. Samson is five
minutes behind but closing fast, Dargassies, Salais and Catteau another five, the latter chewing ferociously on a chicken
leg as he gets under way again.

After another 20 kilometres, the leaders cross back to the
north bank of the Loire via of the Pont de Beaugency, its 24
arches spanning almost 500 metres across the river. Passing the
flying control, Samson has bridged back up to the front, where
ten riders are disputing the lead. The favourites are also still
present, as is the surprising figure of François Beaugendre,
whose hometown of Orléans is now little more than two dozen
kilometres upstream.

By the time the front group approaches Orléans, news that
Beaugendre is within it has already reached the throng around the
control at the Hôtel du Berry. That information had been greeted
with a huge cheer, and there's an even louder one a few minutes
later when, according to the local paper, 'Ten grey and dusty
demons force a path through the crowds at high speed and burst
like a whirlwind into the narrow corridor of the Hôtel de Berry.'

L'Auto's correspondent can't contain his exhilaration.
'They've surprised everyone with their courage, their fierce
energy, their matchless endurance and I don't know who we
should admire the most, those who came up with the idea and
have put together such a grandiose event or those who dared,
stupefying and marvellous human machines that they are, to
compete in it right to the finish?' His hyperbole goes on and on,

until he finally records that Garin, Samson, Beaugendre, Muller, Foureaux, Pothier, Augereau, Girbe, Jean Fischer and Kerff signed in at two minutes to eight, the control witnessing the usual madness as they try to grab what they can even as they were running back out of the hotel's door.

Dargassies, Salais and Josef Fischer arrive half an hour later. Behind them, the rest of the field passes in ones and twos. Catteau is battling fatigue, Pasquier the effects of his injuries, Millochau is quite fresh and, with a smile, points out to the officials that he has neither money nor a seat in his trousers, but that he will be pressing on once his racing companion Lechartier has been attended to. The other rider hobbles in, his left knee a bloody mess after his earlier fall in Saumur. He is helped through to the officials' room and spends the next four hours receiving attention to his wounds and resting. Le Vélo reports his abandon, but just before two in the afternoon, Lechartier tentatively lifts his bandaged leg over his bike and pushes away into the last third of the final stage.

At the front of the race, one of the race officials reports Garin's unusually good humour on the road into Orléans, describing him as being on one of his great days, joking with his rivals as if he were still in the salons of Nantes. Regularly at the front of the group, keeping the pace high with the bigger gear he's fitted, it is now he and not Samson who looks the strongest as the leaders finally leave the Loire behind and head north-east across the wide-open expanse of the Beauce plain.

Approaching the final fixed control at Chartres, he offers another demonstration of both his good humour and his form.

Just before the city, the leaders are confronted with a closed barrier at a level crossing. Garin, Muller, Pothier and Augereau manage to scoot through the gate at the side just before the signalman can stop them, leaving the rest gesticulating and bawling furiously. Realising what's happened, Garin, who is not known for such gestures, instructs his three companions to stop and wait until the train has passed. Minutes later, he underlines the edge he has on his rivals by winning the 25-franc prize put up by local businesses, ahead of Muller and Pothier.

After 'burning' most of the earlier controls, the ten riders agree to a temporary truce at Chartres and spend quarter of an hour refreshing themselves in preparation for the closing 84 kilometres of the Tour de France, stuffing themselves with broth, sandwiches and chocolate. While L'Auto's correspondents stick to their mantra of the riders being 'remarkably fresh', a reporter from the local paper describes them as being in 'a pitiful state, covered with mud, dust, sweat, clothes torn, muddy, scarcely looking like men'.

Following the passage almost an hour later of Salais, Josef Fischer and Dargassies, who twirls the ends of his moustache for photographers in what has become trademark fashion, the remainder of the field are an even more dispiriting sight as most of them limp slowly towards Paris. Lechartier is using his good right leg with impressive effect, Pasquier is struggling on even though Le Vélo reports he has climbed into a car and abandoned, while Desvages, although no longer the backmarker, is riding with blood running from a wound on his head after a recent fall. Borot and Millochau are now the last men on the road after the latter had insisted on stopping for a nap at the roadside.

By the final flying control at Rambouillet, Beaugendre and Kerff have lost contact with the leaders. Ahead lies the undulating and heavily forested Chevreuse. Julien Girbe is the next to yield as Garin tries to ride his rivals off his wheel, determined to not only win the Tour but win it in style by clinching his third stage victory. 'Not so fast, we'll be there soon enough!' Muller shouts across to him, as 'The Little Sweep' forges on.

Up ahead, between Versailles and the finishing control point at Ville d'Avray, immense crowds are lining the course. The riders have never seen anything like it. Le Vélo's Alphonse Baugé describes the control at the Restaurant du Père Vélo – the traditional finishing point for Le Vélo's Bordeaux–Paris, but renamed Père Auto for the day! – being 'invaded by a joyous crowd who have lunch while they await the riders'. It could hardly be any more different to the low-key scene at the start of the race 19 days earlier. By half past one, with the front group just half an hour away, Baugé describes how, 'the road is completely filled with pedestrians and cyclists who are discussing the chances of each one of the riders with great animation'.

The scene becomes more chaotic when news of the riders' approach arrives, the mayhem exacerbated by a car bursting into flames and another reversing into a spectator, who is carried away for attention in the Père Velo's garden. When cars begin to arrive and announce the leaders are just minutes behind, the crowds press forwards even more, filling the road. There is no way that traffic of any kind can progress. 'In all honesty, I've

*never seen such a poorly organised attempt at maintaining order,'
says Baugé. 'There are just two gendarmes, who are naturally
powerless to prevent this number of curious onlookers from
being on the road, and we anxiously wonder how the riders are
going to be able to force a way through this human sea.'*

*The answer soon arrives. A handful of kilometres back
down the course at Versailles, Jean Fischer accelerates hard on
the stage's final test, the Côte de Picardie. Fernand Augereau
is the only rider able to hold his wheel. Fischer flies up the
climb and has victory in his sights when a spectator steps into
his path. Fischer's pedal clips the young man's leg, sending the
rider crashing to the road.*

*Somehow Augereau manages to pick a path through between
prone bodies and bike, accelerates away over the top of the hill
and hurtles down the far side with a lead of more than a hundred metres. A fully deserved success is almost within his sight
when, barely a kilometre from the finish, his bike starts to
weave underneath him. He looks down and can't believe his
bad luck: a rear wheel puncture. He tries to continue riding on
the rim, only to slither and fall. He grabs a bike offered by a
spectator, but can't complete the exchange fast enough to prevent Garin racing by in the corridor of bodies only 60
centimetres wide. There is no way past.*

*Once again, good luck as well as form are with the race leader,
and it is Garin who arrives first at the control. He underlines his
signature with a flourish amid a swarm of gentleman waving
their hats and ladies their umbrellas, all desperate to get close to
the short, squat rider who has proved himself the greatest of the*

giants of the road. The pre-race favourite has claimed his third stage, but, far more importantly, he has achieved his season's objective and become the first rider to win the Tour de France. He raises the victor's bouquet aloft, acknowledging the cheers of the crowd, many of whom are in tears.

While Garin begins to receive congratulations from dignitaries and officials, a roar goes up as Augereau and Samson sprint for second place. The Frenchman on his borrowed bike edges out the Belgian, only to career headfirst into a photographer who has set up his tripod and camera in the only clear strip of road. Augereau hits the deck and lies unconscious for a few moments as blood trickles from a cut to his forehead. Thankfully, he comes around quickly and is helped into the restaurant's garden, a spectator-less oasis amid the chaos.

The ill-starred Fischer is fourth, young Pothier is fifth and the Italian Muller sixth. The result brings little change to the overall classification, Augereau taking third behind Garin and Pothier, with Muller fourth, Fischer fifth and Samson sixth, a place ahead of his compatriot Kerff.

One by one, the riders find sanctuary in the restaurant's garden, where the proprietor serves them champagne, they puff on cigarettes and get the chance to smarten themselves up a little before having to continue on to the Parc des Princes. Some, most notably the Tour winner, are reluctant to cover the final few kilometres to the track on their bikes. 'I don't want to end up being killed in this overly enthusiastic crowd,' Garin complains, only relenting when the officials make clear that use of a bike is obligatory.

Now dressed in his trademark white with the addition of a tricolour sash, the race winner receives acclaim from thousands of spectators lining both sides of the road, along the 9-kilometre ride to the Parc, with one or perhaps even two thousand more on bikes following the procession. Shouts of 'Vive Garin! Vive Le Tour!' resound through the capital's streets, until, when they approach the track, a fanfare from the drums and bugles of the band of Paris's 15th arrondissement drowns out the din and heralds the Tour winner's arrival for the 15,000 fans packed into the famous arena.

Géo Lefèvre confesses to a little hyperbole when describing crowds on previous visits to the Parc, but insists he has never seen such an attendance at the track, which has been turning people away. He also acknowledges that the crowd has clearly been distracted during a track meeting featuring most of France's biggest names, including former world sprint champion Edmond Jacquelin. The prospect of seeing the Tour riders has been tugging at their attention.

There's another fanfare, and hearing it Lefèvre rushes to the gates of the arena and looks down the Rue de la Tourelle to see Garin arriving between a corridor of spectators, with many hundreds of cyclists waving their caps in his wake. A third fanfare signals Garin's arrival at the gates of the track, where the crowd are already on their feet, clapping, waving hats and handkerchiefs, and, on the side where the band is gathered, making it very clear to the musicians that they should sit down on the grass to allow a clear view across the track.

Garin conducts his victory lap at the most sedate of paces, a *little peeved by a fall en route to the stadium and perhaps rel-ishing the uncommonly smooth cement below his wheels as he acknowledges the acclaim. Behind him, a boy in a white shirt, shorts and cap on a child's bike weaves his way out of the pack and rides up to join him. It's his eight-year-old son. They com-plete the required two laps of the track, then Garin draws to a halt and dismounts. The Tour is over. He exchanges a few words with track ace Jacquelin before his wife and mother embrace him. With Monsieur Hammond, the beaming dir-ector of La Française at his elbow, he's handed a bouquet, then another, then a third, a fourth and a fifth before being swallowed up by the officials and VIPs in the middle of the track.*

Desperate to experience the atmosphere, 'The Flying Car-penter' Foureaux, who finished seventh and should appear in that position at the Parc, breaks ranks and is the next to com-plete his final kilometre of the Tour. His eyes red with fatigue, he dismounts and immediately asks Lefèvre for the dates of the 1904 race. Watching him take swig after swig from a bottle of Vichy water, as the celebrated masseur Brillouet, a bank worker who is known as the man with the magic hands, rubs life back into his legs, Baugé notes that this experienced roadman has completed the race without assistance from a soigneur and with just one bike. 'Bravo, Foureaux!'

Augereau comes next, appearing on a track bike and giving absolutely all he has left to claim the 100-franc prize for the quickest kilometre at the Parc. Thwarted in so much else – 'I've been hexed in this race,' he tells Baugé – in this at least he is successful. He reveals that he's not drunk a drop of water since leaving Nantes, no doubt fearing an attempt to nobble him.

The commotion calms with no more Tour riders yet in sight, allowing the national 100-kilometre championship behind pacers to take place. By the time Henri Contenet has beaten Jacquelin to the title by a length, the crowd is eager to see a new group of Tour finishers complete their kilometre of honour.

First to do so is Tour runner-up Pothier. As he rolls to a halt, he receives a sash of his own, bearing the words: 'Le Vélo-Sport de Sens à son champion'. His proud father plants kiss after kiss squarely on his lips. Muller, wearing his favourite grey jacket, his blond hair white with dust, completes his laps and is embraced by his mother, brothers and sisters. Then, to the delight of the crowd, he remounts and does another lap.

Girbe, Beaugendre and Kerff give their all during their very final kilometre, but Salais and Dargassies, novices in this kind of racing, are not so keen. Salais rides around on the grass inside the cement track, while 'The Blacksmith of Grisolles', who had joked at Ville d'Avray that 'it is regrettable that there aren't six more stages because I'm just starting to find some form', refuses to risk his well-being. 'Roads yes, but cliffs no. We're not used to them in Grisolles,' he laughs, inevitably twirling his moustache.

Soon after, Josef Fischer demonstrates the wisdom of Dargassies's decision. Negotiating the fiercest of the Parc's bends, the long bars on his road bike clip the cement and send him clattering down to the foot of the track, thankfully with nothing more than his pride damaged. Finally, just as the meeting is ending, Pasquier, Catteau and Payan arrive, the former to some surprise as reports of his death are circulating and officials have been endeavouring to prevent his wife seated in the stands from hearing them. Their 1-kilometre time trials bring the curtain down on the Tour de France's finale at the Parc.

There are, however, still four riders out on the road. The effectively one-legged Lechartier signs in at the Ville d'Avray control just after seven in the evening. Ninety minutes later, Émile Moulin signs for eighteenth place on the stage. It has gone midnight when Georges Borot and Arsène Millochau finish, the latter thereby fulfilling a promise he had made to a mechanic who had repaired his broken wheel near Libourne in the opening kilometres of the fifth stage.

The sun is already well up the next morning when Pierre Desvages arrives, having taken almost twice as long as Garin to complete the route from Nantes. He has gone quick enough, though, to prevent Millochau relegating him to 21st and last place overall.

The first Tour de France is over.

STAGE 6 RESULT

1. Maurice Garin 471km in 18-09-00 (average speed 25.950km/h)
2. Fernand Augereau (Fra) at 0-10
3. 'Samson' (Bel) same time

4. Jean Fischer (Fra) at 1-20
5. Lucien Pothier (Fra) at 1-30
6. Rodolfo Muller (Ita) at 2-00
7. Alexandre Foureaux (Fra) at 2-30
8. Julien Girbe (Fra) at 2-35
9. François Beaugendre (Fra) at 21-00
10. Marcel Kerff (Bel) at 53-00
11. René Salais (Fra) at 1-15-30
12. Jean Dargassies (Fra) at 1-21-20
13. Josef Fischer (Ger) at 1-36-25
14. Gustave Pasquier (Fra) at 1-51-15
15. Aloïs Catteau (Bel) at 2-07-35
16. Ferdinand Payan (Fra) at 2-34-26
17. Isidore Lechartier (Fra) at 5-09-20
18. Émile Moulin (Fra) at 6-35-50
19. Georges Borot (Fra) at 10-46-15
20. Arsène Millochau (Fra) same time
21. Pierre Desvages (Fra) at 16-23-30

Final overall classification

1. Maurice Garin (Fra) 2428km in 94-33-14 (average speed 25.678km/h)
2. Lucien Pothier (Fra) at 2-59-31
3. Fernand Augereau (Fra) at 4-29-24
4. Rodolfo Muller (Ita) at 4-39-30
5. Jean Fischer (Fra) at 4-58-44
6. Marcel Kerff (Bel) at 5-52-24

7. 'Samson' (Bel) at 8-31-08
8. Gustave Pasquier (Fra) at 10-24-04
9. François Beaugendre (Fra) at 10-52-14
10. Aloïs Catteau (Bel) at 12-44-57
11. Jean Dargassies (Fra) at 13-49-40
12. Ferdinand Payan (Fra) at 19-09-02
13. Julien Girbe (Fra) at 23-16-52
14. Isidore Lechartier (Fra) at 24-05-13
15. Josef Fischer (Ger) at 25-14-26
16. Alexandre Foureaux (Fra) at 31-50-52
17. René Salais (Fra) at 32-34-43
18. Émile Moulin (Fra) at 49-43-15
19. Georges Borot (Fra) at 51-37-38
20. Pierre Desvages (Fra) at 62-55-54
21. Arsène Millochau (Fra) at 64-57-08

Prize money

Maurice Garin	6,125 francs
Lucien Pothier	2,450 francs
Fernand Augereau	1,975 francs
Hippolyte Aucouturier	1,800 francs
Rodolfo Muller	1,250 francs
Léon Georget	900 francs
Jean Fischer	795 francs
Julien 'Samson' Lootens	700 francs
Émile Pagie	700 francs
Charles Laeser	700 francs

Eugène Brange	650 francs
Gustave Pasquier	600 francs
Marcel Kerff	475 francs
Aloïs Catteau	225 francs
François Beaugendre	195 francs
Jean Dargassies	145 francs
Ferdinand Payan	145 francs
Julien Girbe	145 francs
Isidore Lechartier	120 francs
Ernest Pivin	110 francs
Ambroise Garin	100 francs
Josef Fischer	95 francs
Alexandre Foureaux	95 francs
René Salais	95 francs
Émile Moulin	95 francs
Georges Borot	95 francs
Pierre Desvages	95 francs
Arsène Millochau	95 francs
Philippe De Balade	95 francs

Note: All riders that earned less than 250 francs in prize money were eligible for the 95-franc daily stipend intended to cover costs during the race.

CHAPTER 17

'THE MOST ABOMINABLY HARD RACE EVER IMAGINED'

The extent of the success of the first Tour de France can be gauged by the enthusiastic response of the country's best-selling newspapers, where sport was usually tucked away in a corner on one of the final pages. The Tour, however, had created such a stir that they could not ignore it, and consequently the race's final stage featured prominently alongside headlining stories such as the wave of deaths across the country caused by the relentless heat and a ministerial crisis within the Spanish government.

Le Figaro, to this point almost silent on the race, declared that *L'Auto* 'fully deserve all of the plaudits it is receiving for the admirable sporting test that they have successfully organised. It was a difficult task, and they have proved that they were up to it.' *Le Matin* concluded that, '*L'Auto* has achieved the result that it was hoping for: to prove that races without pace-makers are much fairer and more logical than races contested up to now.' *Le Petit Parisien* described the Tour as gigantic and explained, 'We say it's gigantic, and the word is not too overblown to describe this race, the most important to have been established within cycle sport.' Each backed their praise up with lengthy reports on the final stage.

Echo de Paris went even further, dispatching journalist G. De Lafrete in a car to watch the final kilometres of the last stage, during which he got close enough to the leading pack to be able to conduct a brief interview with Maurice Garin on the Côte de Saint-Rémy-en-Chevreuse where the rider revealed his joy at the thought of being able to kiss and hold his wife and son in the velodrome. 'These men have an iron temperament and, far from being fatigued by this incredible event, they have finished in better form than they had during the first stage . . . In all honesty, as well as the sporting attraction they offer, these events are of significant physiological interest. Previously, it would never have been believed that human beings are capable of dealing with such fatigue,' wrote De Lafrete.

While De Lafrete's comments about their racers' good condition at the finale seem absurd now, the performance of several of the lower-ranked riders on the final stage and also on those immediately before it suggests that many of the racers were not at all well prepared to compete with the likes of Garin when they first lined up in Paris, but improved as the Tour went on, with the result that the last stage was the most competitive and exciting from a racing perspective.

Newspapers in Belgium, Switzerland and Italy also carried reports, while the Tour even earned a mention in *The New York Herald*, which stated that 'the best man had certainly won' and described 'the fantastic ovation that he received at the Parc des Princes yesterday'.

The reaction to the race in the sporting press was equally enthusiastic. Ernest Mousset's comments in *La Vie au Grand Air* were typical of the response in all of *L'Auto*'s rival publications. 'Now that the Tour de France has finished in triumph, we have to give huge thanks to its organisers, our colleagues at *L'Auto* and its director, Henri Desgrange, for having dared to undertake a task so colossal that it was fair to wonder whether it was possible to carry it out successfully,' he proclaimed. 'All the little criticisms of details . . . have been swept aside by this conclusive result.'

Given the many unforeseen issues and all kinds of factors that made a sporting event of the Tour's immense scale unlikely to succeed, it is hard to argue with these conclusions. As Mousset suggested, the race was beset by disputes, inconsistencies and cheating. But having 60 riders line up in Paris and seeing almost a third of them return to the capital's packed streets three weeks later was an absolute triumph at a time when one-day races often had just a handful of finishers. Bordeaux–Paris, then the biggest race on the calendar, drew just 23 starters that year, 13 of them reaching the finish, while only 27 riders completed Paris–Roubaix.

Unsurprisingly and very deservedly, *L'Auto* didn't hold back when hailing the Tour's success in its 20 July special edition, which sold a record 135,000 copies. Inevitably, Desgrange led the way, confessing that he wished the race could continue indefinitely, so much had he enjoyed it. 'I've had plenty of sporting dreams in my life, but I never imagined that this could turn out to be reality. To send these men out across the whole of France, to remember through their feats the joyous feelings that the bike can and must provide, to awaken hundreds of kilometres of the country that was in an inactive physical slumber, to show those who have become numbed, indifferent or fearful that cycle sport is still thriving, that it is still capable of astonishing us, of sparking the desire for emulation, energy and passion is what the Tour de France needed to do, and that is what it has essentially achieved,' he proclaimed, adding that the race would inspire a new generation of cyclists in the same way he and his peers had been inspired by the feats of those who had ridden the first editions of Bordeaux–Paris.

He continued by, rightly, predicting the likely demise of pace-makers in major events, asserting that their use had increased the likelihood of cheating and had held less well-known riders back. He pointed to the exploits of Pothier, Augereau, Kerff, Samson and others as justification for not allowing their use, and suggested that this also would lead to a boost in the pool of competitive talent within the sport, that anyone could now win the Tour if they had a bike and enough talent and application to make the most of their ability. Interestingly, when the first edition of Paris–Valenciennes took place the following weekend, the organisers stressed they were implementing the same rule as the Tour and prohibiting the use of pace-makers.

Yet, Desgrange wasn't so full of his race's success that he was simply content to crow about it. 'Today, for the first time, everyone, including us, can discuss the imperfections of this first attempt,' he conceded, going on to list changes that would be considered for the following year. He admitted the decision to allow riders to participate in individual stages with the aim of encouraging local riders to test themselves against the established names had been a mistake because not enough locals had come forwards. The implementation of the rules relating to soigneurs would, he said, be more strictly applied. He recognised that there was evidence of riders receiving illegal assistance during stages, but insisted none of these had resulted in any significant change in the standings. Interestingly, he revealed that 'we will be examining at our leisure' one instance that had occurred during the third stage to Toulouse, which seemed to hint at further examination of the incident involving Maurice Garin that *La Provence Sportive* had reported in some detail, but would soon be revealed as involving the race's other star name.

Desgrange also admitted that the system of payments to riders needed to be reviewed. It was unfair, he acknowledged, that a rider could almost be within sight of Paris and end up receiving not a franc because they had not finished the race due to illness or bad luck. While Desgrange said it was largely up to the organisers to address this issue, he revealed that the the Tour had cost *L'Auto* more than 40,000 francs and implored the manufacturers and benevolent 'sportsmen' to consider offers of assistance in this area.

'As a result of these reforms we will end up with a perfect event that won't lend itself to any criticism,' he concluded. In this, it would soon be shown, Desgrange was absolutely wrong.

The elation of reaching Paris infected most of the riders who completed the Tour, several making light of the challenge they had faced and insisting that they were already relishing a repeat experience in 1904. The champion was far more reflective, though. Described by his friend and teammate Rodolfo Muller as the rider that the rest had been fascinated by, 'his white jersey always floating in front of us . . . like a white phantom', Garin had now done and won everything of importance in road cycling. Asked by Géo Lefèvre at the Parc des Princes whether he prized his Tour success more than his victory two years earlier in Paris–Brest–Paris, he asked for an evening to reflect on this.

The next morning, after a night celebrating his victory with his family and teammates, he awoke at half past three, got dressed and went out into the Bois de Boulogne to collect his thoughts. His first was for his feet, which he found were excruciatingly painful in his leather shoes after three weeks of pedal-pounding. Returning to his hotel, he swapped them for his slippers and headed out to *L'Auto* offices to deliver a letter to Lefèvre in which he offered his perspective on the race.

Describing the 2,500-kilometre route as a long grey line

that he could only see in monotone, Garin, hailed by many as an almost superhuman athlete, admitted he had struggled from almost start to finish. 'I got hungry, thirsty, tired, I suffered, I cried between Lyon and Marseille,' he revealed. He described himself as being like a bull in an arena that has been pierced by banderillas, with each of them bearing the name of a rival whose constant harrying he had to endure. Only on the last stage did this feeling of being the target for everyone's attacks finally dissipate, he continued, that sensation the result of his knowledge that he could no longer be beaten and also from the cheers and shouts of spectators.

'Now that I've had a good night's sleep and my mind, like my muscles, has had the chance for a little rest, and now that the Tour de France has finished and I'm no longer obsessed by the next stage, I can tell you very clearly that your race is the hardest, the most abominably hard that could ever be imagined,' he declared, adding that he and his rivals had shown what admirable competitors they were by coming through it. Henri Desgrange would undoubtedly have been delighted to read this, but there was better to come as Garin congratulated the organisers on their decision to prohibit the use of pace-makers: 'You've revolutionised cycle sport and the [first] Tour de France will go down as an important date in the history of road cycling.'

For Géo Lefèvre, Garin's victory offered incontrovertible proof of his belief that 'The Little Sweep' was one of the greatest riders road cycling had ever seen. 'Garin has his detractors. He's reproached for what is effectively his brute strength. They say he is not quick, he shows no brio. He's nothing more than a tenacious battler, stubborn, his dynamism as small as his frame . . . But the Tour winner certainly stands alongside Lesna and Aucouturier as the most impressive roadmen that we have ever had in France. But what puts him on absolutely another level is his consistency as a racer. Garin now seems like a piece of granite against which all of his opponents' energy ends up being smashed,' Lefèvre asserted. For good measure, he added Muller's very brief analysis of his rival's ability: 'When up against Garin, there's simply nothing you can do.'

No doubt Fernand Augereau would have vouched for that having witnessed the lengths Garin was prepared to go to win the Tour. Perhaps it was because of this incident, combined with the ill-luck that seemed to dog him, that Lefèvre was so gushing in his praise. Describing him as one of the riders who had emerged thanks to the decision to ensure the race was contested 'with equal arms', Lefèvre advised *L'Auto*'s readers to remember his name. 'This handsome chap, who is so supple and robust, is a born champion. Augereau has surprised us once and he will surprise us again in the future,' he said, not aware at that point how prescient this prediction would soon prove to be.

Two weeks on from the Tour finale, *L'Auto* published a brief story about the race commissaires' investigation into allegations of rule-breaking made during the race. It said that claims made against Hippolyte Aucouturier's actions on his way to victory from the second group during the third stage to Toulouse had been dismissed due to lack of evidence – there was no mention of *La Provence Sportive*'s claims about Garin on that same stage. It also revealed that that the commissaires had not followed up on the allegations Augereau had made against Garin on stage 5 because, the investigation stated, 'Augereau had spontaneously withdrawn his complaint'.

A few days later, the rider from Châtellerault, under fire from some in his home region for apparently buckling to Garin, sent an open letter to *L'Auto* and his local paper, *Le Mémorial du Poitou,* in which he revealed that he had had a meeting in front of witnesses with the Tour winner in Paris on 5 August, coincidentally the same day the Tour commissaires had published their report. 'I withdrew my complaint when [Garin] agreed to grant me the compensation that I had a right to be given,' Augereau stated. Although some papers, although obviously not *L'Auto*, demanded to know what form this 'compensation' had taken, no further light was shed on the issue. However, it can probably be assumed that Augereau received a significant payment from Garin, with the Tour's commissaires perhaps among those present.

This pay-off may have satisfied Augereau, but by sweeping Garin's heinous offence under the carpet it effectively sent the message to riders that anything goes. The 1904 edition of Bordeaux–Paris, for example, was reduced to a farce. Of the 15 riders who finished, 11 were subsequently disqualified including the first four – Léon Georget, future Tour winner Lucien Petit-Breton, César Garin and Rodolfo Muller – for offences including scattering tacks behind them, being towed behind cars and motorbikes, failing to sign at control points and getting pushed up hills.

Coincidentally, the rider who benefited most from these disqualifications, which included a life ban for Georget later reduced to two years, was Augereau, who was promoted from fifth to first place, with Jean Dargassies the new runner-up. Yet even this proved no deterrent when the second Tour took place a month later. Once again, the top four finishers – Maurice Garin, Lucien Pothier, César Garin and Hippolyte Aucouturier – were disqualified, making 20-year-old Henri Cornet the youngest Tour winner ever.

That was all still in the future, though. Back in the post-Tour glow of radiant success, Lefèvre brought the curtain down on the inaugural race. 'And there we have it! It's all over, the battle has finished,' he wrote. 'And all of you, the triumphant, the vanquished and the victims, I salute you as we have to salute men who have attempted or succeeded in something that is really superhuman.'

When L'Auto's post-Tour issue went on sale on 21 July, those superhuman men were returning to all parts of France and beyond to be acclaimed by their fellow citizens. Garin first travelled with Lucien Pothier and their teammate Muller to the Tour runner-up's hometown of Sens for a banquet where 100 guests fêted the three riders. Apparently destined for a great future on the road, Pothier's first task in the wake of this tribute was to return to his job as a butcher's assistant in the town.

That same afternoon, Samson arrived at Brussels-Midi station to be greeted with some pomp by local dignitaries and members of the Stoempers cycling club. Returning to Tourcoing, Aloïs Catteau also found a crowd of well-wishers waiting for him at the railway station. Eugène Brange had a similar reception in Belleville-sur-Saône, while Jean Dargassies was guest of honour at a banquet and ball in his hometown of Grisolles, where, he informed Lefèvre, he planned to set up a cycling club. 'Everyone here is mad, madder than me. They were all waiting for me at the station with music, bouquets and all kinds of beautiful comments. I'm more fatigued than at a Tour finish and I still have to go to a banquet for 80 people that is being put on in my honour,' he reported.

Naturally, the biggest reception of all was in Lens, to which Maurice Garin was very eager to get back to if only to indulge himself on home cooking and replace the two and a half kilos in weight he had lost on the road to victory. Six days on from his Tour success, a multitude of thousands, held back on the pavements by rows of cyclists, welcomed him and his teammates Muller and Pothier. The trio led a procession from the station into the Place de la Gare, where Garin was presented with a bronze trophy. After that came a reception hosted by the mayor and the council, followed by a parade through the town's streets.

'Garin's reception in Lens was something unimaginable.

You needed to see it, experience it, only the famous return to Longchamp in the era of General Boulanger can be compared to it,' cooed *L'Auto*'s correspondent Fafiotte, evoking the reception given to the Third Republic military hero in 1886. Paying tribute during the official reception, the mayor, Émile Basly, told Garin, 'You were the pride of all of the people of Lens . . . and you were the pride of the French people, who were astonished by your endurance and courage, and exalted by your exploit, which reached the sublime.'

Offering a very interesting insight into the mindset of many French people at that time, the mayor continued, 'My dear Garin, your victory glorifies our bicycle industry, which provides so many improvements to the well-being of the working classes, for whom the bicycle constitutes a marvellous machine for getting around.'

Too choked to respond, Garin allowed his manager Delattre and friend Muller to respond on his behalf, the latter announcing, 'I am happy to be Maurice's friend, happy to feel the joy that he has unleashed today thanks to *L'Auto*, the organising newspaper of the Tour de France . . .' Escorted by 2,000 cyclists, Garin was then driven around the town and eventually to his shop on the Rue de Lille, where another huge throng was waiting.

In the days following the Tour, the sporting press published letter after letter that not only praised the riders but also provided evidence of the inspiration they had provided, of France being shaken out of his physical lethargy. New cycling clubs and societies were established right across the country, and most noticeably in the towns and villages of *France profonde*, where the bicycle opened up new horizons and very quickly became the sporting instrument of choice. It was no coincidence that many of France's future cycling greats would emerge from places such as these that were often little more than an insignificant point on the map, from which the bicycle offered the most obvious chance of escape and, for some, adulation and riches.

CHAPTER 18

'A TOUR THAT HAD EVERYTHING'

Four days after the first Tour de France had ended in Paris, as *L'Auto*'s editorial focus began to spread once again into realms beyond the race that had been its focus for the previous month, the paper's front page lead was headlined 'The Monorail'. Over the next column and a half, Octave Uzanne outlined plans being drawn up to build a high-speed monorail link between Liverpool and Manchester.

According to Uzanne's report, the monorail, which would be based on an existing system that had been running since 1888 between Listowel and Ballybunion in Ireland and a temporary one set up at the Brussels Exhibtion of 1897 designed by F. B. Behr, would see trains running at 225km/h, cutting the journey between the two northern powerhouses to a mere 18 minutes. Costing 30 million French francs, the system already had the support of the chambers of commerce in both cities, who were backing a feasibility project.

Uzanne hailed the ingenuity of the project and declared that France needed to invest in similar schemes in order to boost its industrial standing. Such a system would, he pointed out, reduce the journey between Paris and Marseille to just five hours.

The monorail project, of course, never saw the light of day. The fastest trains take 45 minutes to travel the 35 miles between Liverpool and Manchester, although high-tech and very high-speed French trains can now cover the close to 800 kilometres separating Paris and Marseille in a little over three hours. Yet what Uzanne's fascinating story emphasises above all is the widely pervading sense within the belle époque period that it was possible to get almost any cutting-edge or perhaps even madcap project off the ground given the correct combination of cash and commitment.

The Tour de France was undoubtedly a prime example of this. Tending far more towards the wacky end of the innovation scale, the Tour changed not only cycling's competitive landscape, but also that of sport in general, and not only within France. While other popular sports struggled with the conflict between professionalism and amateurs, cycling accepted and accommodated it. Already embraced during the early days of road racing and, much more fully, during track-racing's late nineteenth-century heyday, professionalism provided a solid foundation for events such as the Tour by offering bike and associated manufacturers a shop window for their products.

From this perspective, the sport remains much the same now as it was in 1903. Indeed, there is a good deal of substance to the argument that cycling, and particularly the Tour de France, is an exercise in marketing as much as it is a race. As was very much the case in the early twentieth century, the race remains a tool for promoting the products of team sponsors, the race's backers and, more than anything, France itself.

There is absolutely no better way of promoting the country than via a race that makes a point of visiting its great sights, its little-known wonders and highlighting its cultural and historical treasures. Initially, reports in *L'Auto* and other newspapers showcased the country to a French population enjoying more leisure time and spending power and looking for entertainment, particularly of the sensationalist kind. Nowadays, when the television broadcasts, Internet coverage and social media have expanded the race's commercial reach and importance hugely, it reaches out to a daily audience of tens of millions located in almost 200 countries.

While it is difficult to assess to what extent the Tour contributed towards Henri Desgrange's goal of revitalising French manhood and restoring national pride, the event's role and success in establishing road cycling as the country's favourite sport is certainly beyond dispute. Quite unwittingly, Desgrange and Géo Lefèvre stumbled on to the public's desire for entertainment at its most extreme, a contest that pushed the participants to their physical limits. Previously most evident in six-day races on the track and similarly lengthy endurance events in other sports, the Tour stood out because it was unparalleled in the spectacle it offered and its physical demands.

In addition, rather than being restricted to a stadium, theatre or music hall, the Tour delivered that spectacle directly to its audience, in their towns and villages, on the roads that went past their homes. While it's true that some would have witnessed races such as Bordeaux–Paris or Marseille–Paris beforehand, these events had a fixed itinerary. The Tour, on the other hand, not only chimed with the public's experience of serial entertainment, which had previously been limited to stories of that type that appeared in newspapers, but also delivered it on a national stage to a large but very dispersed population. France became the arena and, in a way that Desgrange and Lefèvre never imagined, the French people embraced it with immense enthusiasm.

Groundbreaking in so many ways, the Tour became an epic journey that celebrated the French nation and its people. As a result, it earned a place in the country's mythology, able to attract not only cycling fans, but also many who had no interest in sport whatsoever and thereby gaining universal acceptance and become France's first national sport and, indeed, its first mass spectator sport. 'It was the first activity of a modern, standardised kind which made an impact in the countryside as well as in the town. It began by providing amusement for the culturally deprived masses of the large cities and ended by penetrating the hitherto closed world of rural entertainment,' says Richard Holt.

Although road cycling and the Tour's status has waned within France over the last three decades and more, when football has undeniably taken its mantle as the country's favourite sport, largely due to the outstanding successes achieved by the national team on the international stage during a long period when French cyclists have been almost completely eclipsed by their foreign rivals, the race remains as important now to cycle sport as it ever has been. It maintains almost religious reverence, which contrasts quite obviously with the uncertainty that characterised its launch.

Planned by Desgrange and Lefèvre as a five-week race that would take place in June but which failed to attract a substantial field, the event mocked by *Le Vélo* as 'the phantom race' was eventually shifted to three weeks in July and has remained essentially unchanged ever since. It still fills that same slot and has, ever since the 1903 edition, overshadowed every other event in the season, leaving the cycling calendar looking rather lopsided, with its competitive highlight at its mid-point rather than at the finale.

This peculiarity is far from the only way that the 1903 Tour has continued to have an impact on the modern-day race. Even though the Tour has developed in ways that the original participants might not have imagined, with the high mountains and time trials now regarded as the key strategic points and tactics changed beyond recognition, the Tour remains the race that most defines professional cyclists.

Apart from many riders in Dutch-speaking Belgium, most pros still view the Tour as the season's racing highlight, peaking for July in the same way that Maurice Garin did for the first edition.

The language used to describe and define it also it also has its roots in that inaugural race, when Desgrange, Lefèvre and all of their peers focused on the attrition and suffering to shape the public perception of the race, fostering the cult of survival. The roads, tactics and the equipment that the riders use may have improved hugely, but, largely thanks to the addition of multiple stages in the high mountains, the Tour remains the ultimate test of physical and mental endurance in cycling and, many would argue, within sport. While Garin's successors as Tour champions continue to take the largest slice of the glory, every rider who lines up in the race and especially all those who reach Paris, has achieved a feat of huge sporting significance.

Has doping undermined such achievements? Certainly, in the eyes of many, and particularly in France, where viewing figures and spectator numbers have dropped away, sponsorship has become harder to find and numbers participating at cycling's grassroots have fallen. However, those issues are probably just one French Tour de France victory away from being reversed.

It should also be remembered that although doping didn't taint the first Tour nor indeed many that followed on either side of the Great War, there is little doubt that it was taking place. In addition, other forms of cheating were rife and employed on the same industrial scale as injections of blood-boosting hormones in races on either side of the millennium. The fact that there's historical evidence of cheating within cycling going back to the first Tour doesn't make it acceptable, but it does underline that those who cheat now aren't besmirching a lilywhite sport.

In much the same way, the Tour's ability to draw an audience remains as strong as it was in 1903. The make-up of that audience may have changed from all-French to a roughly even split of French and foreign spectators, but modern-day fans turn out for essentially the same reasons as their predecessors did in 1903: looking for spectacle against the ever-changing and usually captivating backdrop of France. The essence of that spectacle hasn't changed either. While it includes a large pinch of athletic excellence, it also comprises a good dose of suffering. Without this suffering – riders battling on after multiple punctures, coping with illness and psychological stresses, trying to avoid finishing outside the time limit, pushing themselves to their physical limit in order to better or stay with their rivals – the Tour wouldn't have been such a popular sensation in 1903 and remained so over the decades since. Removing it would diminish the Tour, perhaps fatally.

Looking more specifically at the 1903 race, it is impossible to understate the groundbreaking role that all those involved in it played in popularising road cycling. On the organisational side, Henri Desgrange and Géo Lefèvre were cycling's William Webb-Ellis's, creating a new sport out of an existing one, although they exceeded the achievement of rugby's founder by making their new discipline greater than its antecedent. Driven on by zeal and, due to their newspaper's plight, desperation, together with complete unawareness of what they were getting themselves into, the two men and their staff at *L'Auto*, together with officials, correspondents and volunteers all over France, pulled off a feat that surpassed Garin's in winning the Tour.

The first Tour de France produced not only a popular sensation, but also eclipsed the 1900 Paris Olympics, drawn out over four months and run in conjunction with the Paris World Fair, as the greatest sporting event the world had ever seen from a logistical and organisational perspective. As Desgrange confessed, it did have flaws, but these were primarily related to the rules. Enabling 60 riders to race on dusty and rutted roads, often through the night, and ensuring, for the most part, that they stuck to the route and the regulations when the lack and general unreliability of motor vehicles made tracking them almost impossible was an astounding achievement.

More than the joy and relief they must have felt at seeing 21 riders reach Paris, Desgrange and Lefèvre's reward was securing the long-term future of *L'Auto*. After the sale of 135,000 achieved by its final Tour special edition, the paper's circulation fell dramatically to around 70,000 per day. This, however, was between two and three times the number that Desgrange's title had been selling prior to the Tour. At the same time, the circulation of rivals *Le Vélo* and *Le Monde*

Sportif, which had also reached record levels during the Tour, fell back much more to 35,000 and 25,000 a day, respectively.

The balance of power had changed, and not even Pierre Giffard's return to *Le Vélo*'s helm in 1904 could reverse this. Having lost a good part of its staff to *Le Monde Sportif* in the first months of 1903 and then more than half of its readership to *L'Auto* during the Tour, *Le Vélo* closed in November 1904, having been unable to gain any advantage from the *Le Monde Sportif*'s closure in February of that same year. Consequently, when the 1905 season began, *L'Auto* had no significant rivals to deal with and continued to grow in strength and circulation as the Tour's popularity soared. In the end, Count de Dion and Henri Desgrange had achieved exactly the result they wanted.

As for the riders, while their fitness, tactics and speed were lacking, their exploits should not be devalued. The best of them may have had an inkling of what this new race had in store for them as a competitive and physical test, but most didn't. That a third of them survived to see Paris is extraordinary. Indeed, events on that final stage into the capital emphasise that it took several stages for most of them to fully realise the extent of their ability.

Some may have laughed about what they had gone through on the road to Paris, but all would certainly have agreed with Garin's description of Desgrange's new race as 'the hardest, the most abominably hard that could ever be imagined'. Absolutely unparalleled in terms of the challenge it offered, the Tour extracted the very best from its participants. Although the competitive level may not have compared to Tours even a handful of years later, it should be considered as one of the greatest events in sporting history. It was a Tour that had everything and, to an extent, every single Tour that has followed has been a rerun of that first race, featuring the same endeavour, courage, determination, rule-breaking and, most importantly, spectacle. The first Tour de France is every Tour de France. What a race it was and is.

WHAT BECAME OF THE 1903 TOUR'S STAR NAMES

MAURICE GARIN: 'The Little Sweep' successfully defended his title in 1904, only to be stripped of the victory later that year when he was among eight riders the French federation disqualified for cheating. Banned for two years, he never raced again, retiring to run a garage in Lens. He did continue to follow cycling, though, and set up a professional team under his own name following the Second World War. Its leader, Wim van Est, won the Tour of Flanders and two editions of Bordeaux–Paris in Garin's red-and-white colours. Garin died in 1957 aged 85. In 2007, the local velodrome, which had been named in Garin's honour in 1933, was knocked down to make way for the Lens offshoot of the Louvre museum.

GUSTAVE PASQUIER: Made one more appearance at the Tour, abandoning on stage 3 in 1905. He retired from racing that year, became the French federation's representative in Reims and devoted himself to engineering. In 1907, he designed a new transmission system for automobiles. In 1908, inspired by the Wright Brothers, he turned to aeroplane design. He died in 1965, aged 87.

LUCIEN BARROY: The former acrobat, clown and trapeze artist made one more Tour appearance in 1909, abandoning on the second stage. He set up a cycling and automobile business in Boulogne-sur-Seine, but was declared bankrupt in 1911. He died in 1974 aged 89. In October 2016, a pair of his trapeze shoes sold for €11.50 on eBay.

ALEXANDRE FOUREAUX: 'The Flying Carpenter' adopted his nickname for the name of his business in Paris and opened a bike manufacturing business next door. He never raced again.

HIPPOLYTE AUCOUTURIER: Winner in 1904 of Paris–Roubaix, the first edition run without pace-makers, 'The Hercules of Commentry' finished fourth in the Tour that year, only to be disqualified along with Garin and six others. He returned to win three stages and finish second overall to Louis Trousselier in 1905. His career declined after this and the former grocer and inspector of banks' telegraph machines retired in 1908.

MARCEL KERFF: The Belgian veteran never raced again. He was executed by the Germans in the Belgian Ardennes in August 1914 after being arrested for spying.

LÉON GEORGET: The rider from Châtellerault who ran out of steam and lay down to sleep on stage 5 went on to become 'The Father of the Bol d'Or', winning the 24-hour track endurance race nine times. Suspended for two years after being disqualified from Bordeaux–Paris in 1904, he didn't ride the Tour again until 1906, finishing eighth, three places behind brother Émile.

JEAN FISCHER: 'The Climber' only appeared at the Tour on one more occasion, abandoning in 1905. More than a century would pass before another rider from Alsace finished in the top ten of the Tour, Thomas Voeckler achieving that feat in 2011 when he reached Paris a place higher than Fischer.

ÉMILE PAGIE: Having emerged from near-obscurity as a journeyman racer, 'The Prince of Mines' returned there. He won Paris–Valenciennes the week after the Tour finished but rarely competed at the top level again.

JEAN DARGASSIES: One of the stars of the 1903 race, the blacksmith from Grisolles returned in 1904 and finished fourth following the disqualification of six riders above him in the top ten. He failed to finish in 1905 and 1907. On the latter occasion, he and Henri Gauban rode as guides/pace-setters/domestiques for rich landowner Henri Pépin. As the race was by then decided by points rather than time, the trio stopped wherever they wanted during stages, dining well and sleeping in good hotels, all at Pépin's expense. None of them finished the race, and Dargassies became a grocer and then a bike shop owner and died aged 93 in Grisolles, where a monument outside the tourist office commemorates him.

JULIEN 'SAMSON' LOOTENS: The Belgian veteran rode the next three Tours, only finishing the 1905 edition when he came twentieth. He rode Paris–Brest–Paris in 1901, 1911 and 1921, completing all three editions, the last of them at the age of 45.

RODOLFO MULLER: The Italian-born rider who spent most of his life in France was another of the riders suspended in the 1904 edition of Bordeaux–Paris. Muller, who spoke four languages, turned his attention to journalism and to hiring out motor vehicles. Winner, in 1902, of the first race to the summit of the Tourmalet pass in the Pyrenees, he became one of France's leading cross-country runners in his late thirties. From 1904, he also showed some talent in motor racing. He continued to live in France and died in Paris in 1947 aged 71.

LUCIEN POTHIER: 'The Butcher of Sens' finished second again in 1904, but was handed a life ban for cheating. After this had been reduced to three years, he returned to racing in 1907 and rode the Tour on five further occasions, the last of them in 1921, when he finished 32nd at the age of 38. He later ran a cafe in Troyes called Au Tour de France, and is buried in his home village of Cuy, where the main square is named in his honour.

FERNAND AUGEREAU: Winner of Bordeaux–Paris in 1904 after the four riders who finished ahead of him were disqualified, he competed until 1911 but never appeared at the Tour again. He went on to serve in the French artillery during the Great War and died in his home region of Poitou-Charentes in 1958 aged 75.

PIERRE DESVAGES: The penultimate rider in the overall standings in 1903, Desvages participated in the next seven editions of the Tour but didn't finish any of them. He continued racing until the early 1920s, finishing seventh in Bordeaux–Paris at the age of 53.

FRANÇOIS BEAUGENDRE: Months on from abandoning the 1904 race, he was declared the winner of the fourth stage following the disqualification of the two riders ahead of him. That decision also put him into the race lead. As he quit on the next stage, he was effectively the first rider to abandon the Tour when leading. He finished a career-best fifth at the Tour in 1907.

JOSEF FISCHER: The German veteran continued racing until 1904, then worked as a chauffeur to French aristocrats. Forced to leave Paris when the First World War broke out, he died in Munich in 1953 at the age of 88. He remained the only German to win Paris–Roubaix until John Degenkolb took the title in 2015.

CHARLES LAESER: The first foreign winner of a Tour stage, the rider from Geneva started the 1904 race but abandoned on the opening day. He never participated in the Tour again.

LOUIS TROUSSELIER: Although he didn't start the 1903 race after submitting his registration, 'Trou-Trou' became one of its pre-war legends, taking the title in 1905, when mountains appeared on the route for the first time, and winning 13 stages. He famously lost his winnings playing dice with fellow riders the same evening the race had finished in Paris.

HENRI ELLINAMOUR: Actually surnamed Collet, the young Frenchman's racing career failed to take off after he abandoned the Tour. His next brief foray into the headlines was in 1908, when he was one of a gang of thieves operating in Paris and well beyond who were arrested for stealing wallets from the coats hung up in cafes.

ARSÈNE MILLOCHAU: The last rider to finish in Paris, bike mechanic Millochau had ridden and finished all of the great races on the French calendar before lining up at the Tour. By then he was 36. He continued racing intermittently into the post-war years, mixing competitive commitments with work in the kitchen-cum-workshop of his home on Rue de Charonne. Reputed as a lady's man who was twice married, he participated in Paris–Brest–Paris in 1921 when he was 54, failing to finish. Interviewed in 1947 by *Miroir Sprint*, he said he still preferred his bike to the metro and described the modern-day Tour as 'a walk in the park'. He died the following year aged 81.

ALOÏS CATTEAU: Third in 1904 following the disqualification of the top four finishers, the Belgian showed great consistency in the race over the next few seasons, finishing sixth in 1906 and ninth a year later when part of the powerful Alcyon team that usurped La Française's position as the dominant force in the pre-war years.

LUCIEN PETIT-BRETON: Like Trousselier, Petit-Breton, or Mazan as he was actually known – he took the name Breton to hide his identity from his family when racing and added Petit as there was already another rider called Breton – registered for the 1903 Tour but didn't start. Similarly to Trousselier, he proved a complete adept when he did finally appear at the Tour, finishing fifth in 1905, fourth a year later and then winning the title in 1907 and 1908. The

French-born, Argentinian-naturalised rider also won the inaugural edition of Milan–Sanremo in 1907.

GÉO LEFÈVRE: The originator of the Tour de France, Lefèvre stayed with *L'Auto* for several years and played a key role in establishing cyclo-cross as cycling's winter discipline. After serving and being decorated during the First World War, he went on to work for motoring titles and had a significant part to play in the establishment of the Le Mans 24-Hour Race. Following the Second World War, he worked for several years as a correspondent of *L'Auto*'s successor, *L'Équipe*, retiring in 1955 on his 78th birthday. He died six years later.

PIERRE GIFFARD: After returning as *Le Vélo*'s editor late in 1903, he was at the helm when the title he had founded folded a year later. He went on to work for *Le Matin*, covering the Russo–Japanese war for that title in 1905, and *Le Figaro*. Invited by Henri Desgrange to become a correspondent for *L'Auto* in 1910, he continued to work on that title and produced many books and essays until his death in 1922.

COUNT JULES-ALBERT DE DION: The motoring tycoon whose money and drive led to the founding of *L'Auto* devoted himself largely to politics, becoming a right-wing member of parliament in 1902 and a senator in 1923, holding that position until the German invasion in 1940. His car manufacturing company focused increasingly on luxury models in the pre- and post-war eras. Hit by the crash of 1929, it turned to the production of buses and road-sweepers. A marquis in later life, de Dion died in 1946 aged 90.

HENRI DESGRANGE: Soon dubbed 'The Father of the Tour', Desgrange was the dominant figure in road cycling for the three decades following the race's establishment. Founder in 1904 of the Audax movement catering to amateurs who wanted to test themselves in long-distance events, Desgrange's iron will made the Tour and *L'Auto* hugely successful, although his determination to impose his desires on riders and teams often resulted in conflict. In the pre-war years *L'Auto* regularly sold more than a quarter of a million copies during the Tour and its sales were often double that in the post-war period. In 1917, aged 52, Desgrange volunteered for service in the French army, earning the Croix de Guerre for his conduct. Forced to undergo a prostate operation in the weeks prior to the 1936 Tour, Desgrange went against doctor's orders and followed the race as usual in the lead car for the opening two stages, when the pain forced him to quit the race and hand over the reins to Jacques Goddet. Desgrange retired to the Mediterranean and died in 1940 aged 75, just weeks after Germany occupied France. He is remembered by a monument near the top of the Galibier pass in the French Alps, by a Tour prize awarded to the first rider to cross the highest pass in the race, and by his initials on the yellow jersey. The 2016 version won by Britain's Chris Froome featured the following dedication on the back: 'In 1903 Henri Desgrange created the greatest cycling event of all time'.

BIBLIOGRAPHY

Most of the details used to piece together the run-up to the 1903 Tour de France and, particularly, events that took place during it appeared in the pages of *L'Auto*, *Le Vélo*, *Le Monde Sportif*, *L'Écho de Paris*, *Le Figaro*, *La Revue Sportive*, *Le Matin*, *Le Petit Journal*, *Le Petit Parisien* and *La Vie au Grand Air*. I would like to express my gratitude to the staff of the Bibliothèque Nationale de France in Paris for helping me access these publications.

For further insight into that Tour and the state of the French nation in the late nineteenth and early twentieth century, I also referred to:

Chany, Pierre, *La Fabuleuse Histoire du Cyclisme* (Éditions ODIL, Paris, 1975)

Chany, Pierre, *La Fabuleuse Histoire du Tour de France* (Éditions de la Martinière, Paris, 1995)

Faccinetti, Paolo, *Tour de France 1903: La Nascita della Grande Boucle* (Ediciclo Editore, Portugruaro, Italy, 2003)

Goddet, Jacques, *L'Équipée Belle* (Robert Laffont/Stock, Paris, 1991)

Holt, Richard, *Sport and Society in Modern France* (Macmillan Press, Basingstoke, 1981)

Lablaine, Jacques, *Desgrange Intime* (CD, 2013)

Rapaud, Didier, *L'Incroyable Épopée de Marseille-Paris 1902* (Éditions Cristel, Saint-Malo, 2003)

Sergent, Pascal, *Les Pionniers du Cyclisme* (Alan Sutton, Saint-Cyr-sur-Loire, 2005)

Thompson, Christopher S., *The Tour de France: A Cultural History* (University of California Press, Berkeley, 2006)

Vespini, Jean-Paul, *Le Premier Tour de France* (Éditions Jacob-Duvernet, Paris, 2009)

ACKNOWLEDGEMENTS

I owe particular thanks to Fran Jessop, my editor at Yellow Jersey, for the many insights she offered during the writing and editing of this book, which is a much-better work for these suggestions. My thanks also to everyone else at Yellow Jersey who has assisted and to Justine Taylor for her forensic edit of the book and delivering its first – and very promising! – review. I would also like to express my gratitude to my literary agent, David Luxton.

I received significant help and support while working on this book from Brian and Barbara Crabtree, and from Gill, Jim, Pedro and Dougie at Bordebasse in the Aude, an inspirational place where this book came together.

Finally, my love and gratitude goes to my wife, Elaine, and my children, Lewis and Eleanor, at the start of our own little French adventure.

LIST OF ILLUSTRATIONS

1. The front page of the 1 July 1903 edition of *L'Auto*; Henri Desgrange; Géo Lefèvre

2. Maurice Garin; Pierre Desvages and Jean Dargassies at a stage start; Hippolyte Aucouturier (Spaarnestad Photo); Charles Laeser

3. The opening stage of the Tour de France on the front page of *L'Actualité*; Charles Laeser on his way to victory in Bordeaux

4. Léon Georget signs in at a stage start; Hippolyte Aucouturier sprints to win the second stage in Marseille

5. Spectators on the Toulouse–Bordeaux stage; Géo Lefèvre and Maurice Garin; Jean Dargassies on the fifth stage

6. Géo Lefèvre directing Maurice Garin; Garin and Léon Georget at a stage finish (Spaarnestad Photo); the Ville d'Avray control point in Paris

7. Spectators at the finish at Ville d'Avray; Maurice Garin with his victory garlands (Getty Images)

8. Maurice Garin post-race; Henri Desgrange

All images © Offside Sports Photography, except where indicated.

INDEX

Peter Cossins has been writing about cycling since 1993. He has covered more than a dozen editions of the Tour de France.

Photograph by Simon Wilkinson

 The Nation Institute

NATION
BOOKS

Founded in 2000, **Nation Books** has become a leading voice in American independent publishing. The imprint's mission is to tell stories that inform and empower just as they inspire or entertain readers. We publish award-winning and bestselling journalists, thought leaders, whistleblowers, and truthtellers, and we are also committed to seeking out a new generation of emerging writers, particularly voices from underrepresented communities and writers from diverse backgrounds. As a publisher with a focused list, we work closely with all our authors to ensure that their books have broad and lasting impact. With each of our books we aim to constructively affect and amplify cultural and political discourse and to engender positive social change.

Nation Books is a project of The Nation Institute, a nonprofit media center established to extend the reach of democratic ideals and strengthen the independent press. The Nation Institute is home to a dynamic range of programs: the award-winning Investigative Fund, which supports groundbreaking investigative journalism; the widely read and syndicated website TomDispatch; journalism fellowships that support and cultivate over twenty-five emerging and high-profile reporters each year; and the Victor S. Navasky Internship Program.

For more information on Nation Books and The Nation Institute, please visit:

www.nationbooks.org
www.nationinstitute.org
www.facebook.com/nationbooks.ny
Twitter: @nationbooks